REFUGE OF SCOUNDRELS

SCOUNDRELS

BY DAVID HORSEY

ISBN: 1492929891
ISBN-13: 978-1492929895

CARTOON COLLECTIONS BY DAVID HORSEY

Draw Quick, Shoot Straight (2007)

From Hanging Chad to Baghdad (2003)

One Man Show (1998)

The Fall of Man (1993)

Horsey's Greatest Hits of the '80s (1988)

Rude Awakenings (1983)

Politics and Other Perversions (1974)

OTHER BOOKS

Connie: Lessons from a Life in the Saddle (2013)

Chip Shots (2005)

Cartooning AIDS Around the World (1992)

_____

David Horsey's books, museum-quality prints and original cartoons can be purchased at

david-horsey.com

TO JANICE

My wonderful sister and first hero.
She has known me from the day I was born
and, in all those years, we never fought --
unless you count the time I sold her diary
to her junior high boyfriend for 25 cents.

"Patriotism having become one of our topicks, Johnson suddenly uttered, in a strong determined tone, an apophthegm, at which many will start:

'PATRIOTISM IS THE LAST REFUGE OF A SCOUNDREL.'

But let it be considered, that he did not mean a real and generous love of our country, but that pretended patriotism which so many, in all ages and countries, have made a cloak of self-interest."

-- James Boswell, *The Life of Samuel Johnson*, 1791

INTRODUCTION:
BENDS IN THE ARC OF HISTORY

The people came by the hundreds of thousands, filling the streets of Washington like a hundred rivers flowing toward the same sea. They converged on the Mall, massing at the west front of the Capitol and extending far back to the reflecting pool. The air was freezing cold, but the sun was high and bright, lighting the smiling faces of the people who had come to witness the historic moment: the inauguration of the first black man to be elected president of the United States of America.

It felt like a new day, a day when the nation's darkest stain, the long history of slavery and racism, would become more faint, a relic of a time quickly receding. I had brought my wife, daughter and son with me that morning to share in the new beginning. The lines were long and agonizingly slow at the security entrances. If this had been a football game or a pre-Christmas sale, tempers would have flared and fights would have broken out. But on this day in this place, the people were buoyed through the crush of humanity by communal joy.

The young president-elect and his picture-perfect family stepped forward on the flag-draped balcony below the magnificent dome that had been built nearly 150 years before in a time when the country was at war with itself, an era when people who looked like Barack Obama were in chains. But now, as Obama took the oath and became our president, the arc of history did seem, at last, to be bending toward justice.

Somewhat to the disappointment of the 1.8 million citizens who had come to see and hear the man, Obama delivered a speech that was more somber than expected, heavy with warnings that the road ahead would not be easy. On that day, it did not feel that way. When the helicopter carrying the departing president, George W. Bush, rose up behind the dome and headed across the Mall, people were gleeful. The bad days of a botched presidency were over. Everything seemed possible.

And then, too soon, reality set in. The new president was correct, the road would be rugged and victories far from guaranteed. That much was to be expected, after all. New days are really only high points in the unending parade of calamity that forms human history. But the years after that day of hope did not have to be as filled with rage, mendacity, paranoia and division as they have been. No, that was brought upon us by a parade of scoundrels who refused to accept that this new president was legitimate and who worked with all their being, not just to beat him, but to destroy him.

* * * * *

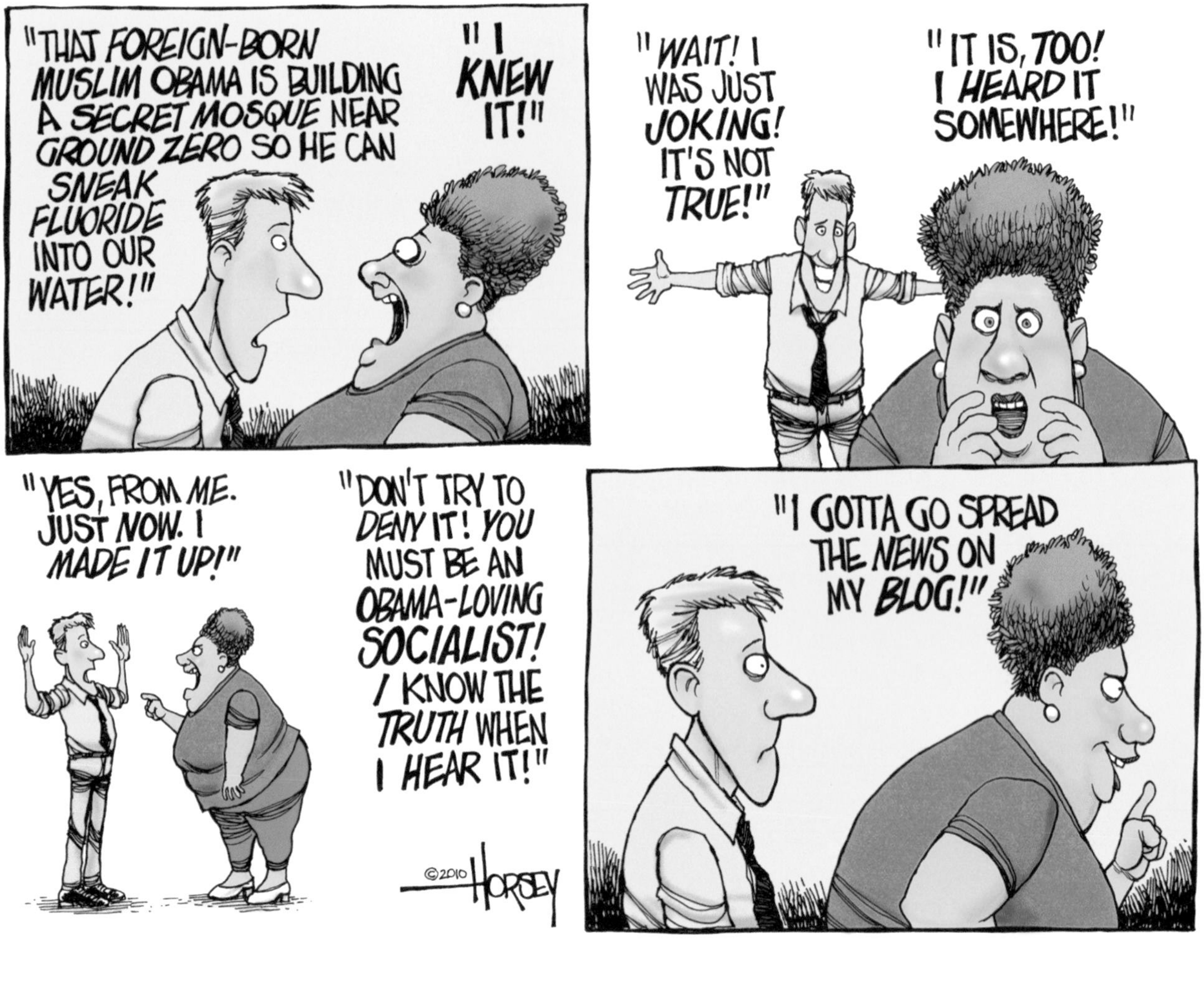

"THAT FOREIGN-BORN MUSLIM OBAMA IS BUILDING A SECRET MOSQUE NEAR GROUND ZERO SO HE CAN SNEAK FLUORIDE INTO OUR WATER!"
"I KNEW IT!"
"WAIT! I WAS JUST JOKING! IT'S NOT TRUE!"
"IT IS, TOO! I HEARD IT SOMEWHERE!"
"YES, FROM ME. JUST NOW. I MADE IT UP!"
"DON'T TRY TO DENY IT! YOU MUST BE AN OBAMA-LOVING SOCIALIST! I KNOW THE TRUTH WHEN I HEAR IT!"
"I GOTTA GO SPREAD THE NEWS ON MY BLOG!"
©2010 HORSEY

My plan was to stay on in Washington for the first hundred days of the Obama administration. I had moved into a basement apartment in a house near the National Cathedral and had my own office at the Hearst Newspapers Washington Bureau. In the first month, I got into a bachelor routine, ate like a college student, missed my family but loved the work. Then, something unexpected happened: My newspaper went and died on me.

Having begun publication in 1863 when Seattle was a muddy, upstart logging town, the Seattle Post-Intelligencer stopped print publication in March 2009. I had been working there 30 years and was having more fun than ever. With a talented young staff and an editor, David McCumber, who knew how to lead them, the P-I was energized. The paper had lost money for years, but my colleagues and I could not imagine a world without the P-I. Of course, that was like whistling past a graveyard. The business model for the newspaper industry had been destroyed by the rise of Internet advertising. Americans were floating in an ocean of information and few wanted to actually *pay* for information anymore.

After the newspaper closed, I was kept on to help launch the fledgling child of the P-I, seattlepi.com, and to do cartoons for other Hearst publications around the country. I learned the new rhythms and demands of online journalism and felt lucky to still have a job, unlike most of my P-I colleagues. Still, on the streets of Seattle, I began to feel as if I were becoming invisible to my former readers.

Meanwhile, 1,200 miles to the south, a different newspaper was being ravaged by a foul-mouthed billionaire from Chicago named Sam Zell -- a man the Washington Post dubbed a "human wrecking ball." In the sort of business deal that would be illegal in any sane society, Zell bought the Tribune Company, owners of the Los Angeles Times, in a leveraged buyout using very little of his own fortune. Now loaded with debt, it took only until the end of 2008 for the company to file for chapter 11 bankruptcy.

Like the hotshot financial wizards who drove the American economy off the cliff that same year, Zell kept his billions, but the LA Times and the other Tribune newspapers were hit with round after round of layoffs as they tried to dig themselves out of the hole in which Zell had dumped them. When I had lunch with Russ Stanton, the editor of the Times, in the summer of 2011, he was bone weary of being forced to kick good journalists out the door. Happily for me, he found a way to bring one in.

On New Year's Day 2012, I took over the political blog, Top of the Ticket, for latimes.com and, not long after, my cartoons began to appear on the Times editorial page. The timing was perfect. It was the start of a big political year and I was working for a big newspaper with an online audience numbered in the tens of millions. I was back in the game on one of the best teams in the country -- not where I thought I'd be back in 2009, but, then, I was not the only one who saw his plans get rearranged.

* * * * *

Barack Obama had opened his presidency with a pledge to move past the toxic partisanship that was dividing the country and crippling Congress. Instead, he became a lightning rod for an even more ruthless brand of partisan warfare. Obama is one of the most sane, level-headed and thoughtful men ever to sit in the Oval Office. Not a hint of scandal has tarnished his marriage. His politics are run-of-the-mill liberal and his policies are practical, not radical. But, if one believed the preposterous tales told about him by his foes on the right, one would think he was a tyrant who needed to be impeached, if not hung from the Liberty Tree.

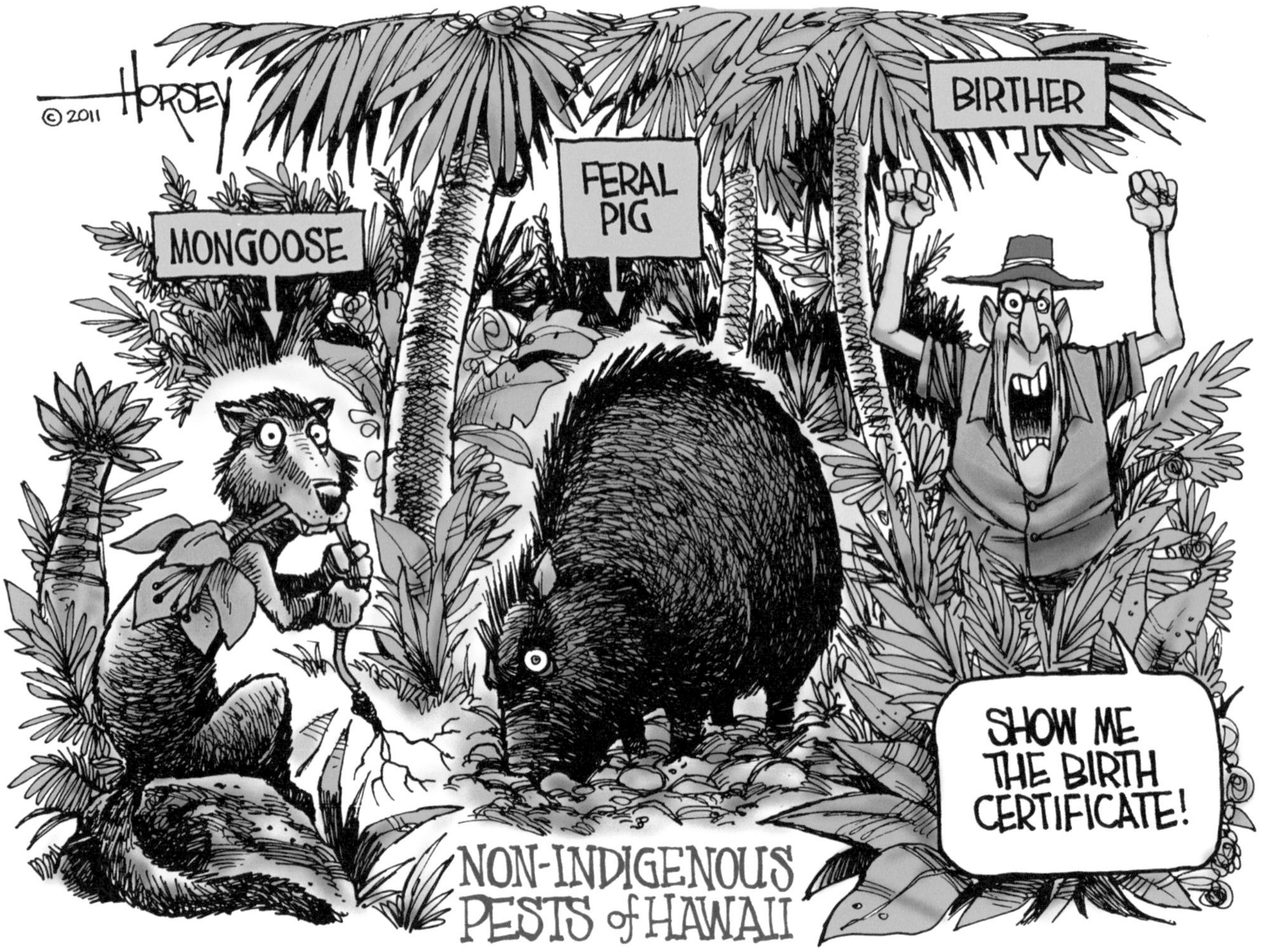

© 2011 HORSEY
MONGOOSE
FERAL PIG
BIRTHER
SHOW ME THE BIRTH CERTIFICATE!
NON-INDIGENOUS PESTS of HAWAII

And, of course, many people do believe. In poll after poll, about a quarter of Americans have expressed the opinion that the president is, variously, a Muslim, not a citizen, a supporter of Islamic terrorists and a radical, third World socialist. Religious web sites hint darkly that he is a devilish "Lord of the Flies," if not the Antichrist himself. His singular legislative achievement, the Affordable Care Act, may have seemed too great a compromise with the insurance industry to many liberals, but, to conservatives, it is nothing less than a government takeover of healthcare that, as expressed in the GOP primary campaign speeches of both Newt Gingrich and Rick Santorum, will turn the USA into a grim, Orwellian welfare state.

The rhetoric has become apocalyptic. No fight in Congress is just about nuances in legislation; every vote is a struggle for the soul of America. Never has so much ferocious anger been unleashed in response to such small provocation. Never have the merchants of spin and mendacity found such fertile ground. Never has the once great Republican Party been so overrun by fervent kooks obsessed with the president's birth certificate and possessed of curious theories about how rape may be part of God's plan.

The bankers, hedge fund managers and high-flying financiers on Wall Street who, through their greed and hubris, brought the American economic system to its knees have yet to mend their ways. A changing climate is revving up the force of weather systems and the country is being hit by monstrous storms, floods and wildfires. The wealth gap between the richest one percent of Americans and everyone else is turning America into a banana republic. Yet, any suggestion that Wall Street needs to be reigned in or the climate challenge confronted or the extreme inequities of wealth addressed is met with knee-jerk denunciations of Big Bad Government.

The election and then the re-election of the first black president has unleashed a visceral revulsion among a fearful but potent minority of white Americans. The fear and loathing are constantly fed by the shrill propagandists at Fox News, the ranters on right wing talk radio, the furious Tea Party screamers with their wealthy industrialist backers and the anonymous Internet trolls spewing paranoid fictions. Their goal is to "take back America" – apparently from those who twice voted for Obama, who feel comfortable with the idea of letting gays and lesbians marry and who think it might be a wise idea to let Latino kids go to college, join the military and become citizens. In other words, they want to take America back from the majority of the American people.

* * * * *

When President Obama leaves office, I suspect he will feel deeply frustrated that his unrelenting, unhinged foes were able to block so much of what he dreamed of accomplishing on that bright inauguration day in 2009. Still, he will be able to claim credit for at least four great things. Number one, in the days after his election and in his first weeks in office, he pulled the country back from the edge of a yawning chasm that could have swallowed up the world economy. Number two, he will have ended the two miserable wars he inherited and brought tough justice to Osama bin Laden. Number three, with the scheme that now unofficially bears his name – Obamacare – he will have given millions of people the chance to get the healthcare they had long been denied.

Last of all, as columnist Andrew Sullivan has observed, he will have done the country a great service simply by being the man who has stopped the right wing crazies from demolishing 100 years of economic, social, environmental and political progress.

Barack Obama is no messiah; just a good man. Sometimes his dearth of governing experience shows. But his flaws pale in comparison to those of his detractors. That is why, during his presidency, I have drawn him so infrequently in my cartoons. My job as an opinion journalist has never been to be neutral, but when our political life was more in balance, I found it much easier to go after both sides. In this bizarre, dispiriting moment of American history, however, I feel compelled to take aim at those who have proven their pose of patriotism to be little more than – in the words of Samuel Johnson -- a "refuge of scoundrels."

If a book of cartoons can be an expression of patriotism and love of country, this book is that for me. I am weary of watching the same battles being fought over and over again, but the truth is the struggle never ends. Martin Luther King, Jr., was right; the arc of history is long. And it bends toward justice only if we stay resolute in the work that makes it turn.

• DAVID HORSEY

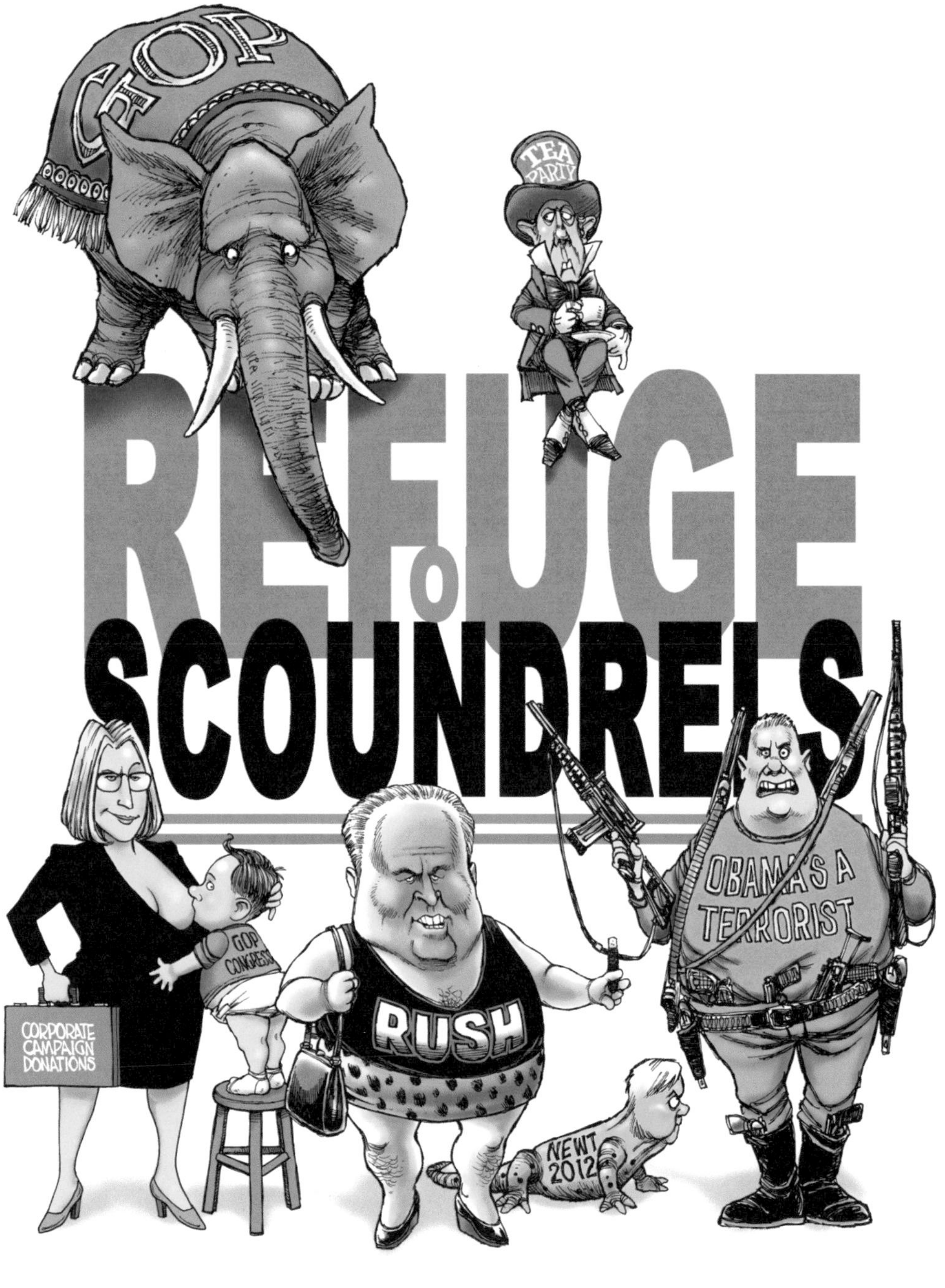
GOP
TEA PARTY
REFUGE
OF
SCOUNDRELS
GOP CONGRESS
CORPORATE CAMPAIGN DONATIONS
RUSH
OBAMA'S A TERRORIST
NEWT 2012

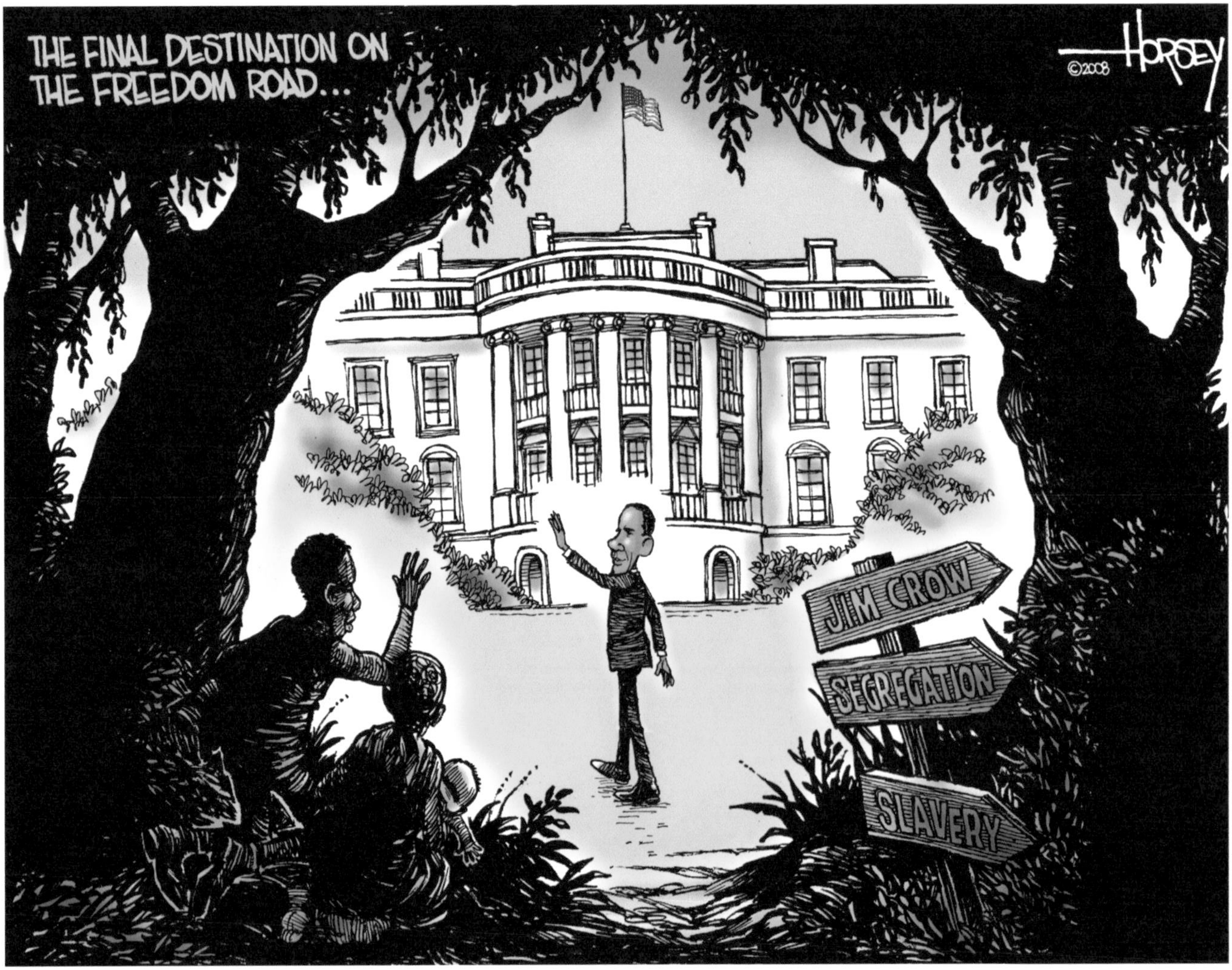
THE FINAL DESTINATION ON THE FREEDOM ROAD...
©2008 HORSEY
JIM CROW
SEGREGATION
SLAVERY

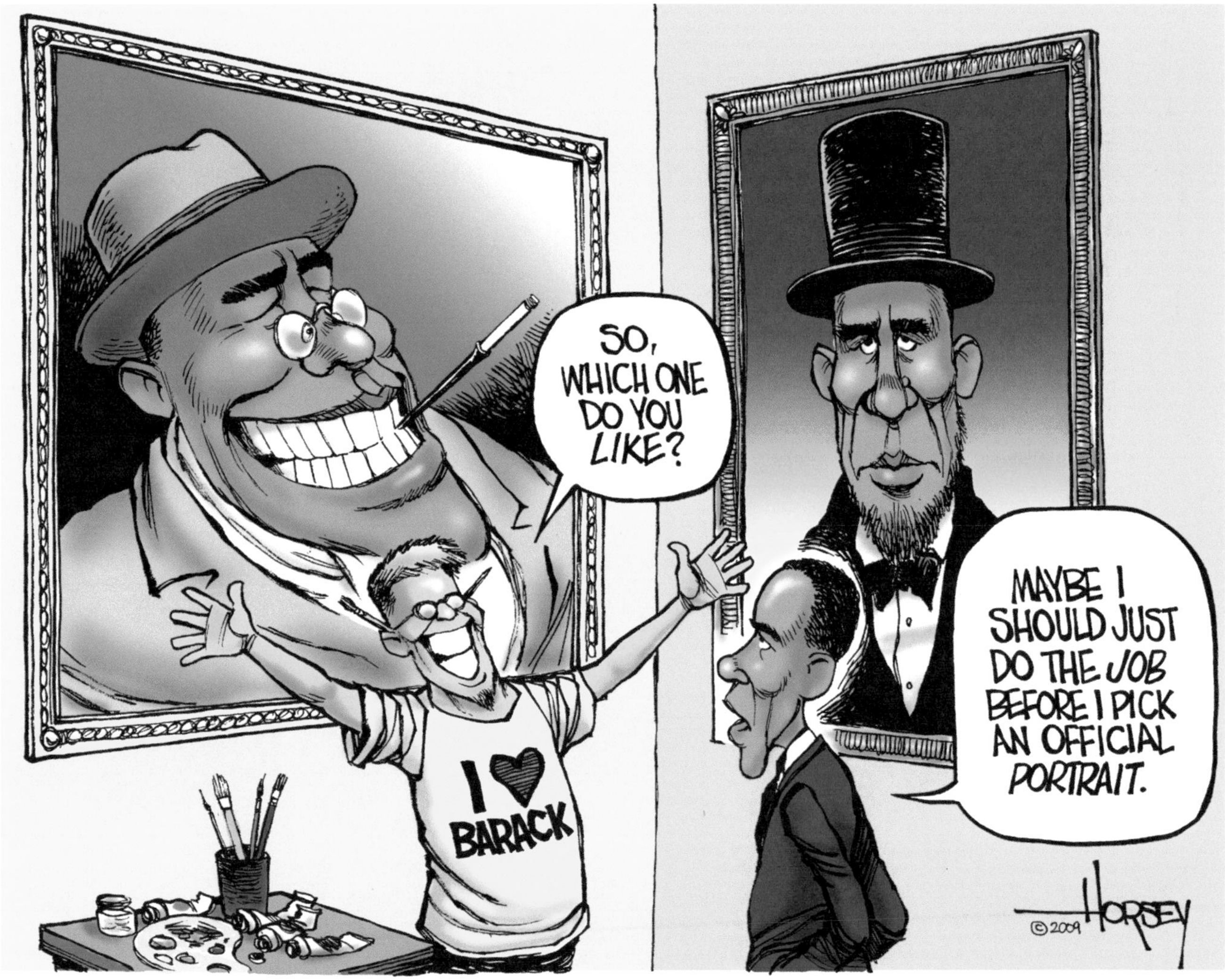
SO, WHICH ONE DO YOU LIKE?
MAYBE I SHOULD JUST DO THE JOB BEFORE I PICK AN OFFICIAL PORTRAIT.
I ♥ BARACK
©2009 HORSEY

· HIGH EXPECTATIONS ·

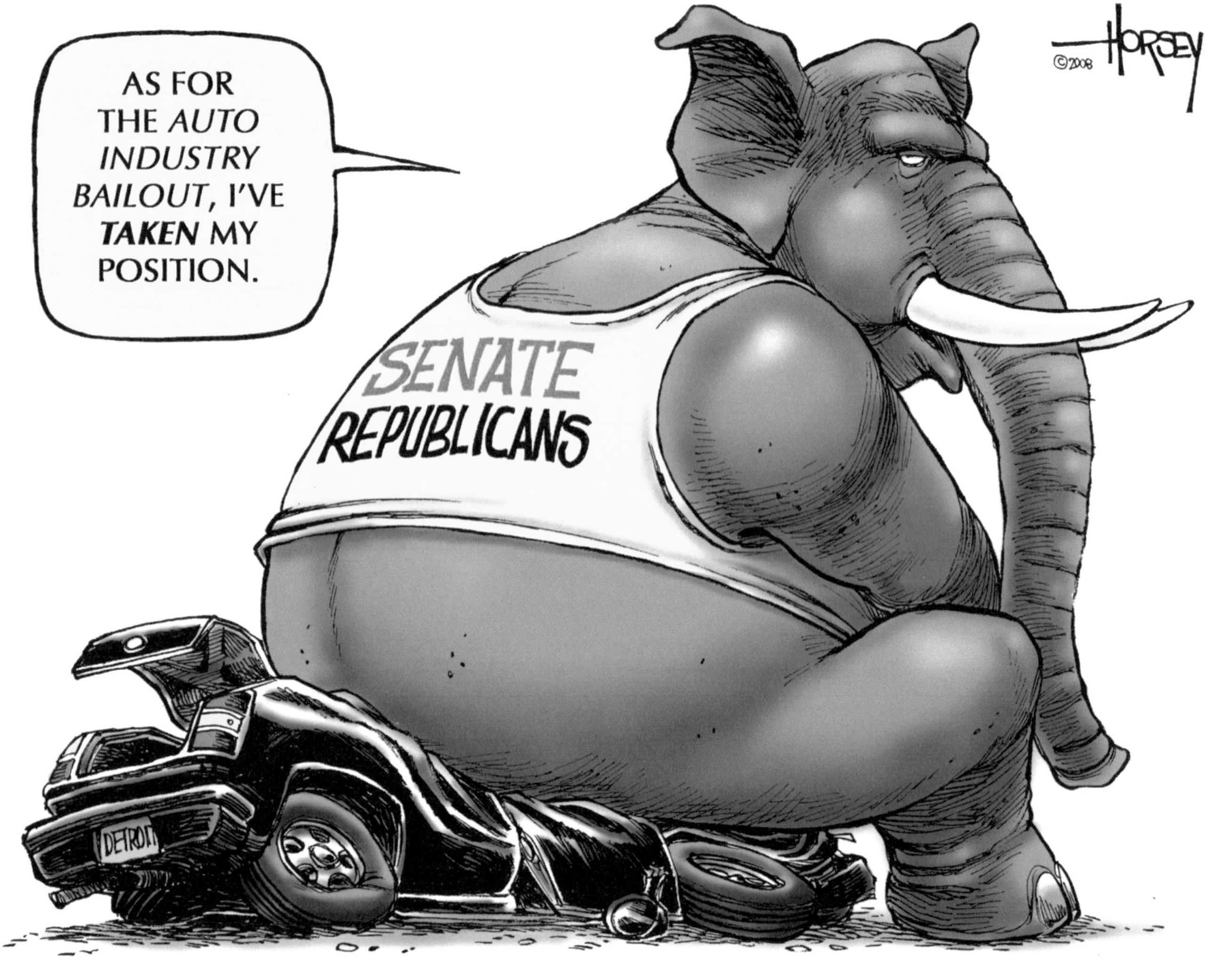
AS FOR THE *AUTO INDUSTRY BAILOUT*, I'VE ***TAKEN*** MY POSITION.
SENATE
REPUBLICANS
HORSEY
©2008

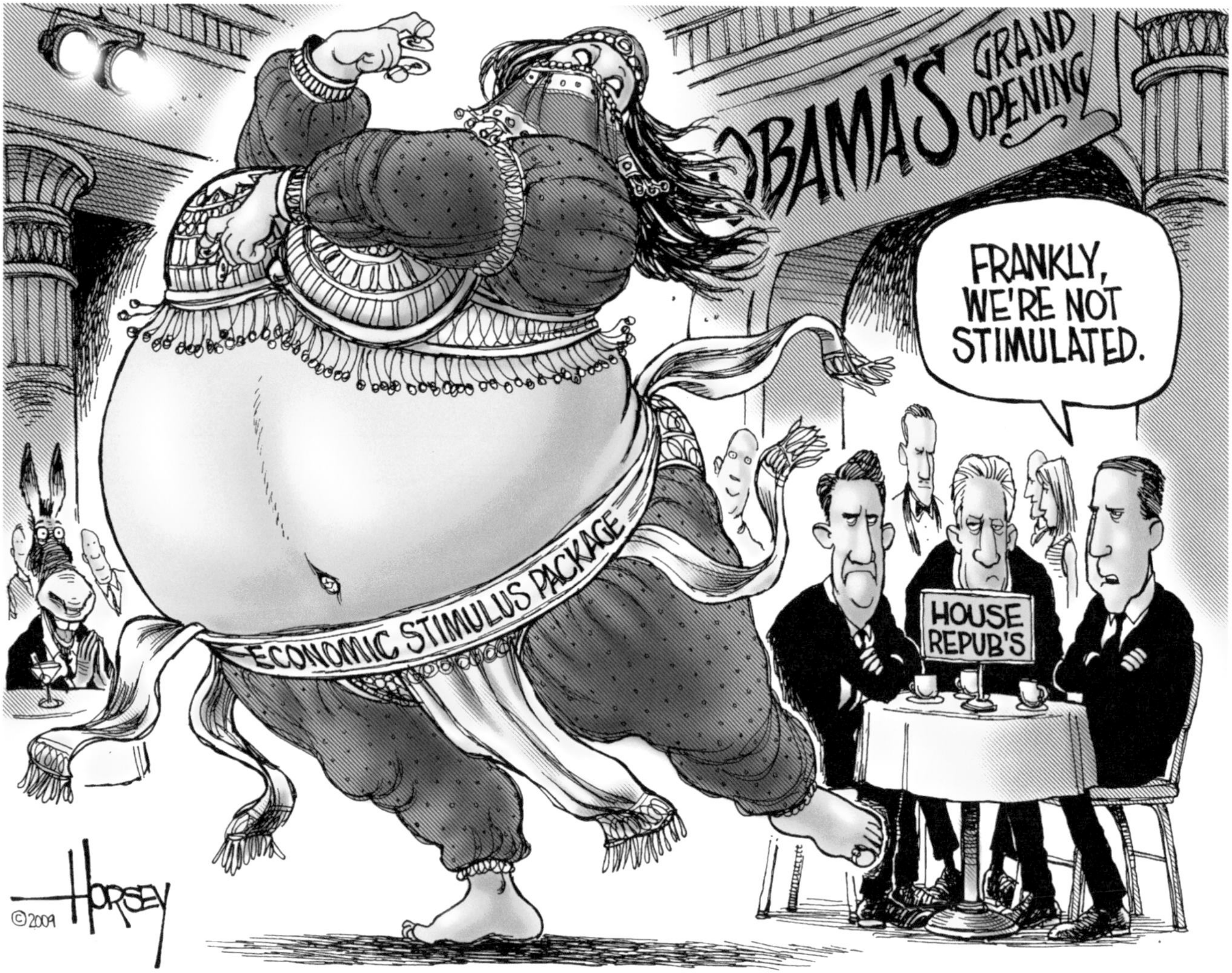
OBAMA'S GRAND OPENING
FRANKLY, WE'RE NOT STIMULATED.
ECONOMIC STIMULUS PACKAGE
HOUSE REPUB'S
©2009 HORSEY

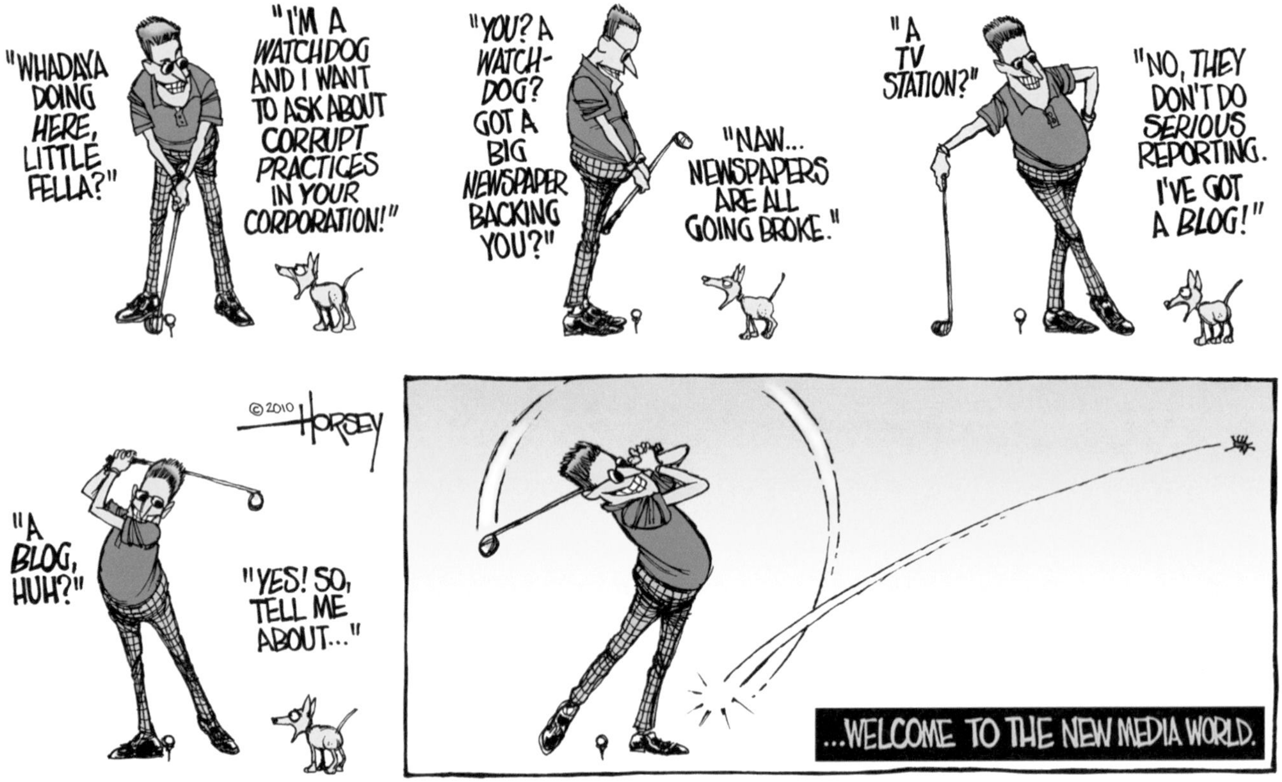
"WHADAYA DOING HERE, LITTLE FELLA?"
"I'M A WATCHDOG AND I WANT TO ASK ABOUT CORRUPT PRACTICES IN YOUR CORPORATION!"
"YOU? A WATCH-DOG? GOT A BIG NEWSPAPER BACKING YOU?"
"NAW... NEWSPAPERS ARE ALL GOING BROKE."
"A TV STATION?"
"NO, THEY DON'T DO SERIOUS REPORTING. I'VE GOT A BLOG!"
©2010 HORSEY
"A BLOG, HUH?"
"YES! SO, TELL ME ABOUT..."
...WELCOME TO THE NEW MEDIA WORLD.

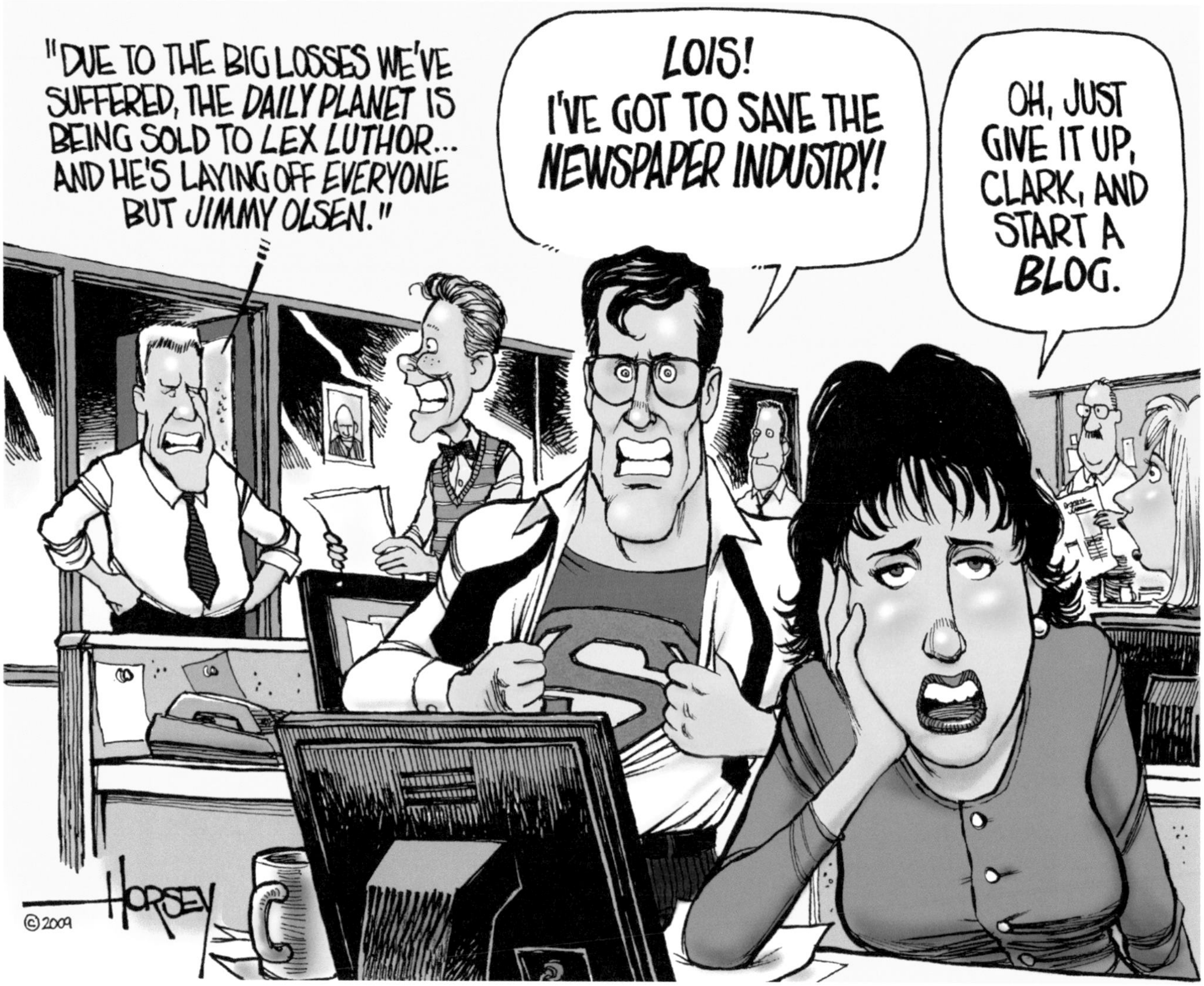
"DUE TO THE BIG LOSSES WE'VE SUFFERED, THE DAILY PLANET IS BEING SOLD TO LEX LUTHOR... AND HE'S LAYING OFF EVERYONE BUT JIMMY OLSEN."
LOIS! I'VE GOT TO SAVE THE NEWSPAPER INDUSTRY!
OH, JUST GIVE IT UP, CLARK, AND START A BLOG.
HORSEY
©2009

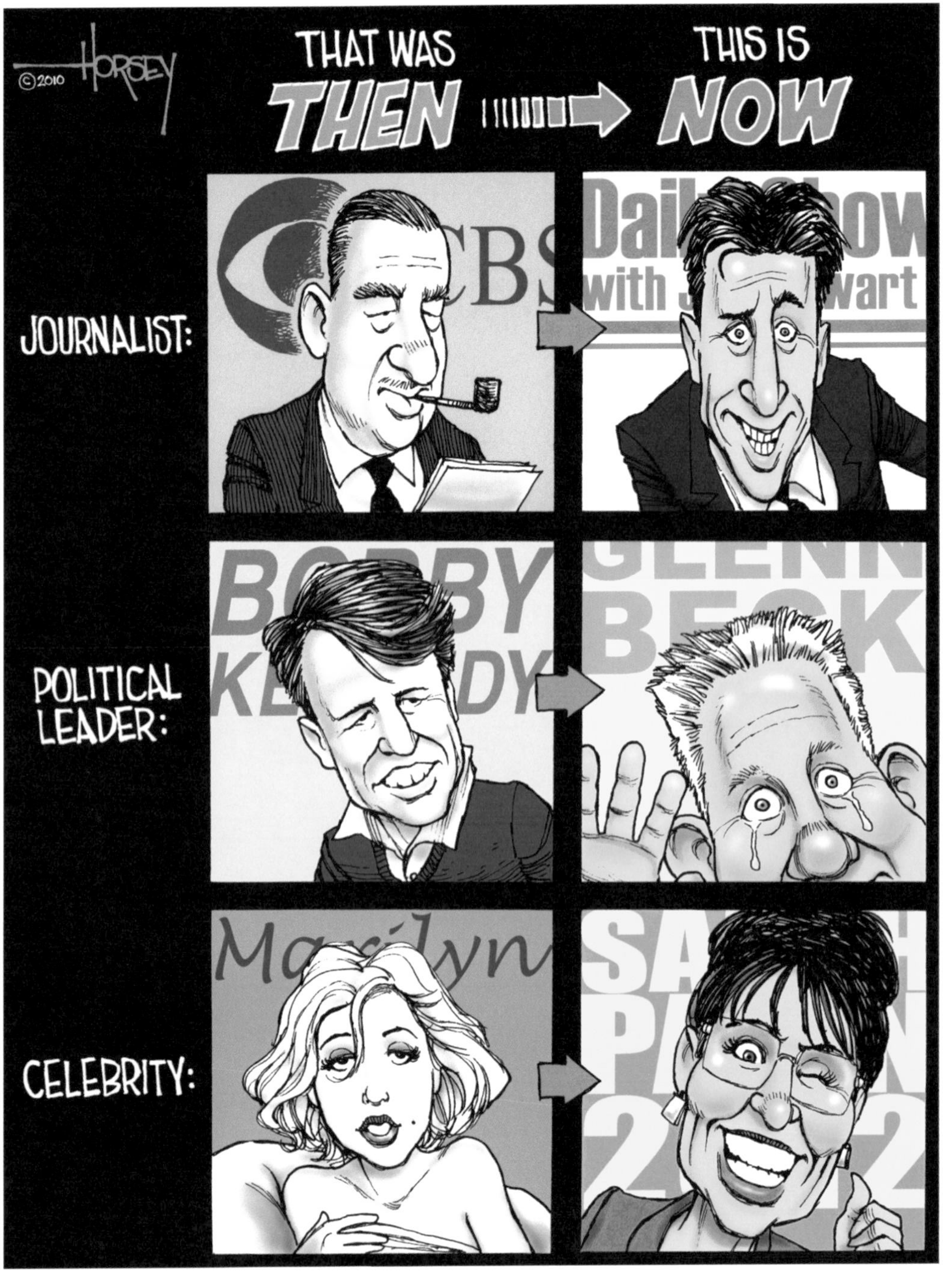
HORSEY
©2010
THAT WAS THEN
THIS IS NOW
JOURNALIST:
CBS
POLITICAL LEADER:
CELEBRITY:

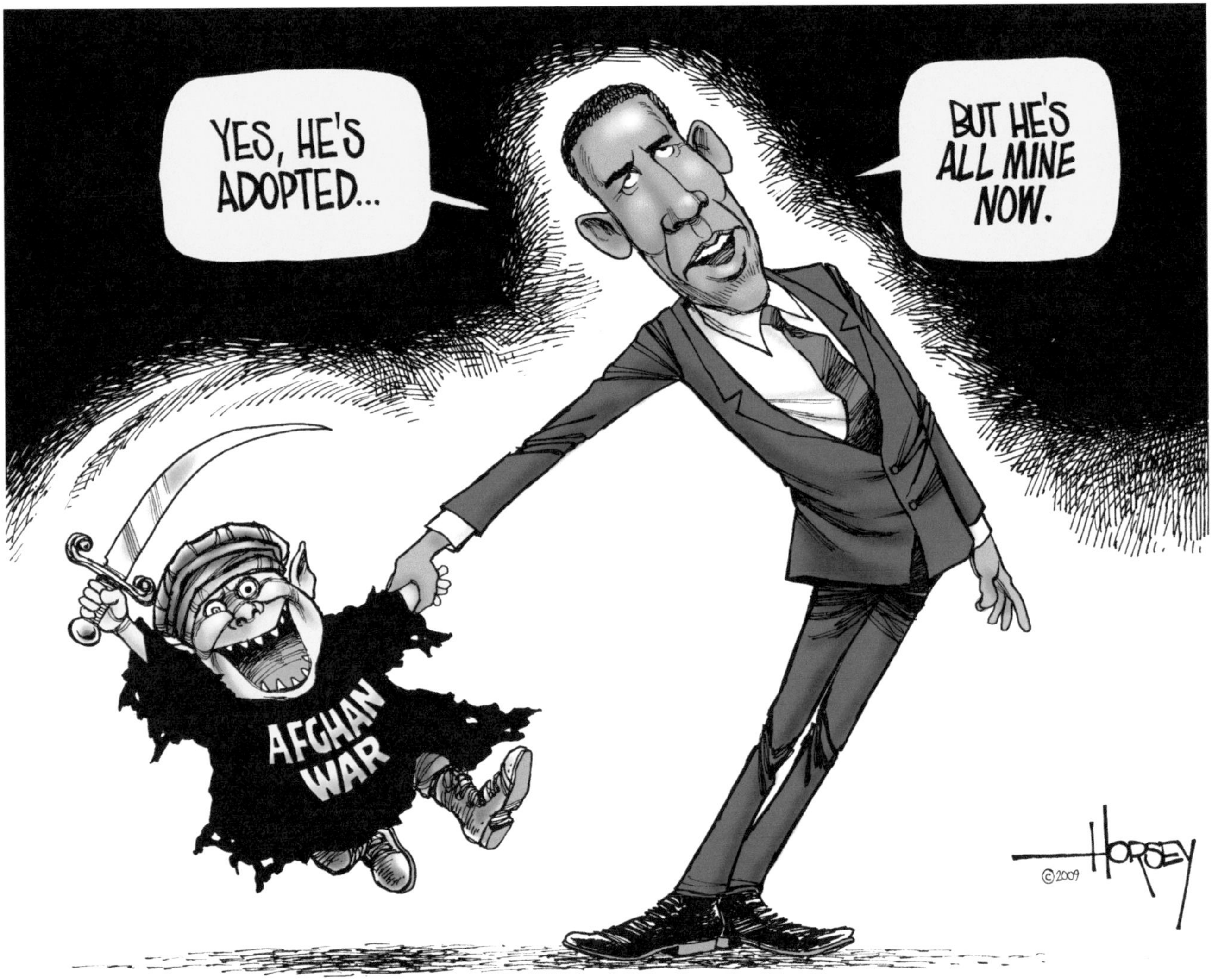
YES, HE'S ADOPTED...
BUT HE'S ALL MINE NOW.
AFGHAN WAR
©2009 HORSEY

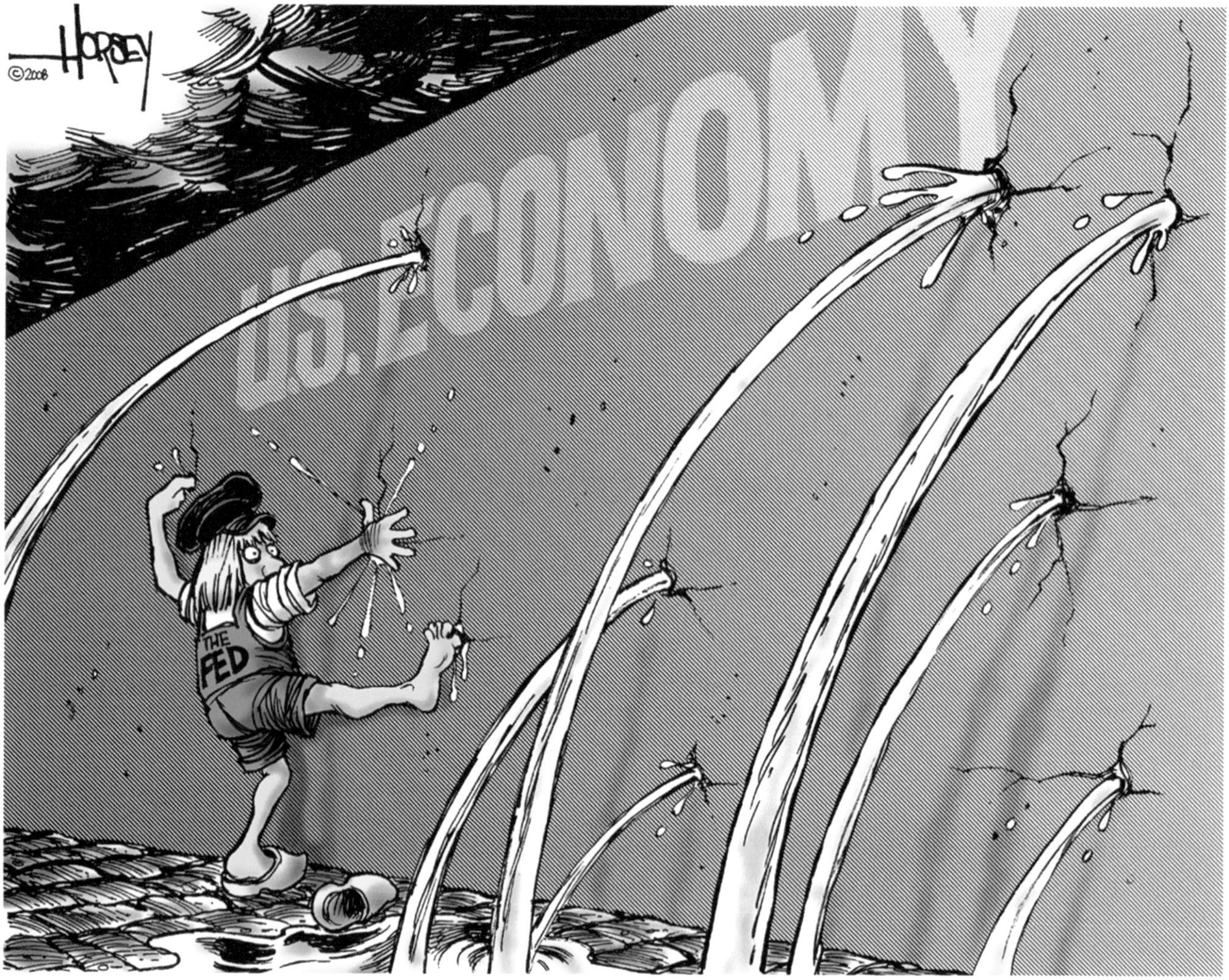
HORSEY
©2008
U.S. ECONOMY
THE FED

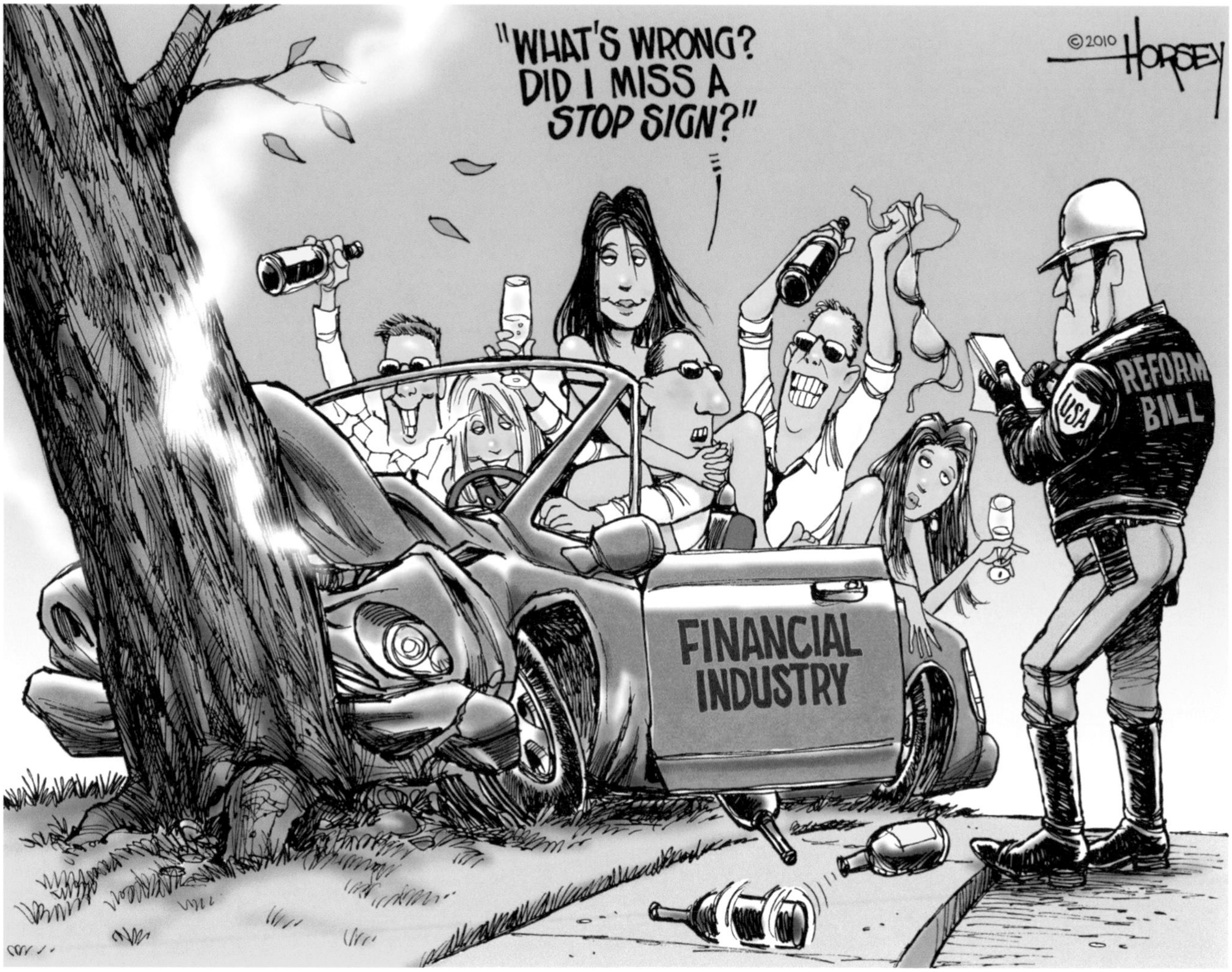
"WHAT'S WRONG? DID I MISS A STOP SIGN?"
©2010 HORSEY
REFORM BILL
USA
FINANCIAL INDUSTRY

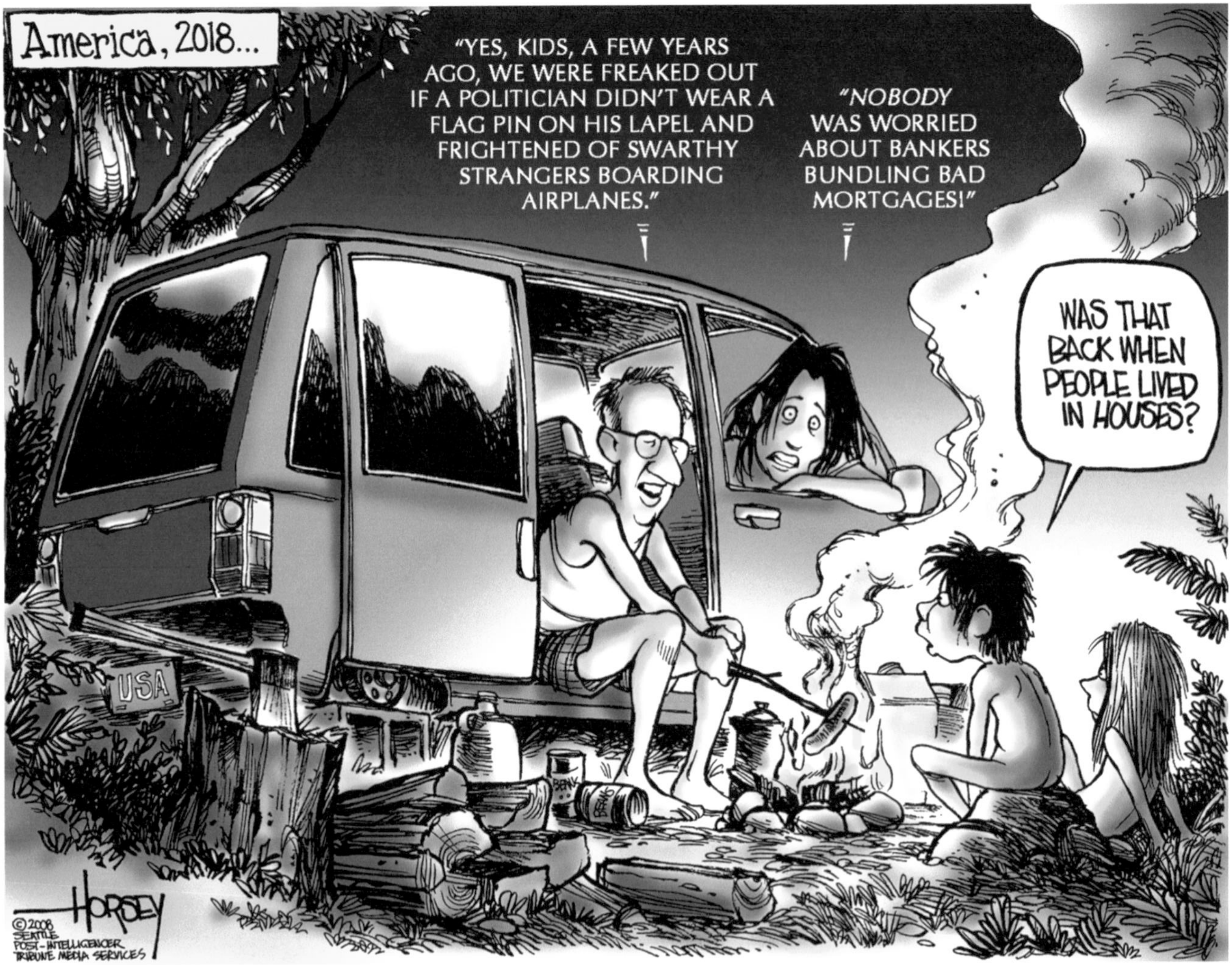
America, 2018...
"YES, KIDS, A FEW YEARS AGO, WE WERE FREAKED OUT IF A POLITICIAN DIDN'T WEAR A FLAG PIN ON HIS LAPEL AND FRIGHTENED OF SWARTHY STRANGERS BOARDING AIRPLANES."
"NOBODY WAS WORRIED ABOUT BANKERS BUNDLING BAD MORTGAGES!"
WAS THAT BACK WHEN PEOPLE LIVED IN HOUSES?
USA
HORSEY
©2008 SEATTLE POST-INTELLIGENCER TRIBUNE MEDIA SERVICES

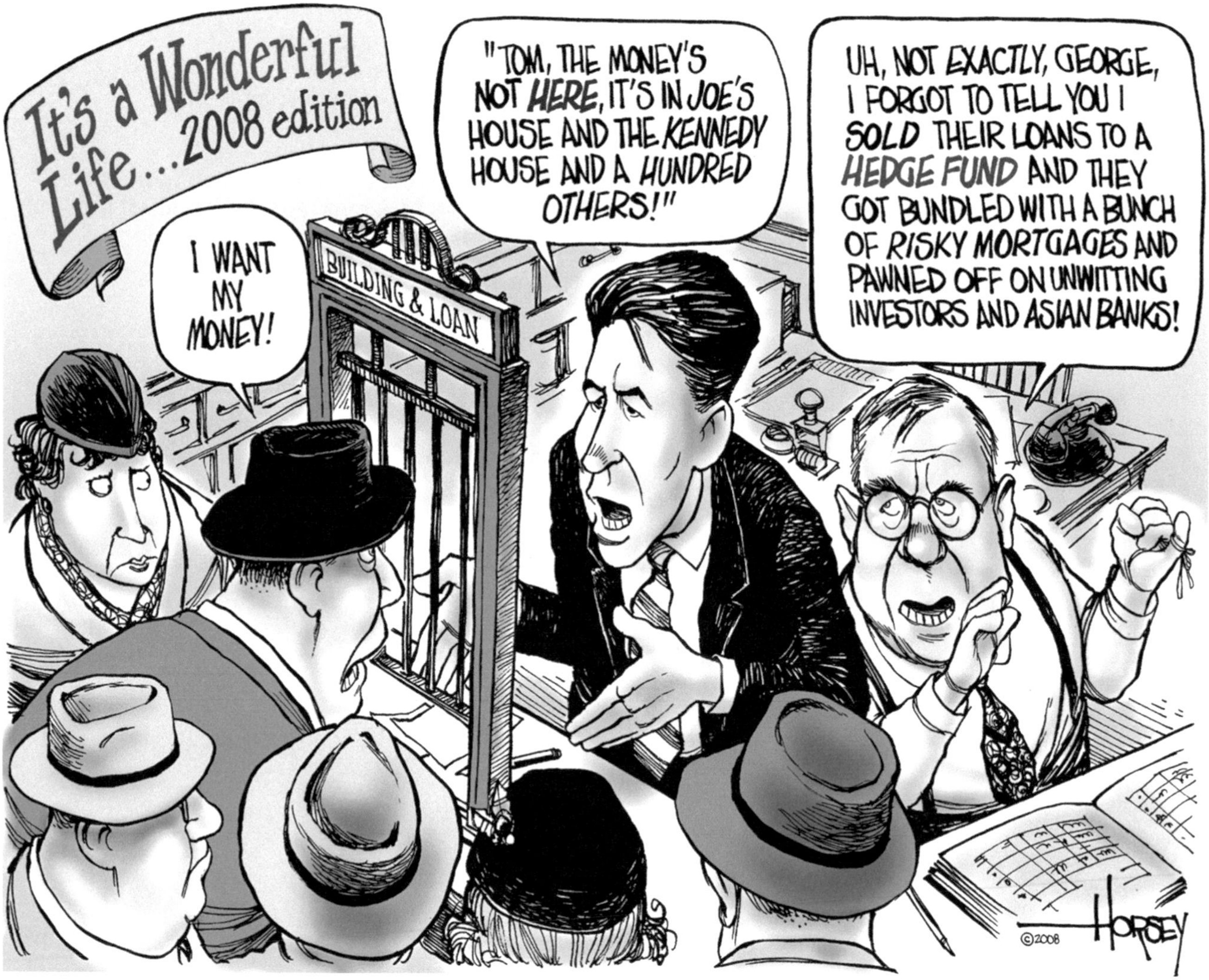
It's a Wonderful Life...2008 edition
I WANT MY MONEY!
BUILDING & LOAN
"TOM, THE MONEY'S NOT HERE, IT'S IN JOE'S HOUSE AND THE KENNEDY HOUSE AND A HUNDRED OTHERS!"
UH, NOT EXACTLY, GEORGE, I FORGOT TO TELL YOU I SOLD THEIR LOANS TO A HEDGE FUND AND THEY GOT BUNDLED WITH A BUNCH OF RISKY MORTGAGES AND PAWNED OFF ON UNWITTING INVESTORS AND ASIAN BANKS!
©2008
HORSEY

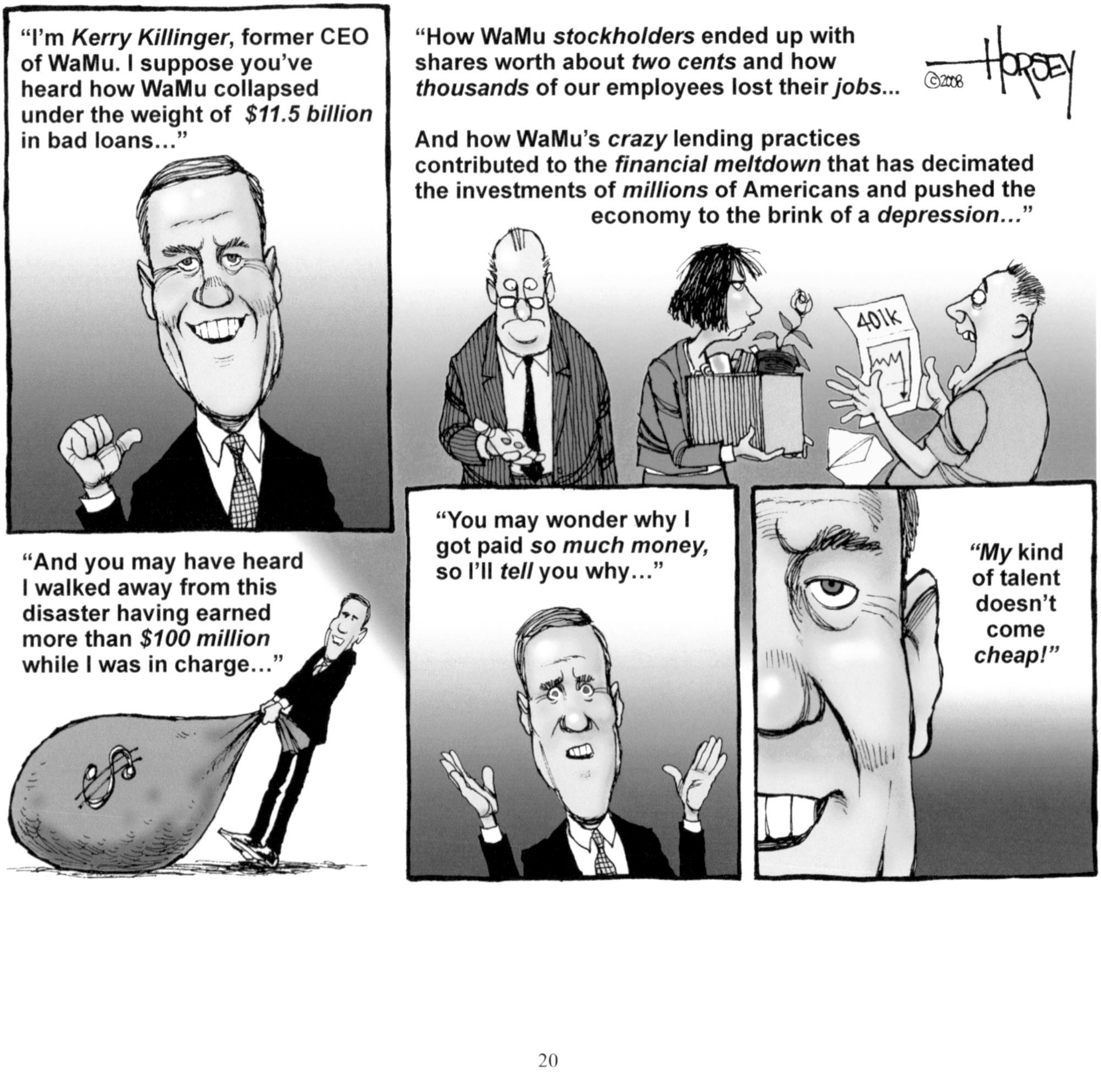
"I'm *Kerry Killinger*, former CEO of WaMu. I suppose you've heard how WaMu collapsed under the weight of *$11.5 billion* in bad loans..."
"How WaMu *stockholders* ended up with shares worth about *two cents* and how *thousands* of our employees lost their *jobs*...
©2008 HORSEY
And how WaMu's *crazy* lending practices contributed to the *financial meltdown* that has decimated the investments of *millions* of Americans and pushed the economy to the brink of a *depression...*"
401k
"And you may have heard I walked away from this disaster having earned more than *$100 million* while I was in charge..."
"You may wonder why I got paid *so much money,* so I'll *tell* you why..."
"*My* kind of talent doesn't come *cheap!*"

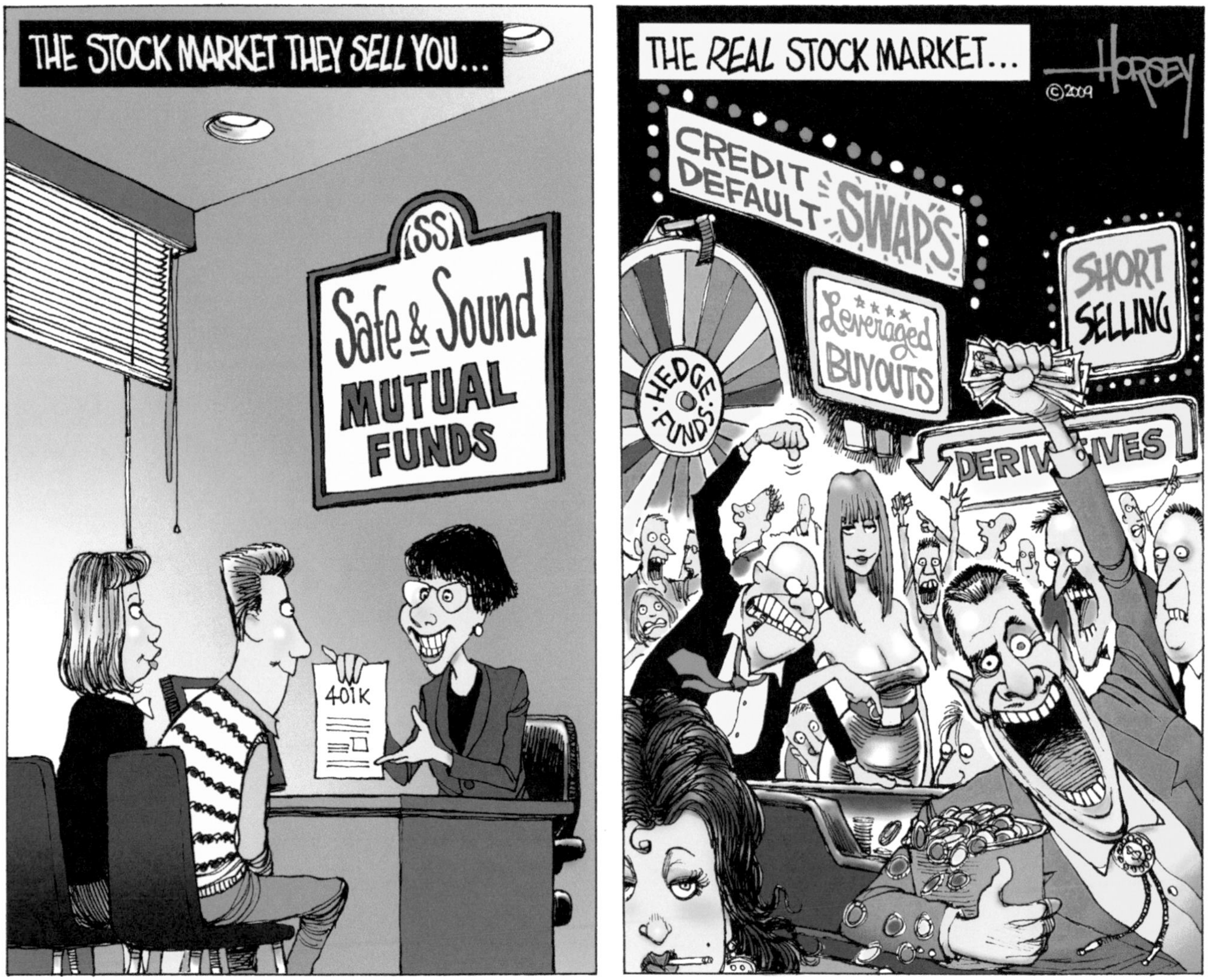
THE STOCK MARKET THEY SELL YOU...
SS
Safe & Sound
MUTUAL FUNDS
401K
THE REAL STOCK MARKET...
HORSEY
©2009
CREDIT DEFAULT SWAPS
SHORT SELLING
Leveraged BUYOUTS
HEDGE FUNDS
DERIVATIVES

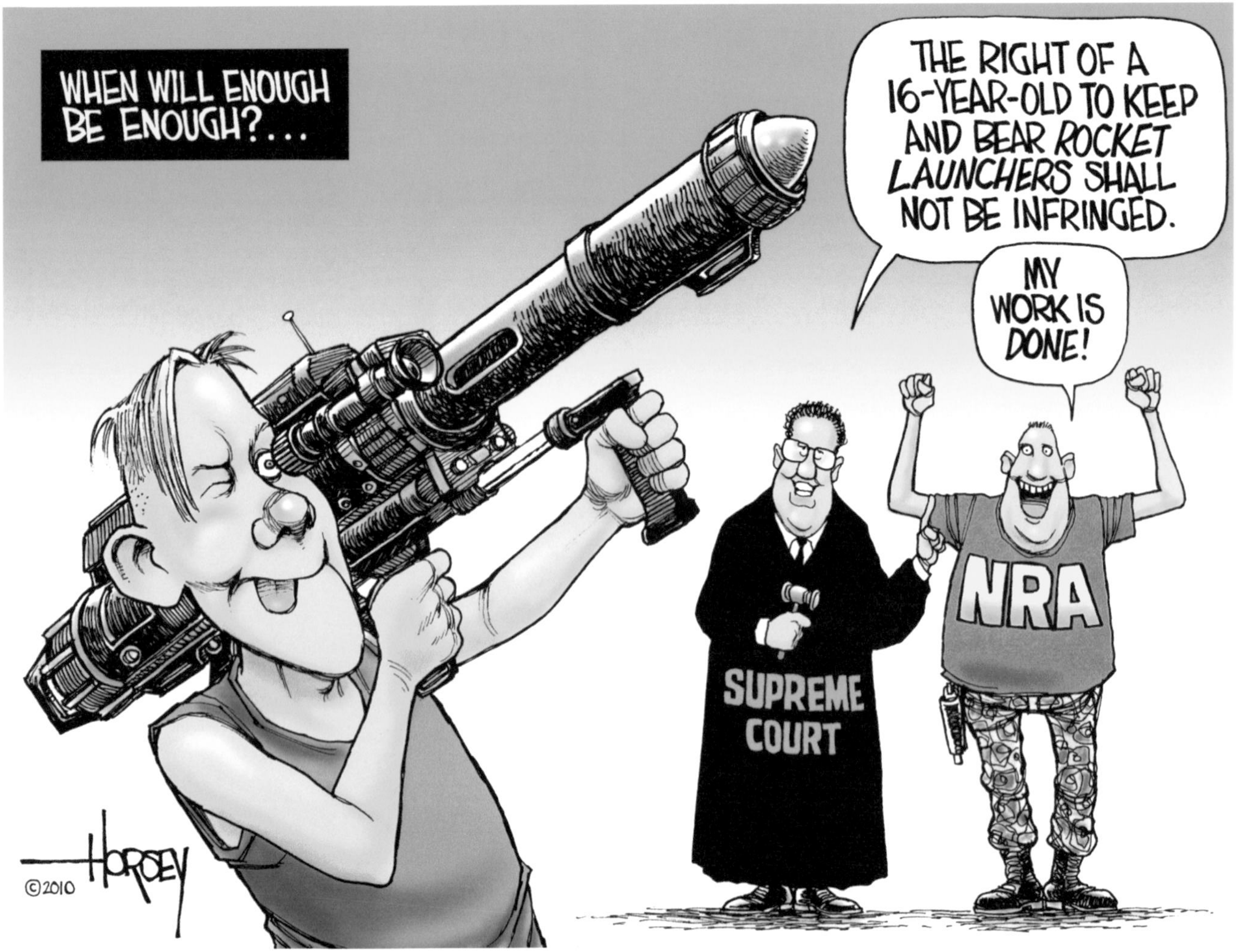
WHEN WILL ENOUGH BE ENOUGH?...
THE RIGHT OF A 16-YEAR-OLD TO KEEP AND BEAR *ROCKET LAUNCHERS* SHALL NOT BE INFRINGED.
MY WORK IS *DONE*!
SUPREME COURT
NRA
©2010 HORSEY

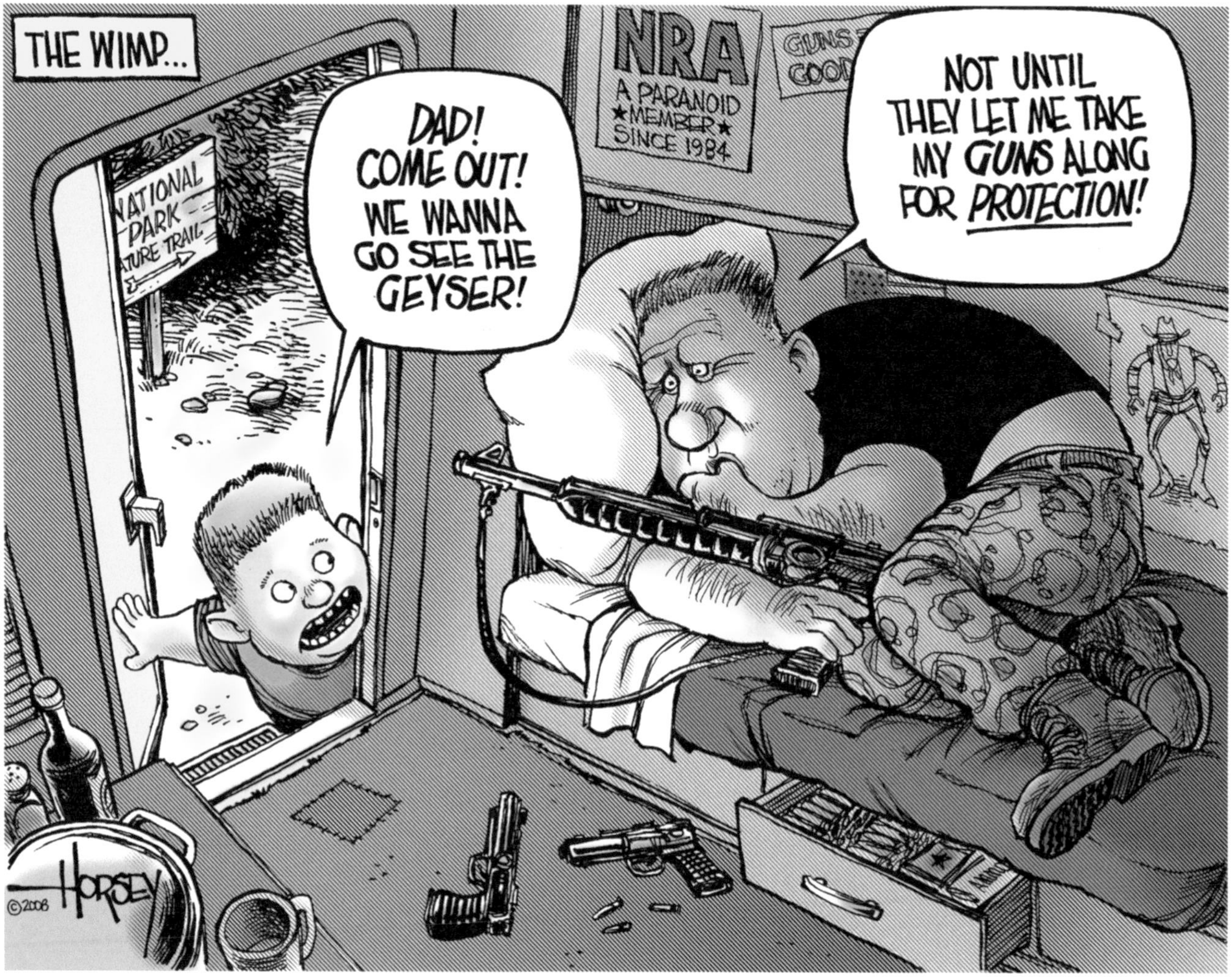
THE WIMP...
NATIONAL PARK NATURE TRAIL
DAD! COME OUT! WE WANNA GO SEE THE GEYSER!
NRA A PARANOID ★MEMBER★ SINCE 1984
NOT UNTIL THEY LET ME TAKE MY GUNS ALONG FOR PROTECTION!
HORSEY ©2008

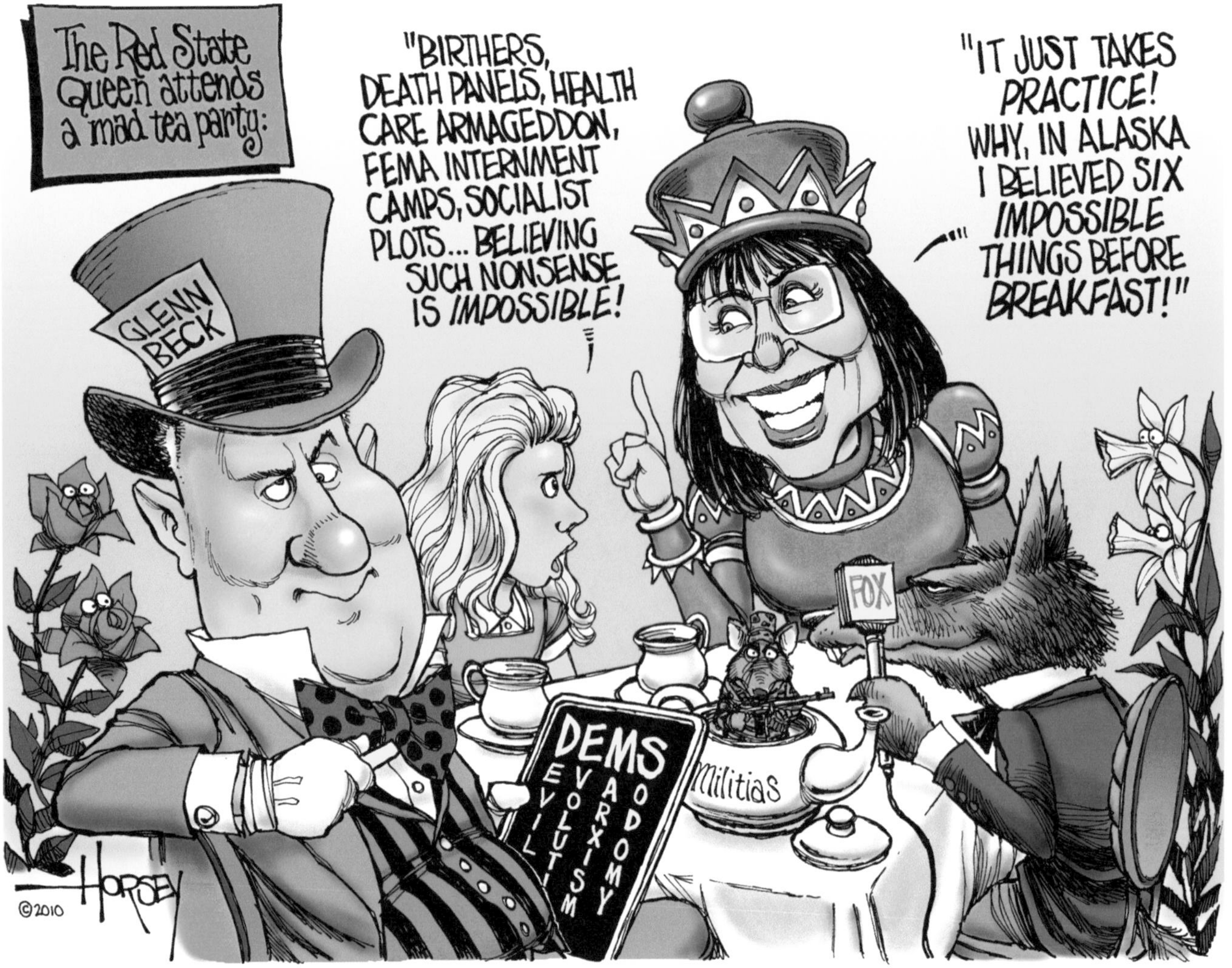
The Red State Queen attends a mad tea party:
"BIRTHERS, DEATH PANELS, HEALTH CARE ARMAGEDDON, FEMA INTERNMENT CAMPS, SOCIALIST PLOTS... BELIEVING SUCH NONSENSE IS IMPOSSIBLE!"
"IT JUST TAKES PRACTICE! WHY, IN ALASKA I BELIEVED SIX IMPOSSIBLE THINGS BEFORE BREAKFAST!"
GLENN BECK
DEMS
EVIL
VOLUTISM
MARXISM
SODOMY
FOX
Militias
HORSEY
©2010

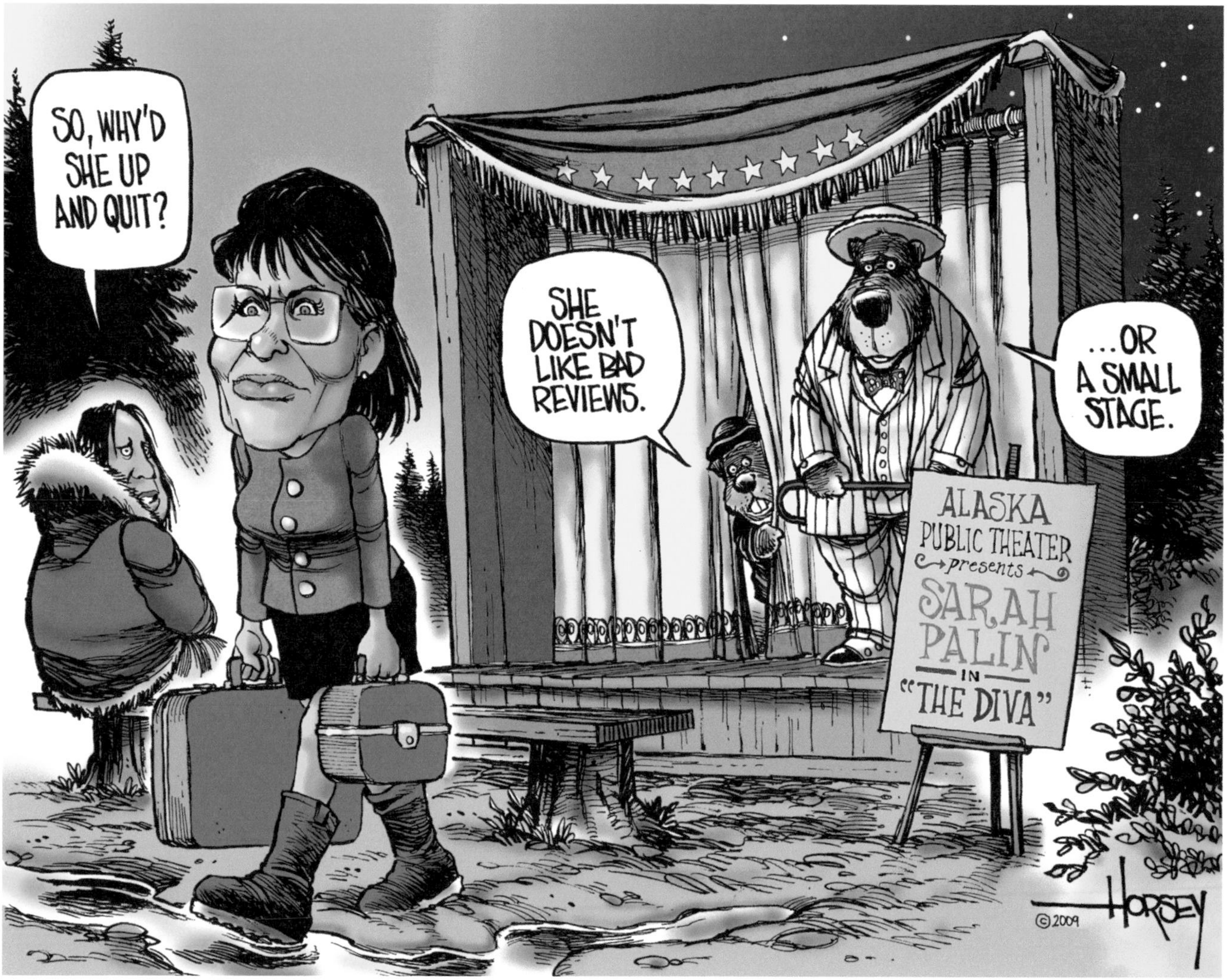
SO, WHY'D SHE UP AND QUIT?
SHE DOESN'T LIKE BAD REVIEWS.
...OR A SMALL STAGE.
ALASKA PUBLIC THEATER presents SARAH PALIN IN "THE DIVA"
©2009 HORSEY

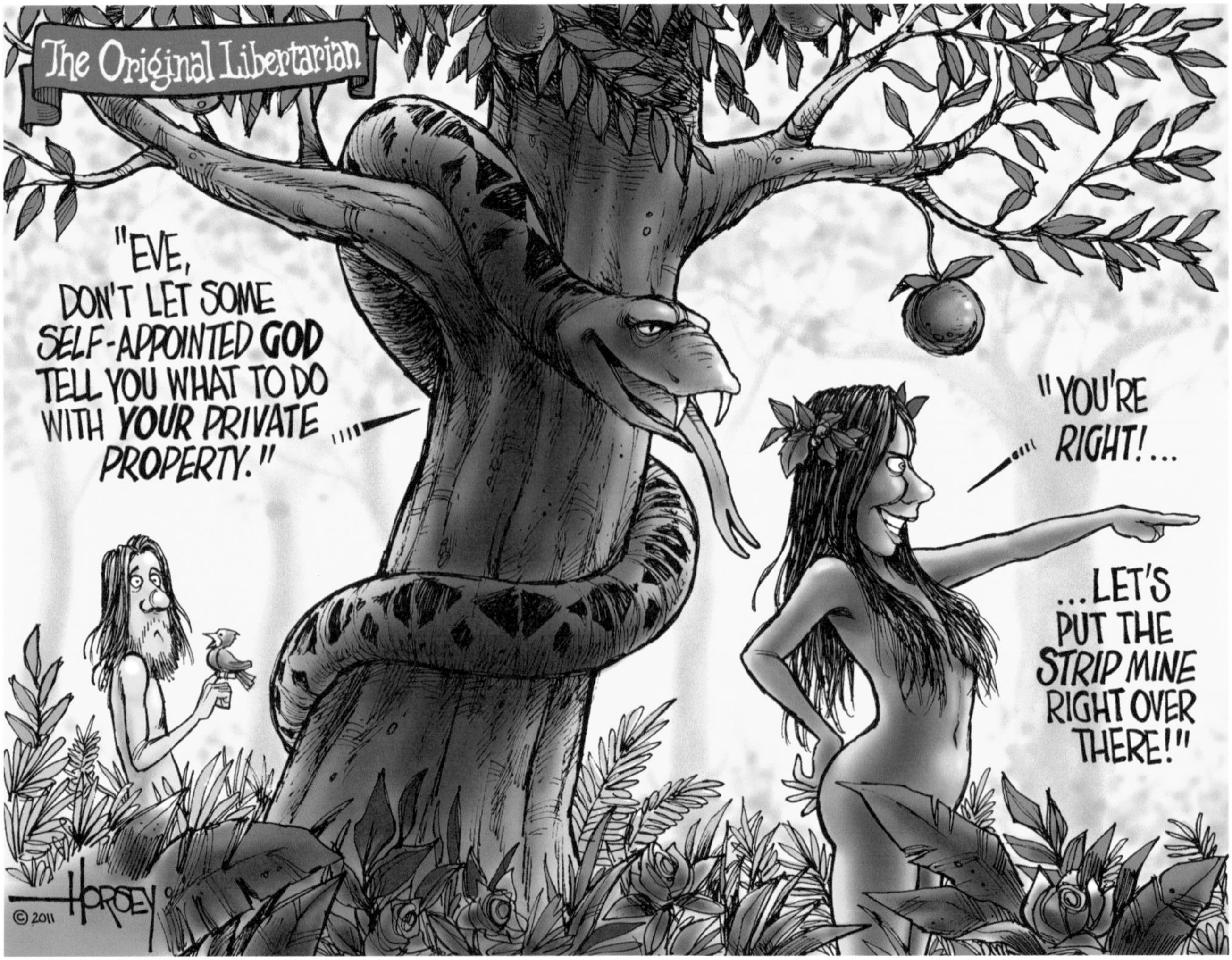
The Original Libertarian
"EVE, DON'T LET SOME SELF-APPOINTED GOD TELL YOU WHAT TO DO WITH YOUR PRIVATE PROPERTY."
"YOU'RE RIGHT!...
...LET'S PUT THE STRIP MINE RIGHT OVER THERE!"
HORSEY
© 2011

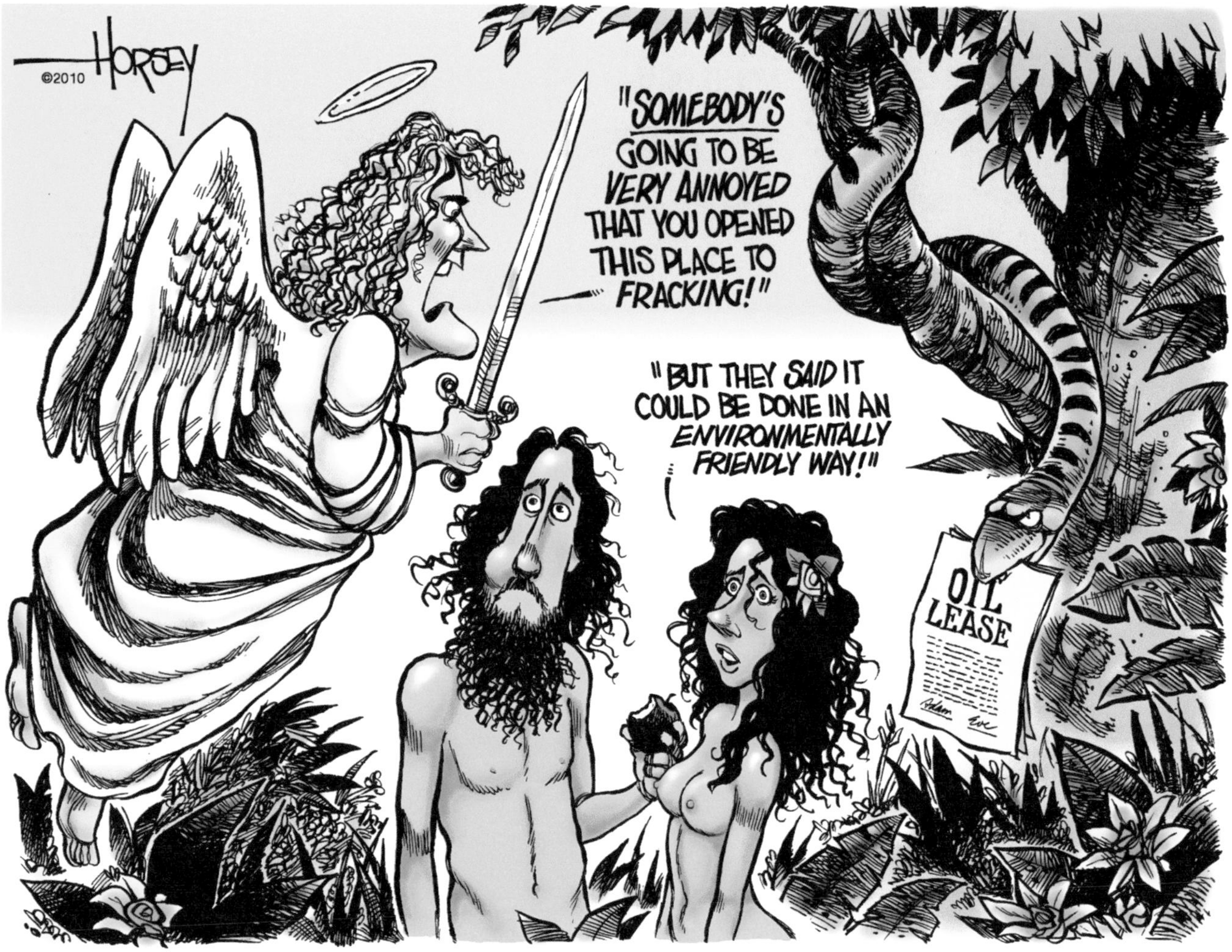
HORSEY
©2010
"SOMEBODY'S GOING TO BE VERY ANNOYED THAT YOU OPENED THIS PLACE TO FRACKING!"
"BUT THEY SAID IT COULD BE DONE IN AN ENVIRONMENTALLY FRIENDLY WAY!"
OIL LEASE

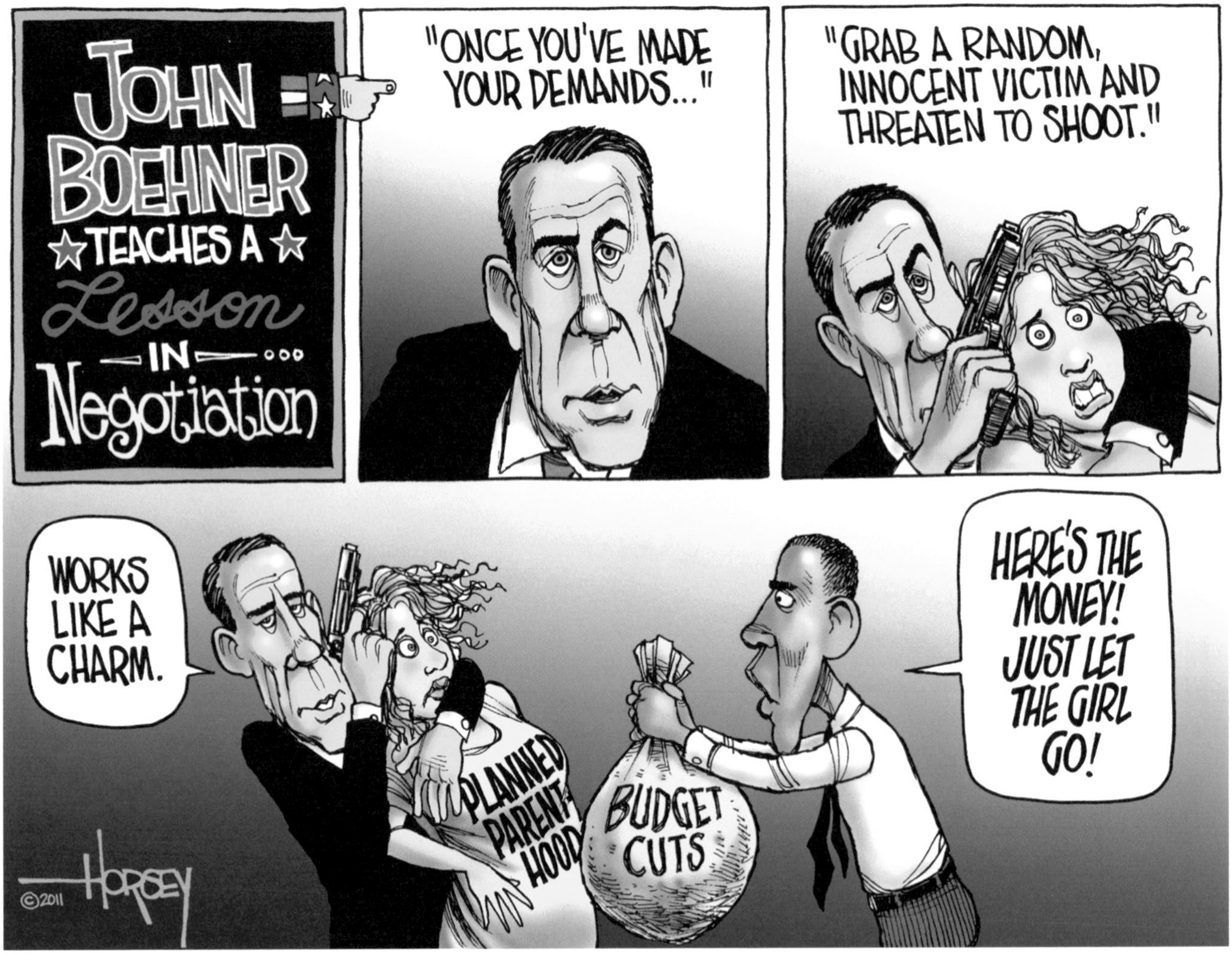
JOHN BOEHNER
TEACHES A
Lesson
IN
Negotiation
"ONCE YOU'VE MADE YOUR DEMANDS..."
"GRAB A RANDOM, INNOCENT VICTIM AND THREATEN TO SHOOT."
WORKS LIKE A CHARM.
HERE'S THE MONEY! JUST LET THE GIRL GO!
PLANNED PARENT-HOOD
BUDGET CUTS
HORSEY
©2011

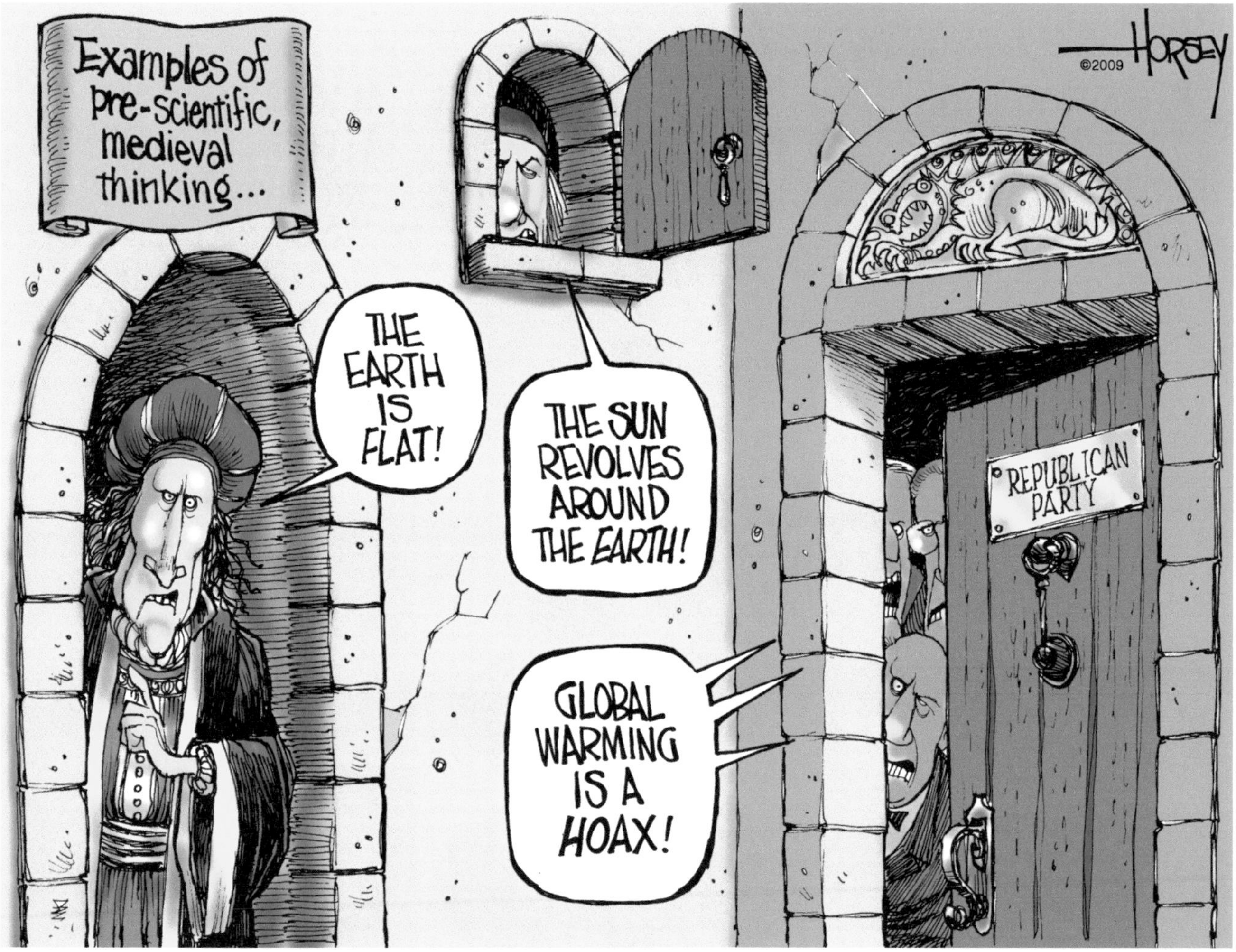
Examples of pre-scientific, medieval thinking...
THE EARTH IS FLAT!
THE SUN REVOLVES AROUND THE EARTH!
GLOBAL WARMING IS A HOAX!
REPUBLICAN PARTY
©2009
HORSEY

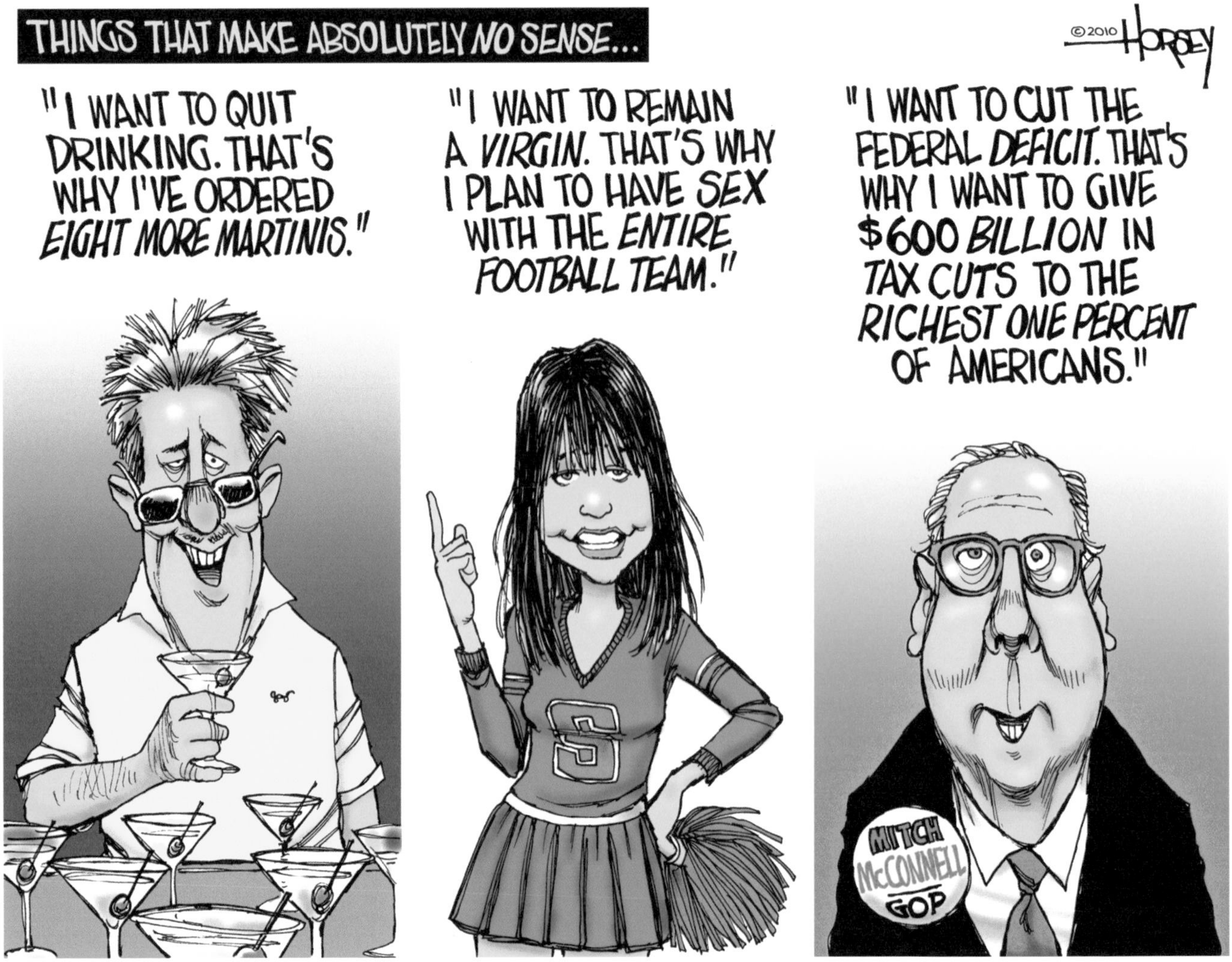
THINGS THAT MAKE ABSOLUTELY NO SENSE...
©2010 HORSEY
"I WANT TO QUIT DRINKING. THAT'S WHY I'VE ORDERED EIGHT MORE MARTINIS."
"I WANT TO REMAIN A VIRGIN. THAT'S WHY I PLAN TO HAVE SEX WITH THE ENTIRE FOOTBALL TEAM."
"I WANT TO CUT THE FEDERAL DEFICIT. THAT'S WHY I WANT TO GIVE $600 BILLION IN TAX CUTS TO THE RICHEST ONE PERCENT OF AMERICANS."
S
MITCH McCONNELL GOP

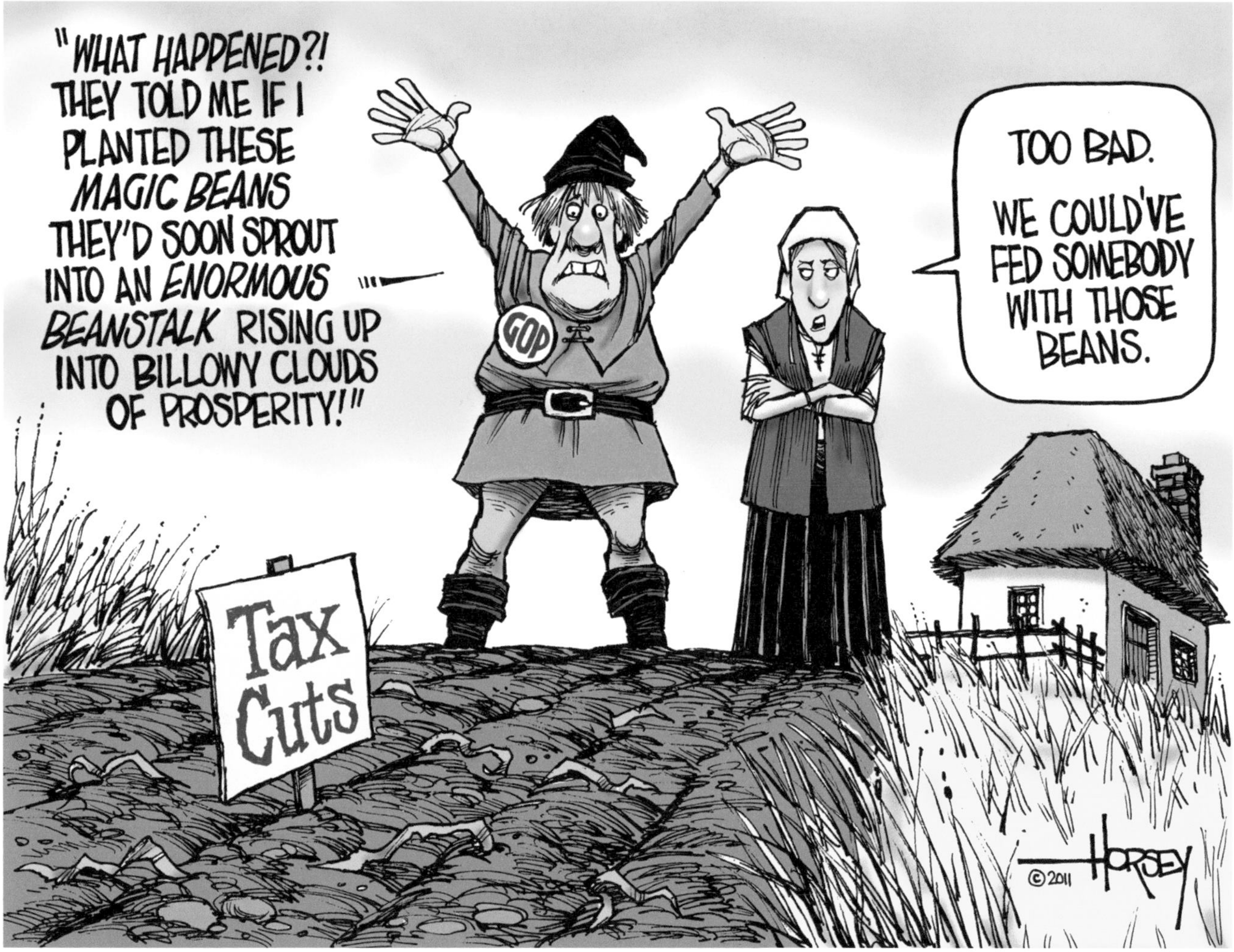
"WHAT HAPPENED?! THEY TOLD ME IF I PLANTED THESE MAGIC BEANS THEY'D SOON SPROUT INTO AN ENORMOUS BEANSTALK RISING UP INTO BILLOWY CLOUDS OF PROSPERITY!"
TOO BAD. WE COULD'VE FED SOMEBODY WITH THOSE BEANS.
GOP
Tax Cuts
©2011 HORSEY

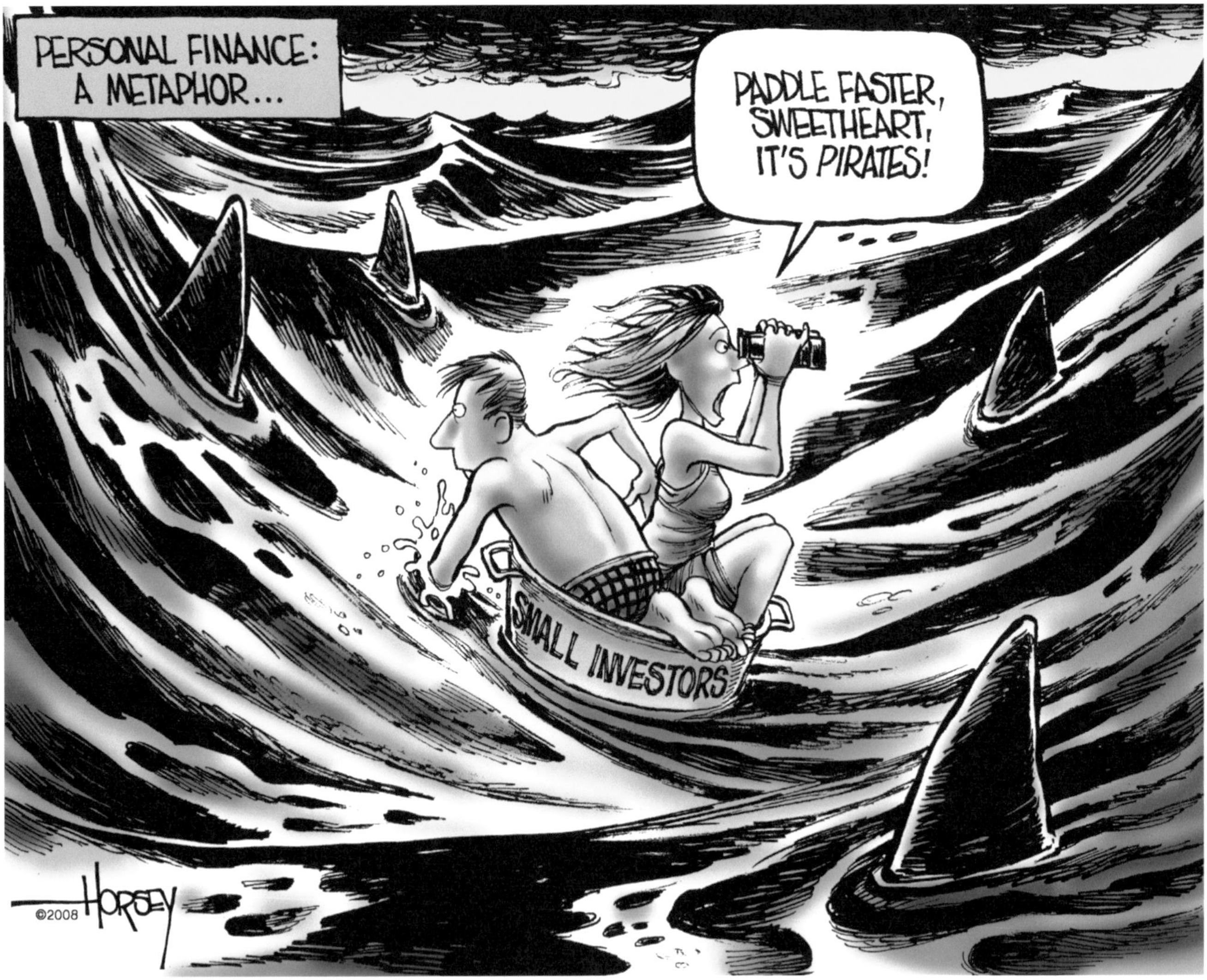
PERSONAL FINANCE: A METAPHOR...
PADDLE FASTER, SWEETHEART, IT'S PIRATES!
SMALL INVESTORS
©2008 HORSEY

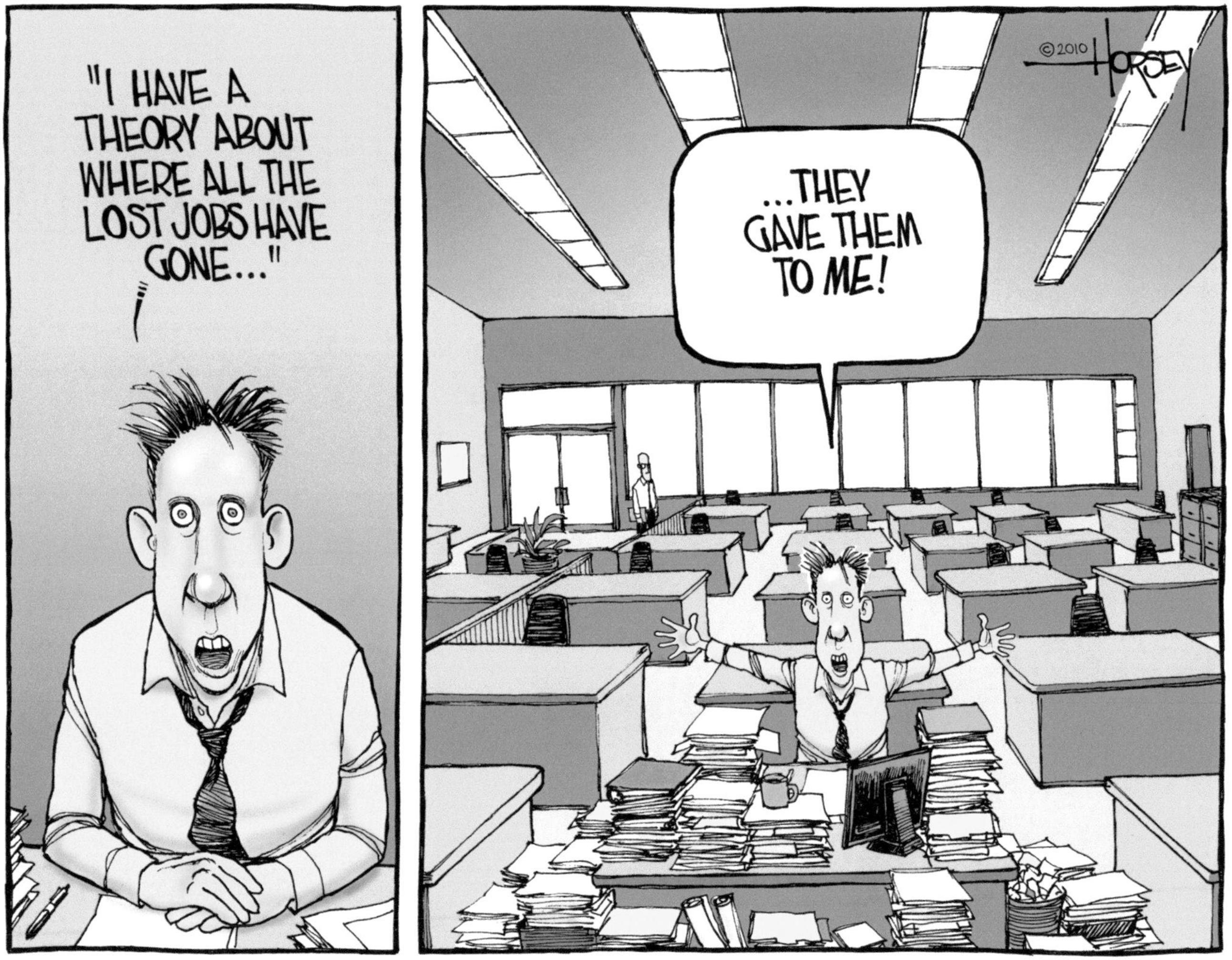
"I HAVE A THEORY ABOUT WHERE ALL THE LOST JOBS HAVE GONE..."
...THEY GAVE THEM TO ME!
©2010 HORSEY

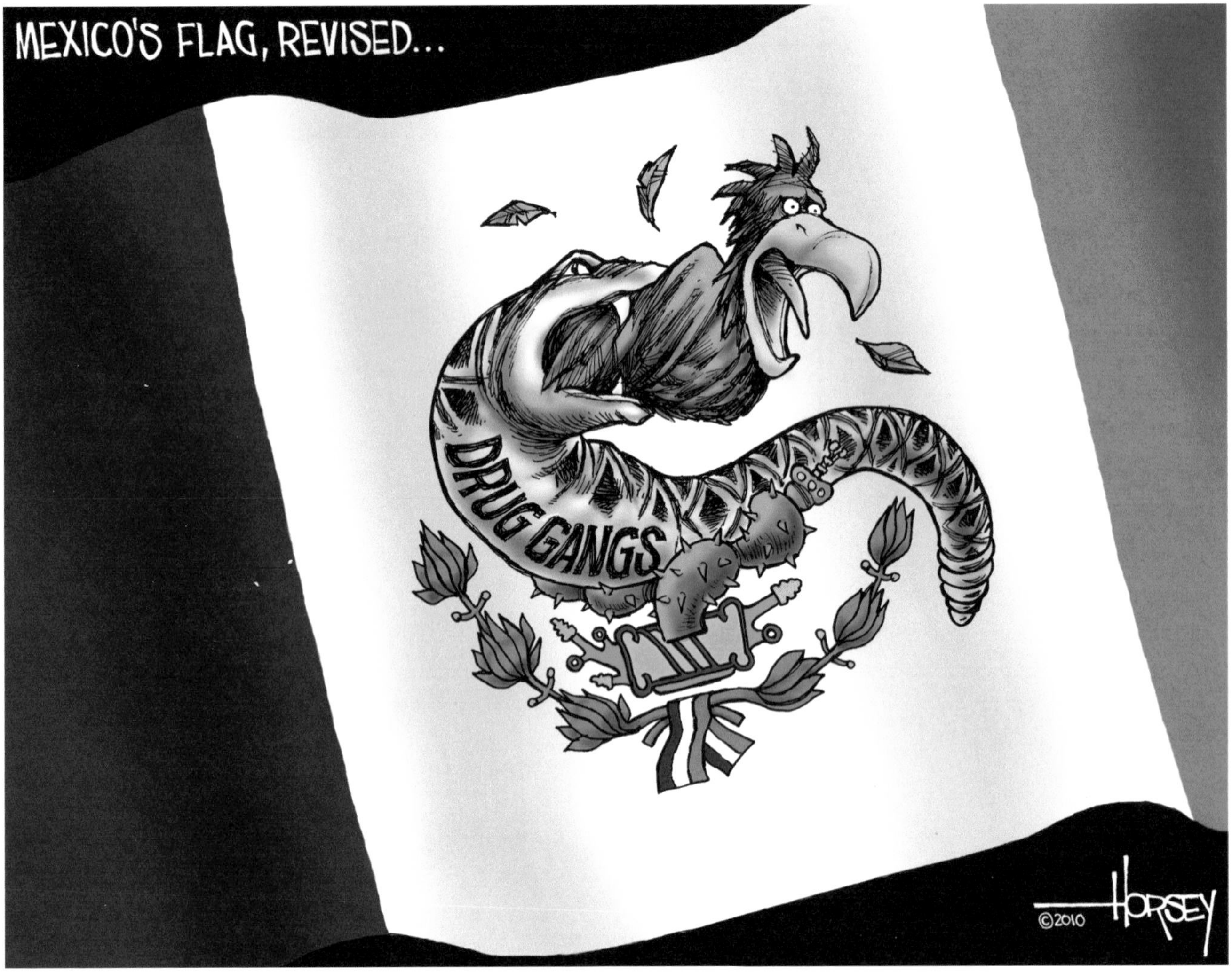
MEXICO'S FLAG, REVISED...
DRUG GANGS
©2010
HORSEY

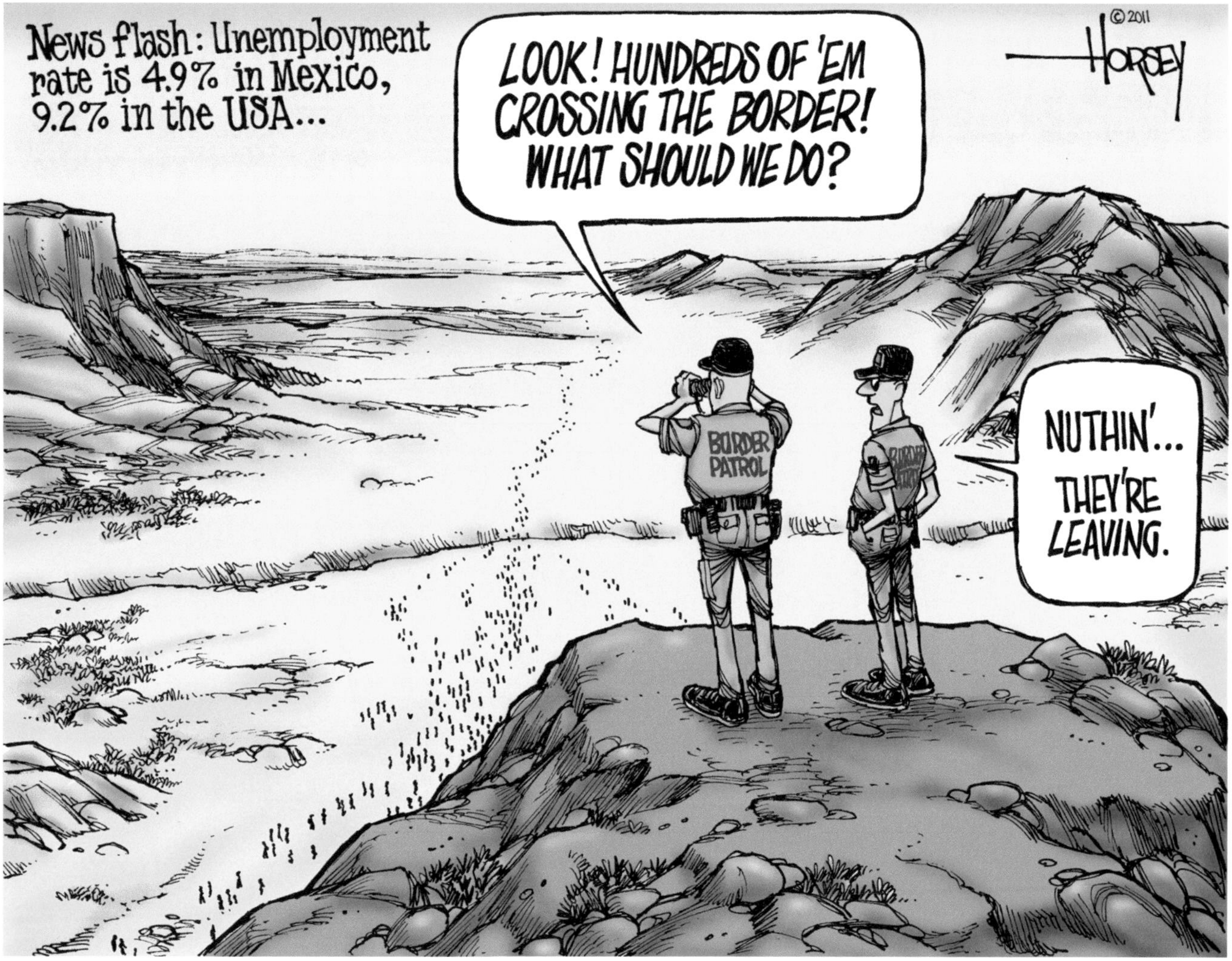
News flash: Unemployment rate is 4.9% in Mexico, 9.2% in the USA...
LOOK! HUNDREDS OF 'EM CROSSING THE BORDER! WHAT SHOULD WE DO?
NUTHIN'... THEY'RE LEAVING.
BORDER PATROL
©2011 HORSEY

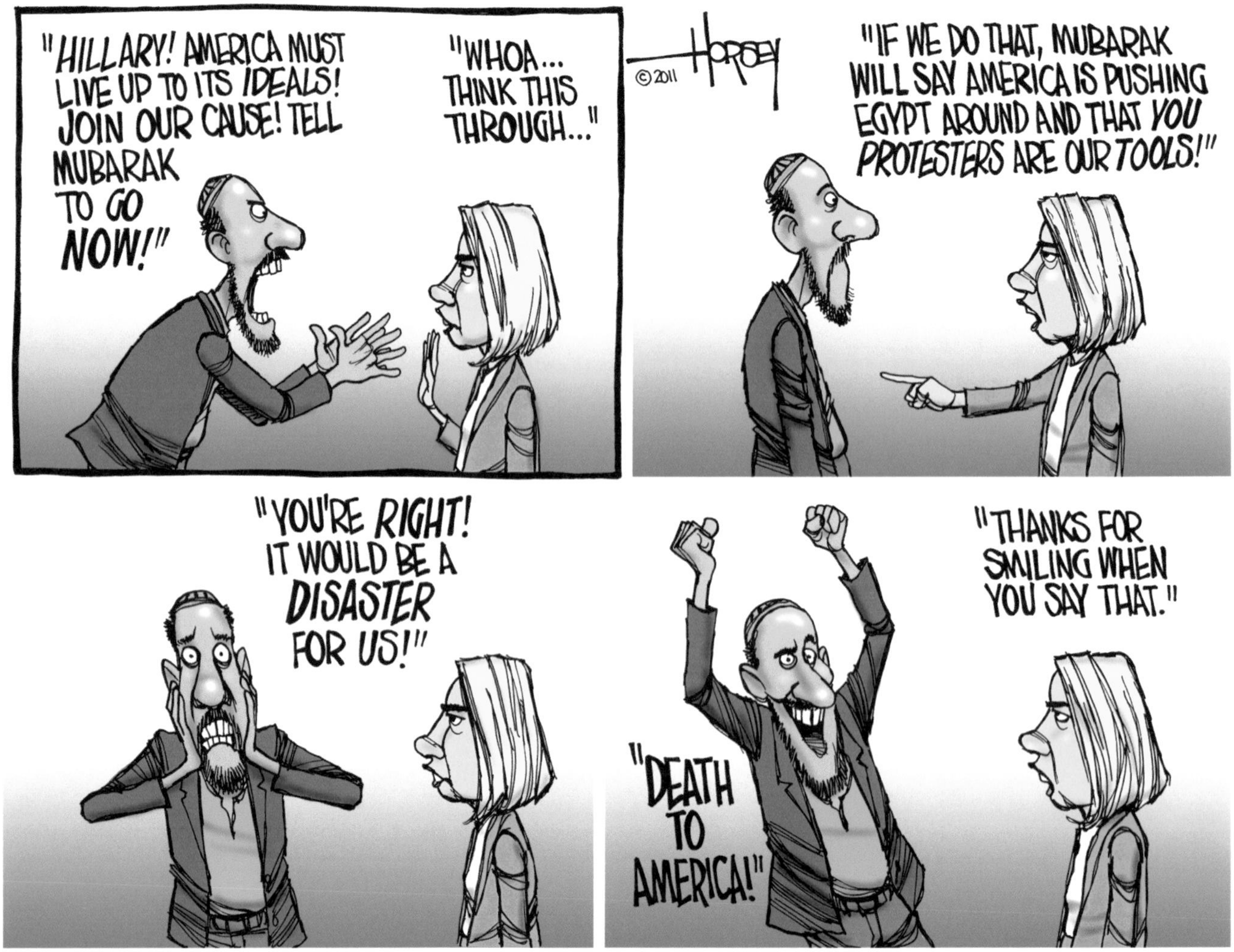
"HILLARY! AMERICA MUST LIVE UP TO ITS IDEALS! JOIN OUR CAUSE! TELL MUBARAK TO GO NOW!"
"WHOA... THINK THIS THROUGH..."
©2011 HORSEY
"IF WE DO THAT, MUBARAK WILL SAY AMERICA IS PUSHING EGYPT AROUND AND THAT YOU PROTESTERS ARE OUR TOOLS!"
"YOU'RE RIGHT! IT WOULD BE A DISASTER FOR US!"
"DEATH TO AMERICA!"
"THANKS FOR SMILING WHEN YOU SAY THAT."

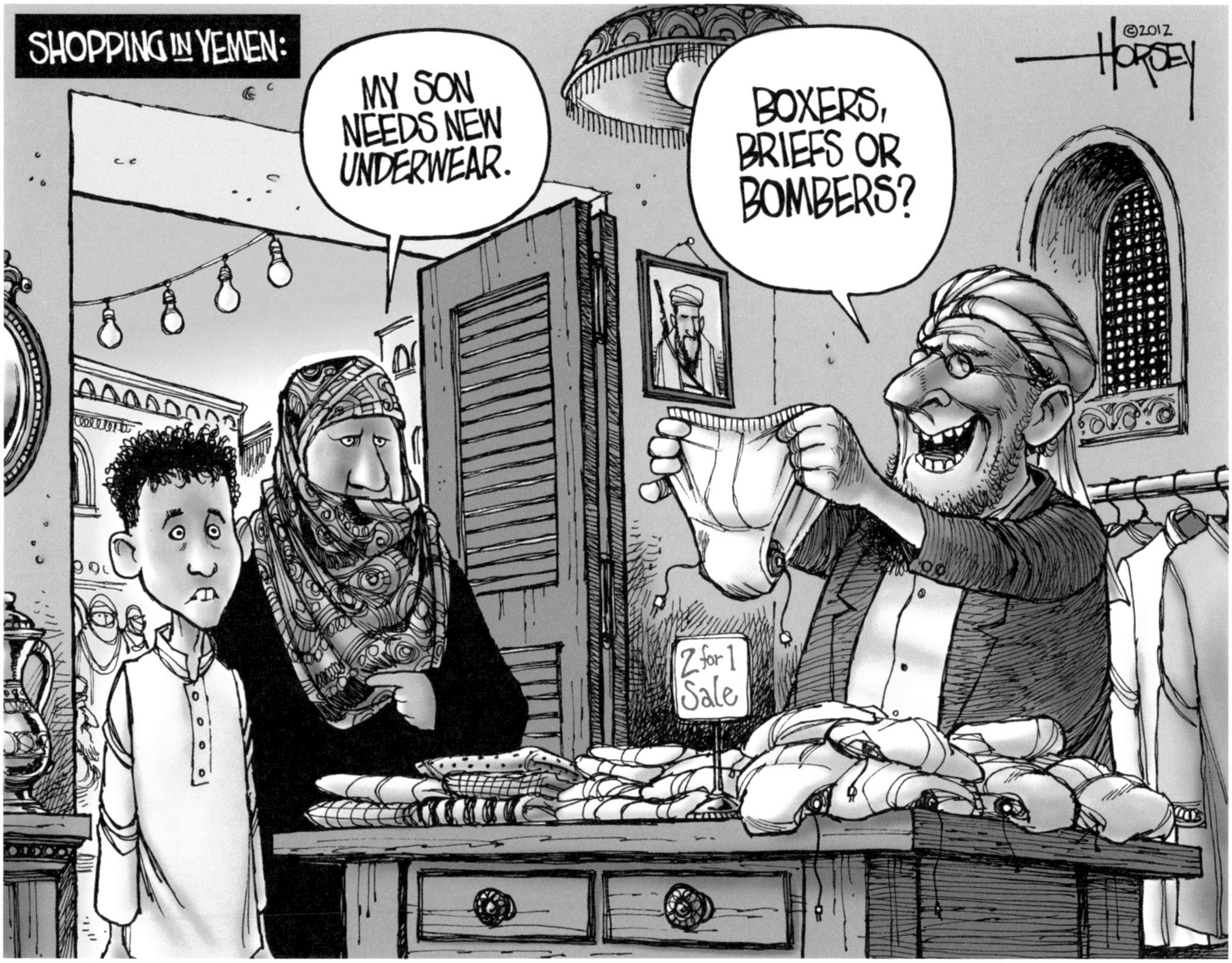
SHOPPING IN YEMEN:
MY SON NEEDS NEW UNDERWEAR.
BOXERS, BRIEFS OR BOMBERS?
2 for 1 Sale
©2012 HORSEY

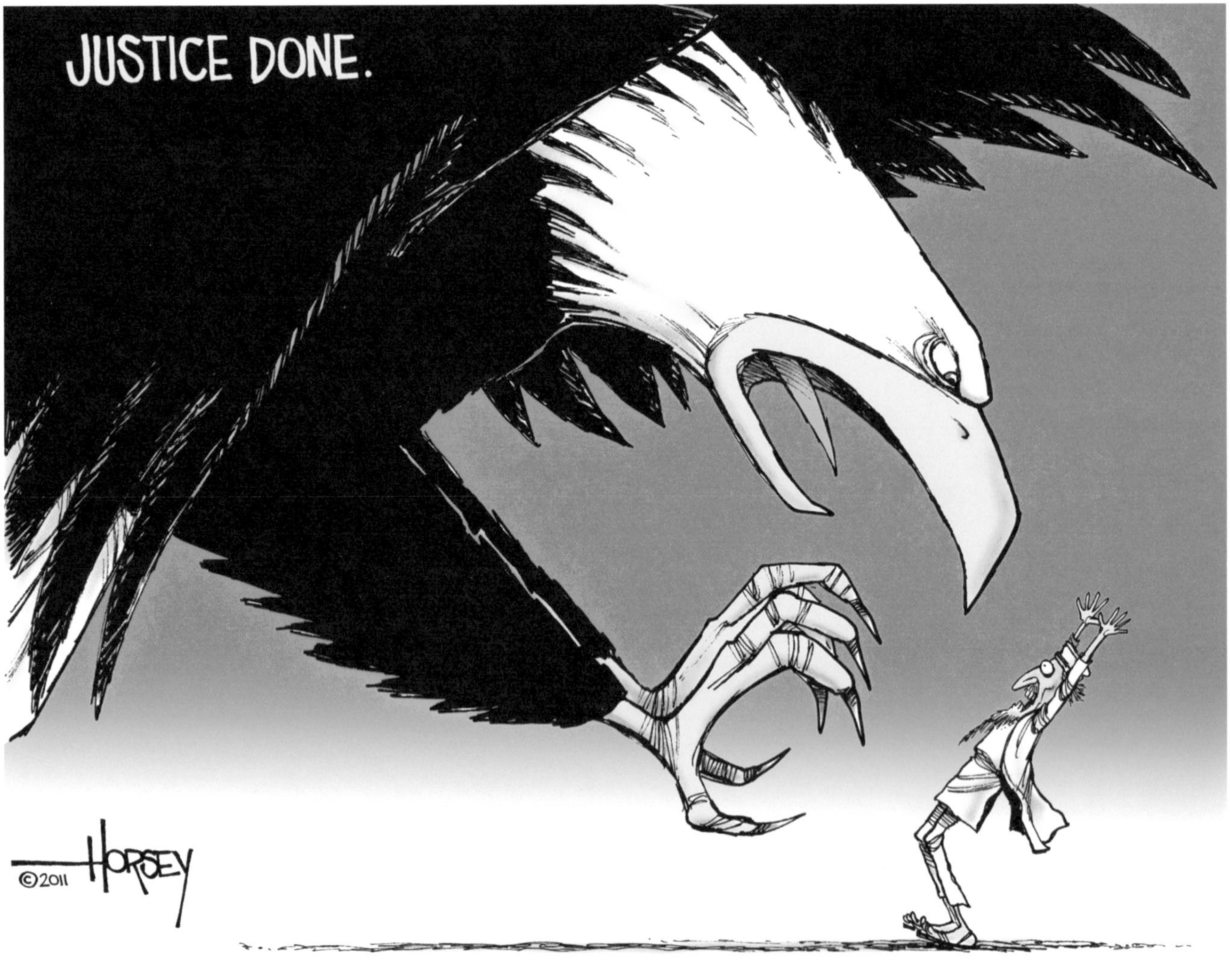
JUSTICE DONE.
©2011 HORSEY

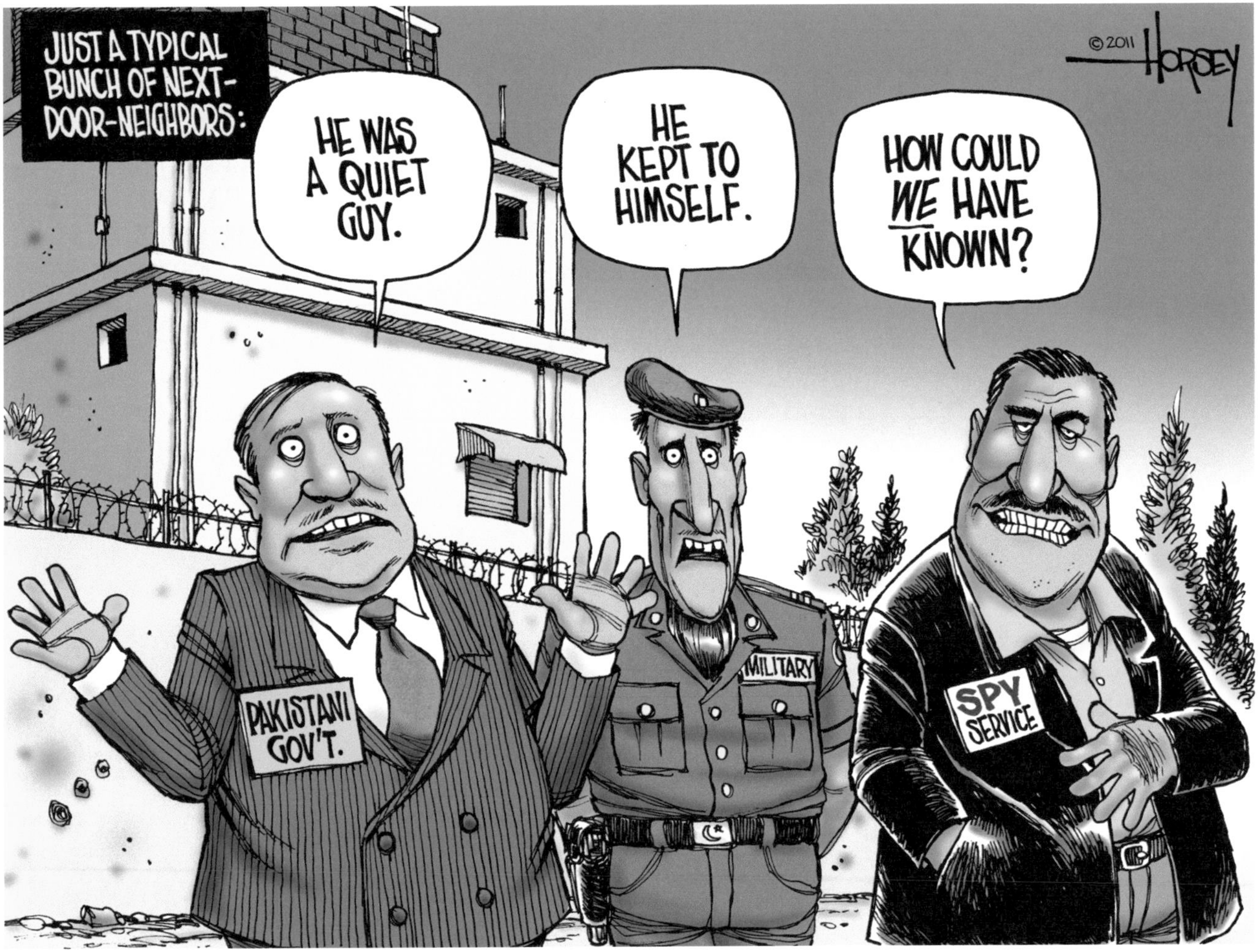
JUST A TYPICAL BUNCH OF NEXT-DOOR-NEIGHBORS:
HE WAS A QUIET GUY.
HE KEPT TO HIMSELF.
HOW COULD WE HAVE KNOWN?
PAKISTANI GOV'T.
MILITARY
SPY SERVICE
©2011 HORSEY

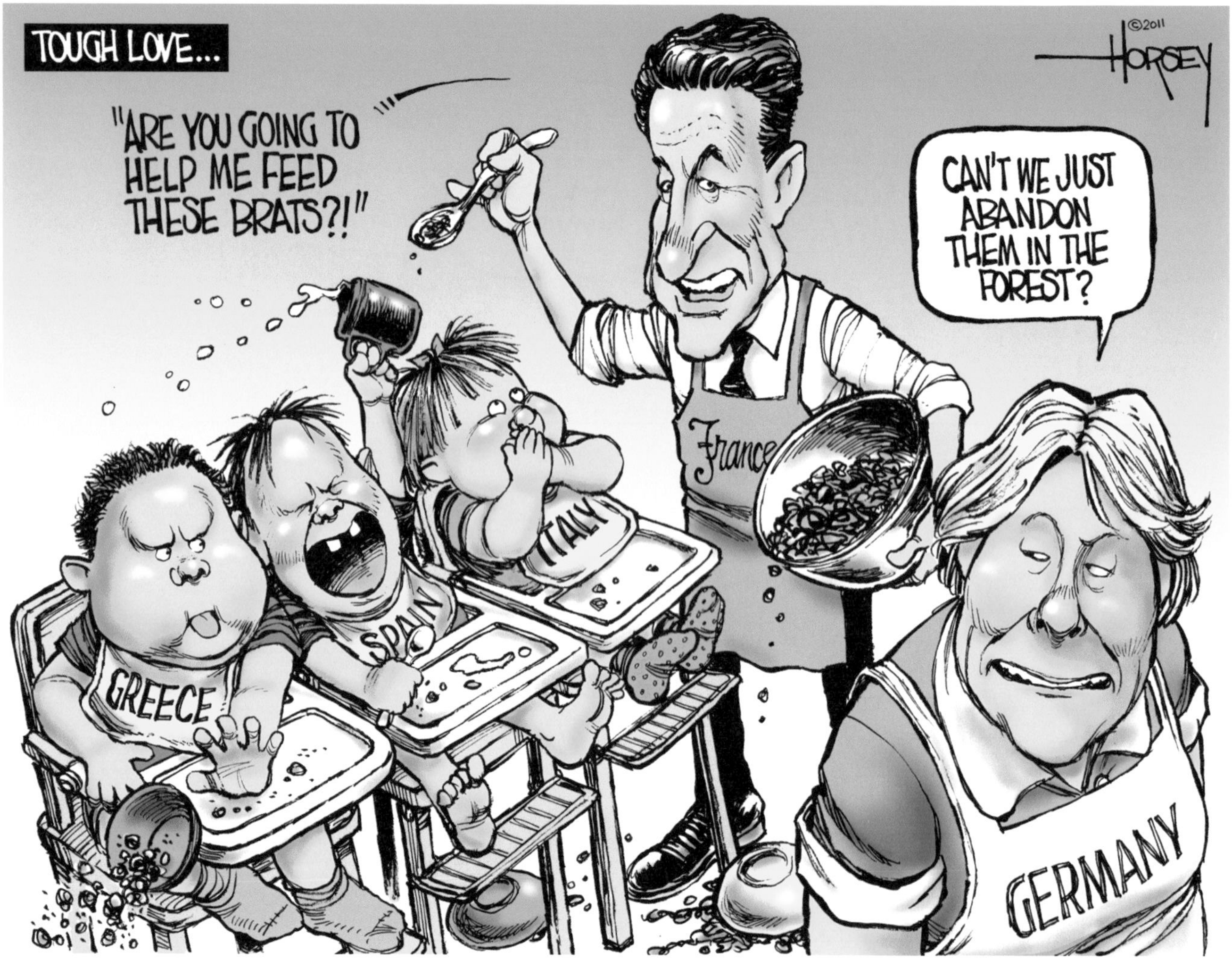
TOUGH LOVE...
©2011
HORSEY
"ARE YOU GOING TO HELP ME FEED THESE BRATS?!"
CAN'T WE JUST ABANDON THEM IN THE FOREST?
France
ITALY
SPAIN
GREECE
GERMANY

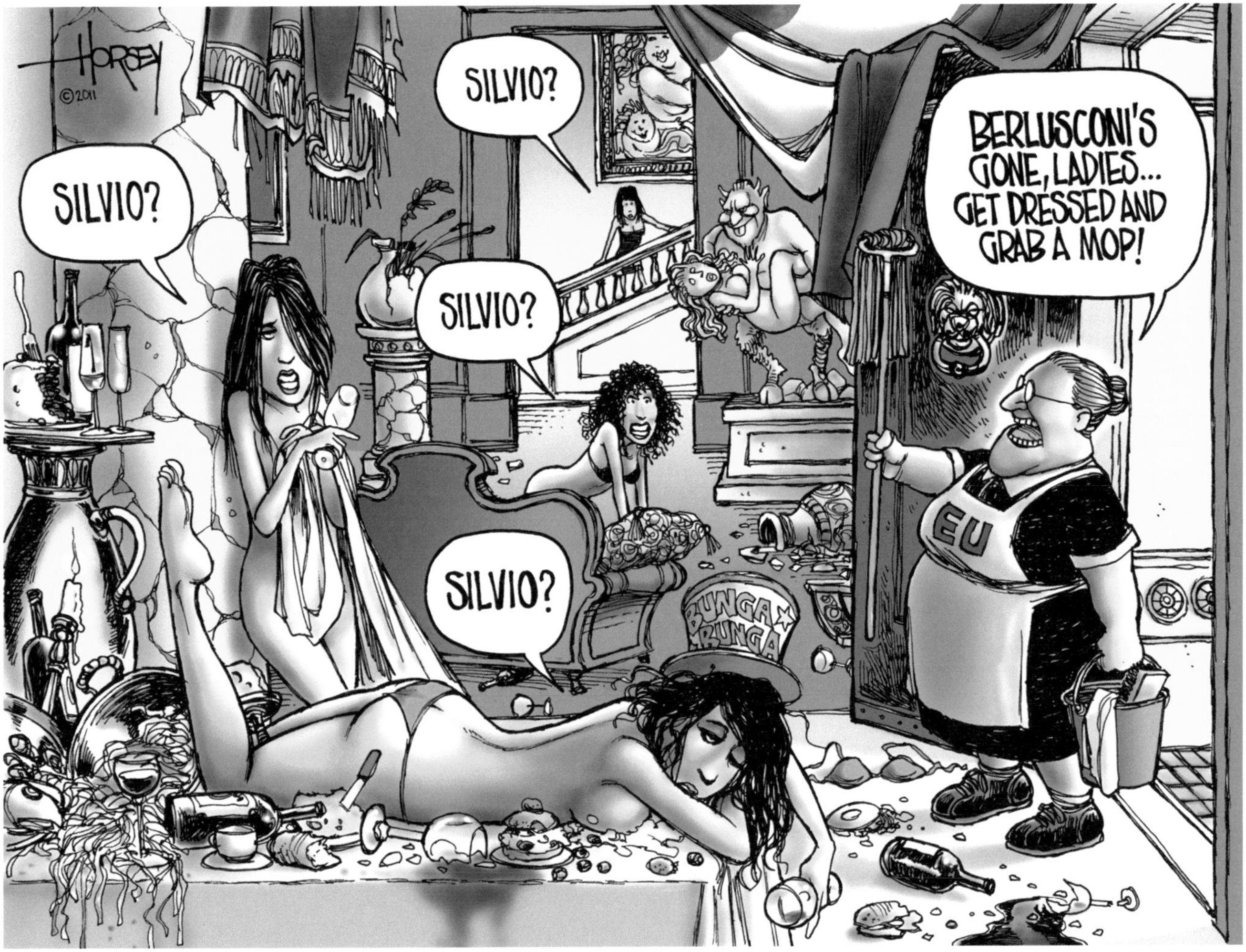
HORSEY
©2011
SILVIO?
SILVIO?
SILVIO?
SILVIO?
BERLUSCONI'S GONE, LADIES... GET DRESSED AND GRAB A MOP!
BUNGA BUNGA
EU

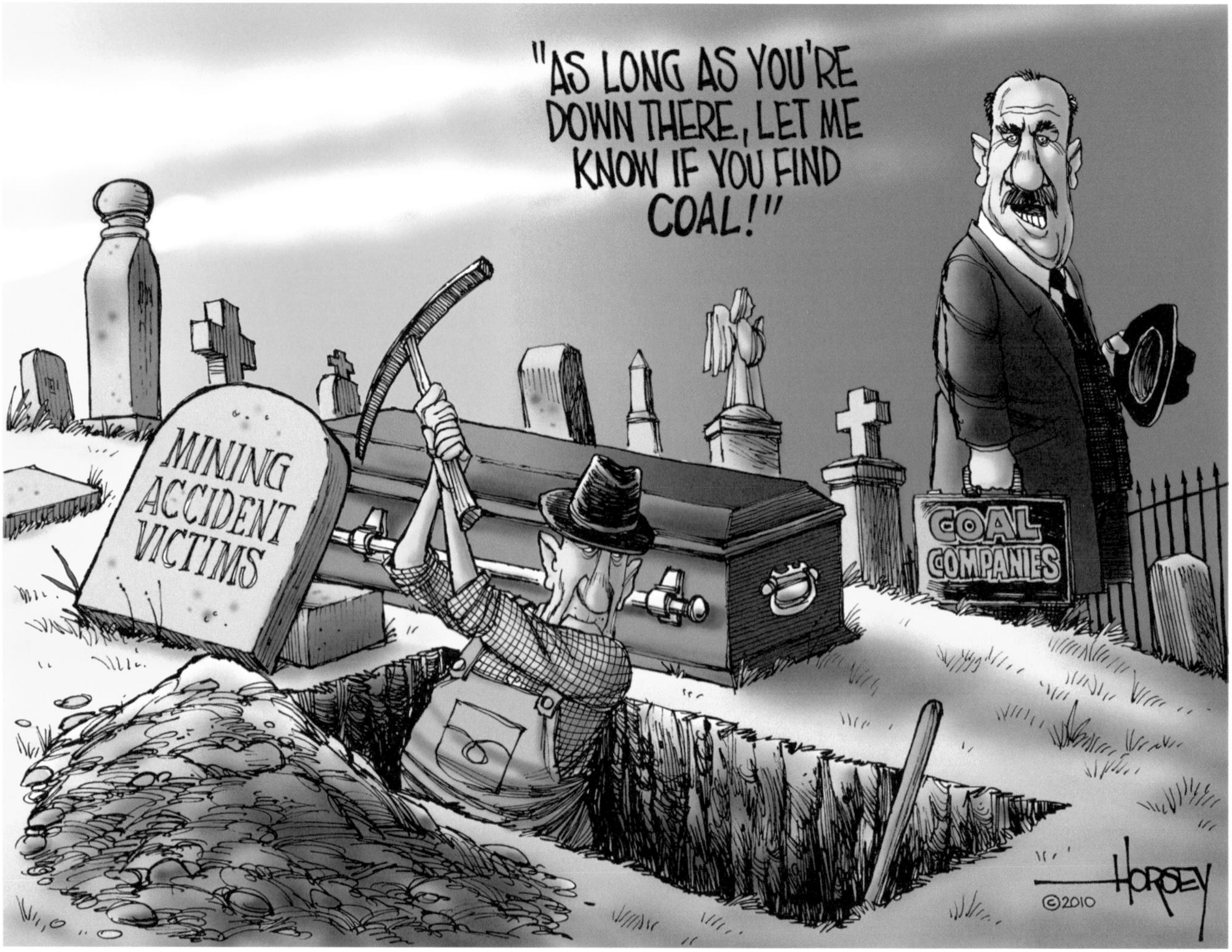
"AS LONG AS YOU'RE DOWN THERE, LET ME KNOW IF YOU FIND COAL!"
MINING ACCIDENT VICTIMS
COAL COMPANIES
HORSEY
©2010

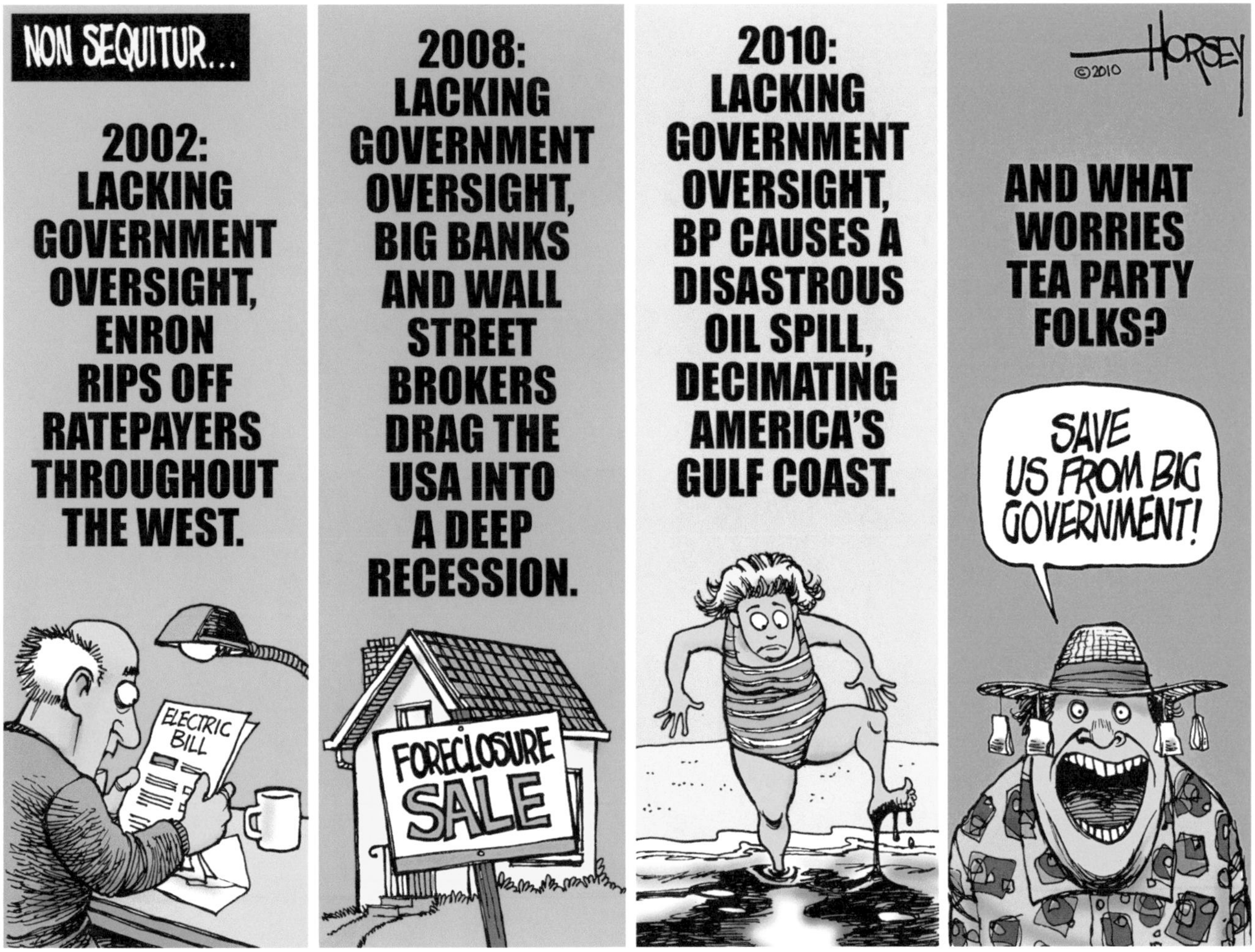
NON SEQUITUR...
2002: LACKING GOVERNMENT OVERSIGHT, ENRON RIPS OFF RATEPAYERS THROUGHOUT THE WEST.
ELECTRIC BILL
2008: LACKING GOVERNMENT OVERSIGHT, BIG BANKS AND WALL STREET BROKERS DRAG THE USA INTO A DEEP RECESSION.
FORECLOSURE SALE
2010: LACKING GOVERNMENT OVERSIGHT, BP CAUSES A DISASTROUS OIL SPILL, DECIMATING AMERICA'S GULF COAST.
HORSEY ©2010
AND WHAT WORRIES TEA PARTY FOLKS?
SAVE US FROM BIG GOVERNMENT!

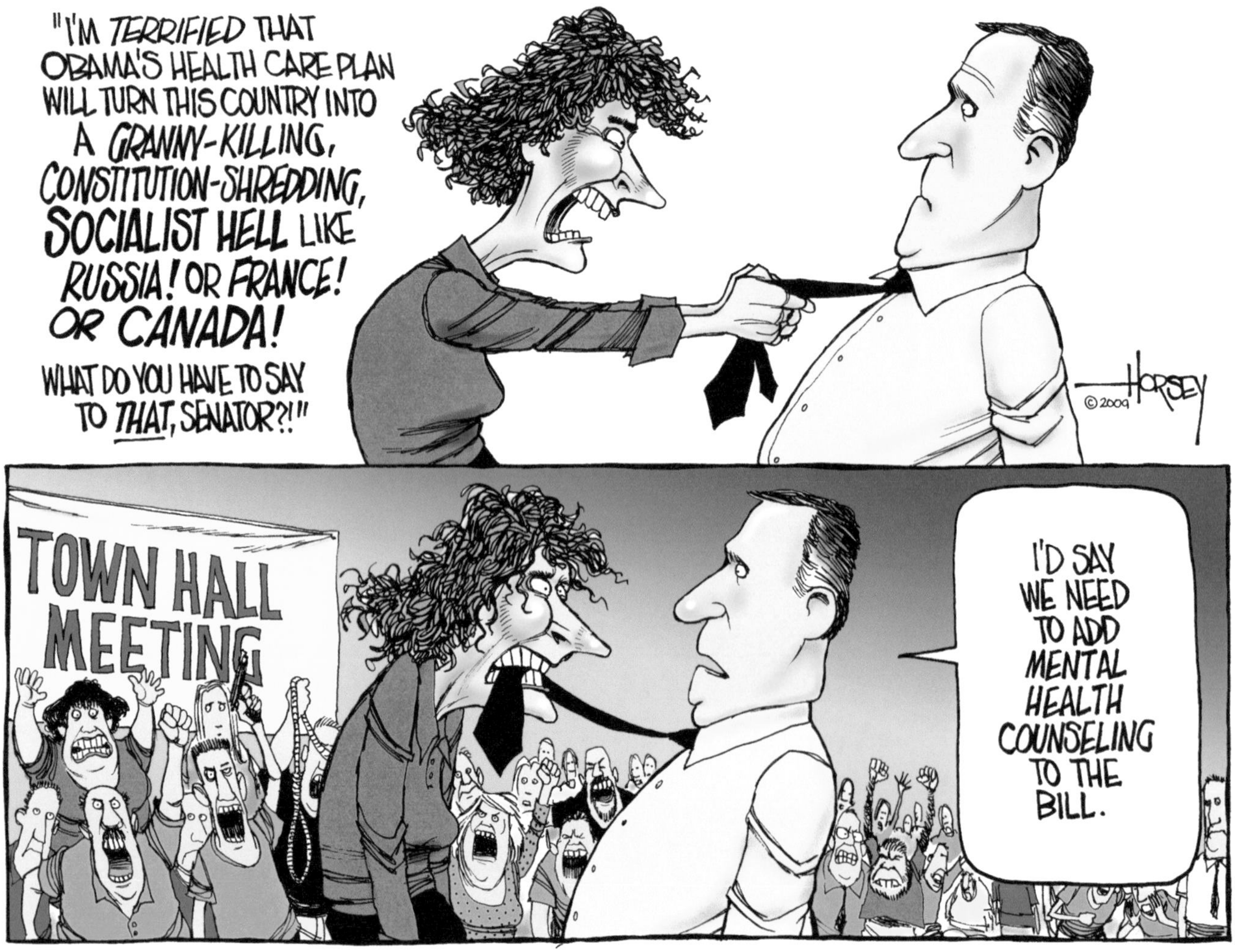
"I'M TERRIFIED THAT OBAMA'S HEALTH CARE PLAN WILL TURN THIS COUNTRY INTO A GRANNY-KILLING, CONSTITUTION-SHREDDING, SOCIALIST HELL LIKE RUSSIA! OR FRANCE! OR CANADA!
WHAT DO YOU HAVE TO SAY TO THAT, SENATOR?!"
HORSEY
©2009
TOWN HALL MEETING
I'D SAY WE NEED TO ADD MENTAL HEALTH COUNSELING TO THE BILL.

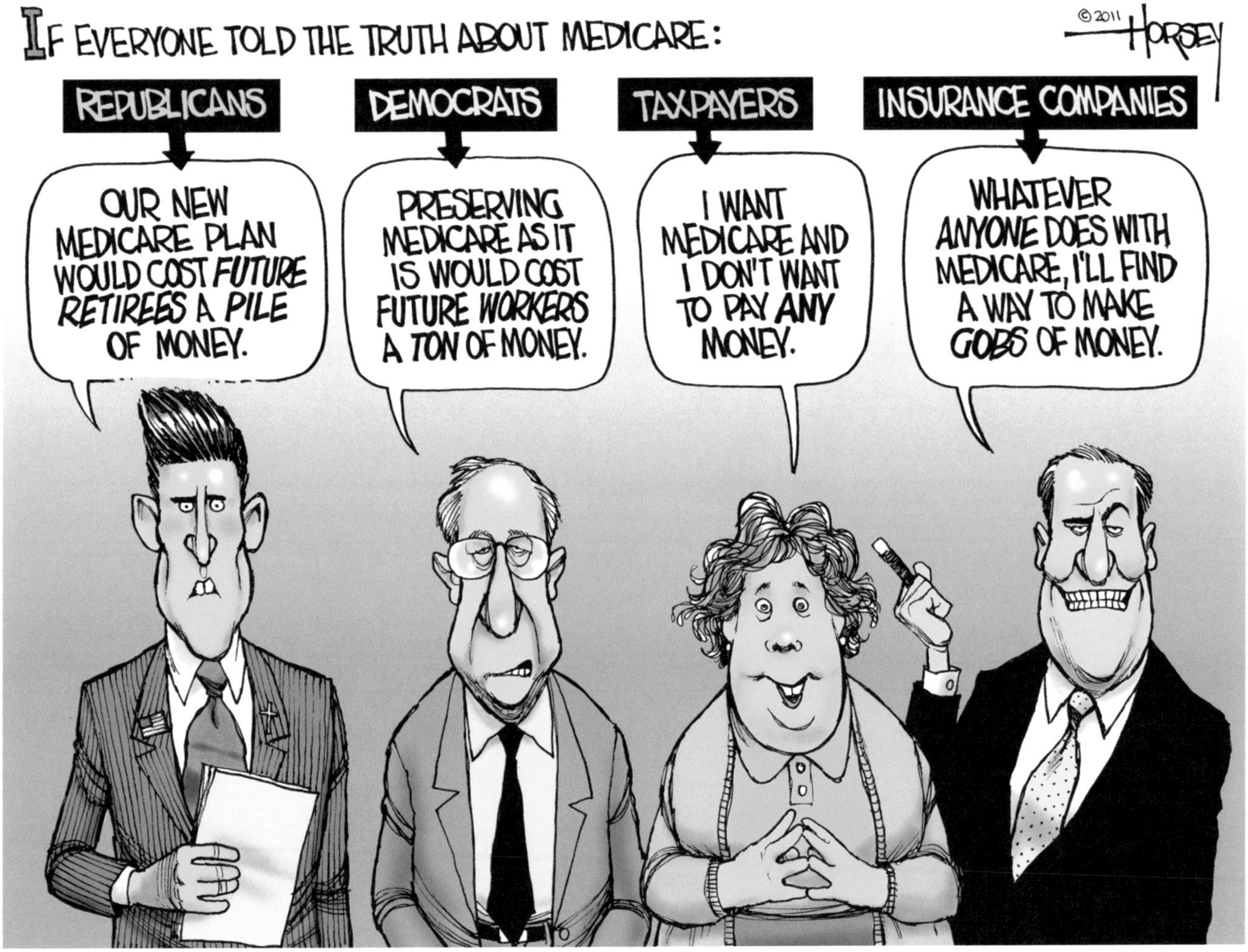
IF EVERYONE TOLD THE TRUTH ABOUT MEDICARE:
©2011 HORSEY
REPUBLICANS
OUR NEW MEDICARE PLAN WOULD COST *FUTURE RETIREES* A *PILE* OF MONEY.
DEMOCRATS
PRESERVING MEDICARE AS IT IS WOULD COST FUTURE *WORKERS* A *TON* OF MONEY.
TAXPAYERS
I WANT MEDICARE AND I DON'T WANT TO PAY *ANY* MONEY.
INSURANCE COMPANIES
WHATEVER *ANYONE* DOES WITH MEDICARE, I'LL FIND A WAY TO MAKE *GOBS* OF MONEY.

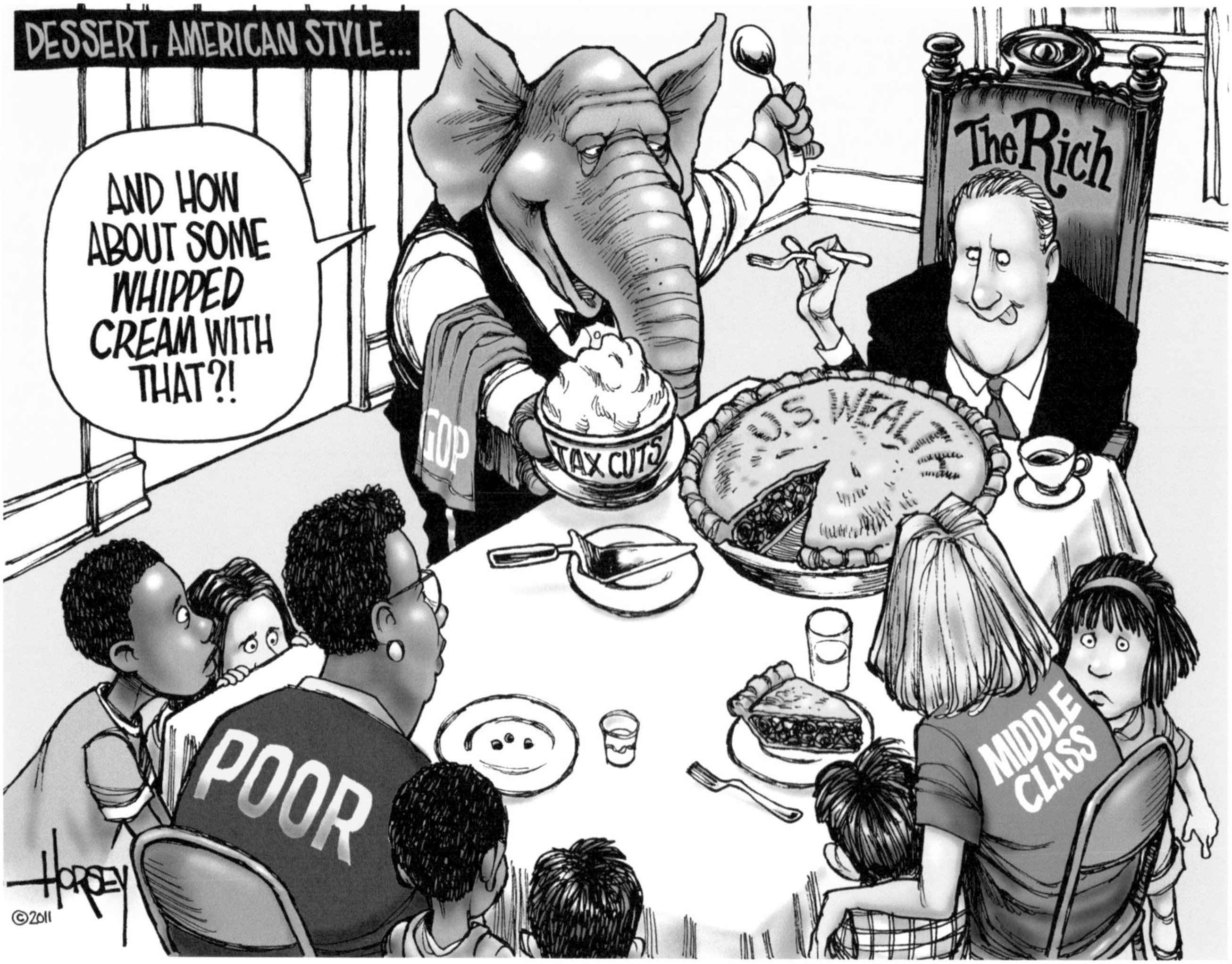
DESSERT, AMERICAN STYLE...
AND HOW ABOUT SOME WHIPPED CREAM WITH THAT?!
The Rich
GOP
TAX CUTS
U.S. WEALTH
POOR
MIDDLE CLASS
HORSEY
©2011

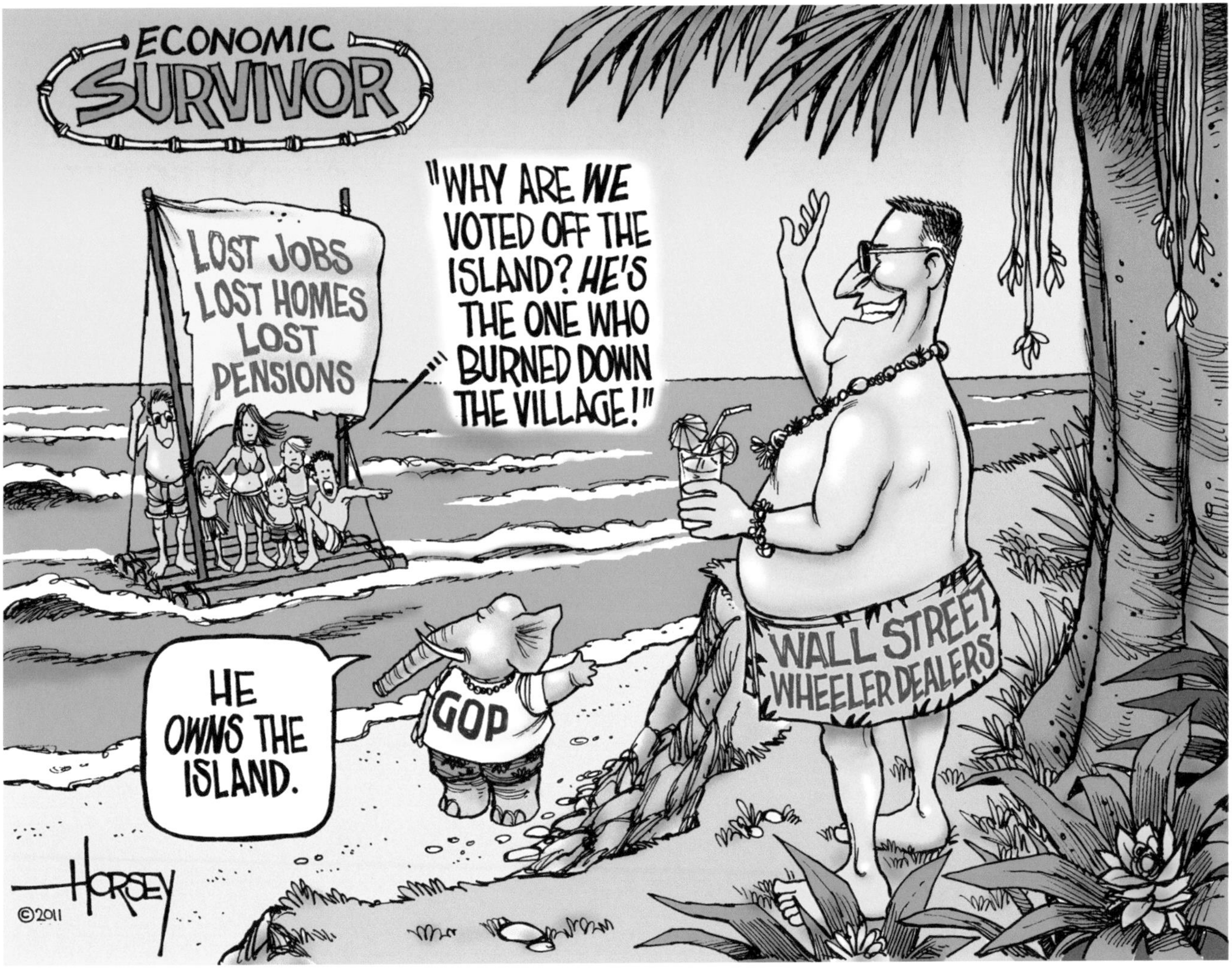
ECONOMIC SURVIVOR
LOST JOBS LOST HOMES LOST PENSIONS
"WHY ARE WE VOTED OFF THE ISLAND? HE'S THE ONE WHO BURNED DOWN THE VILLAGE!"
HE OWNS THE ISLAND.
GOP
WALL STREET WHEELER DEALERS
HORSEY ©2011

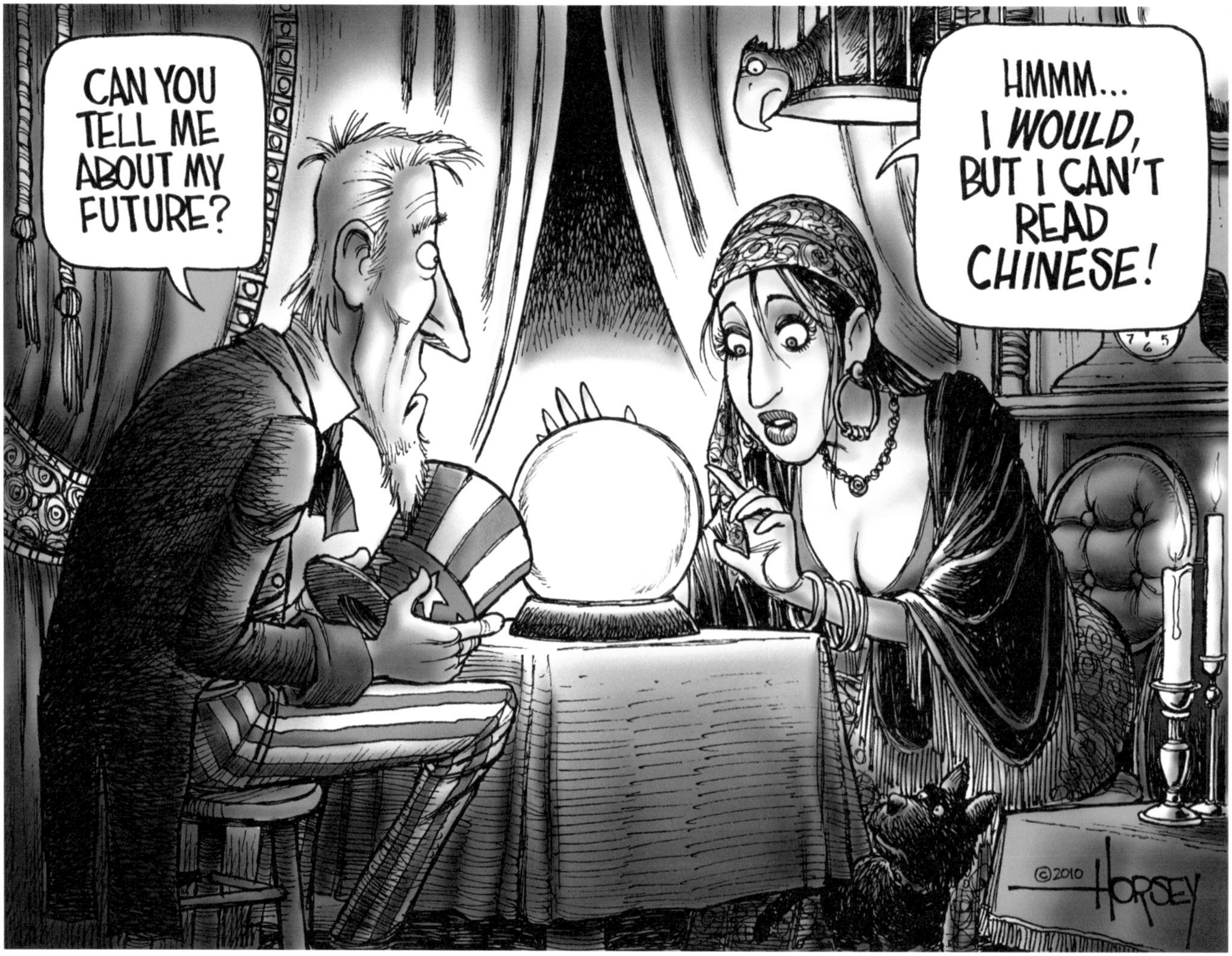
CAN YOU TELL ME ABOUT MY FUTURE?
HMMM... I *WOULD*, BUT I CAN'T READ CHINESE!
©2010 HORSEY

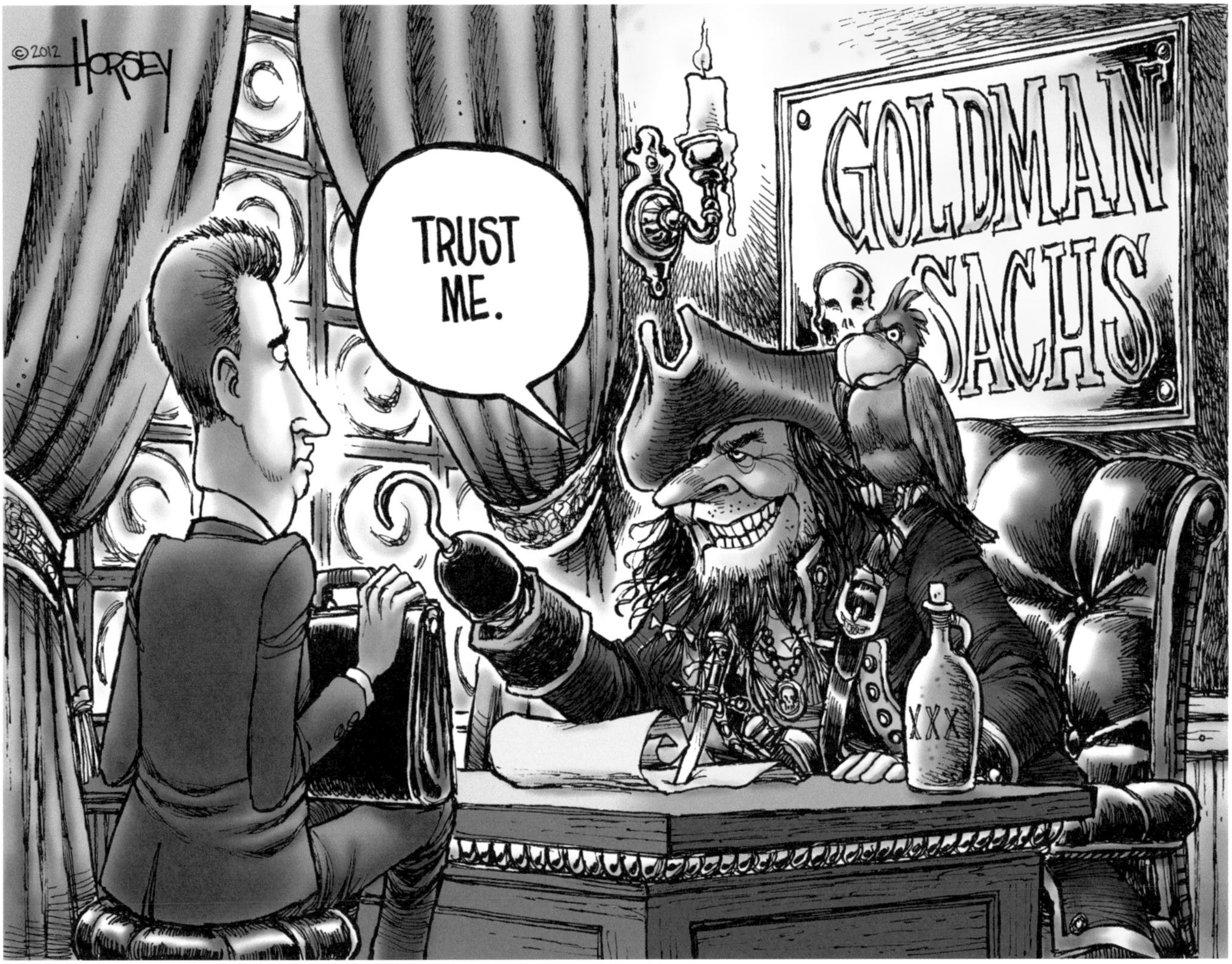
©2012 HORSEY
GOLDMAN SACHS
TRUST ME.
XXX

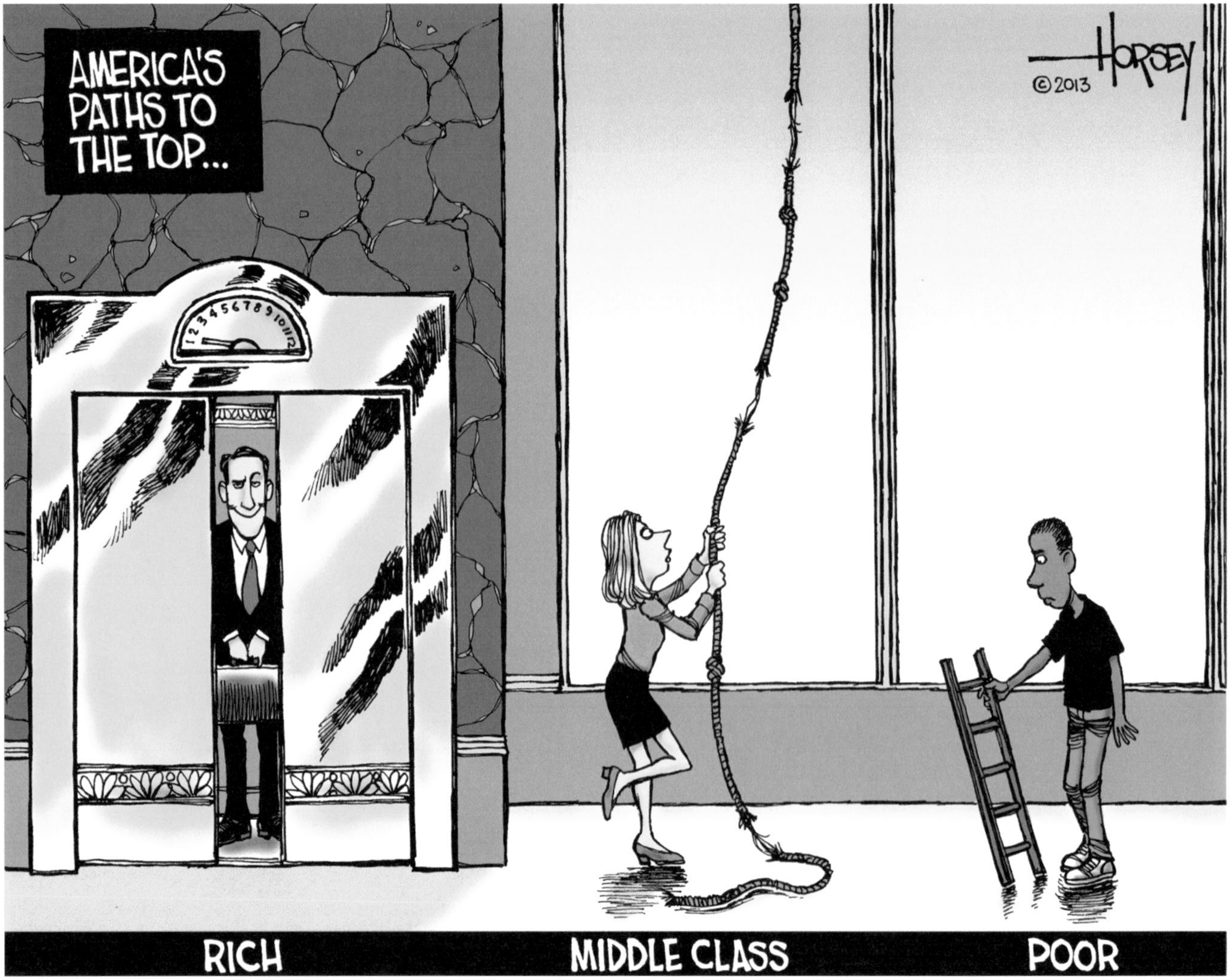
AMERICA'S PATHS TO THE TOP...
HORSEY
©2013
RICH
MIDDLE CLASS
POOR

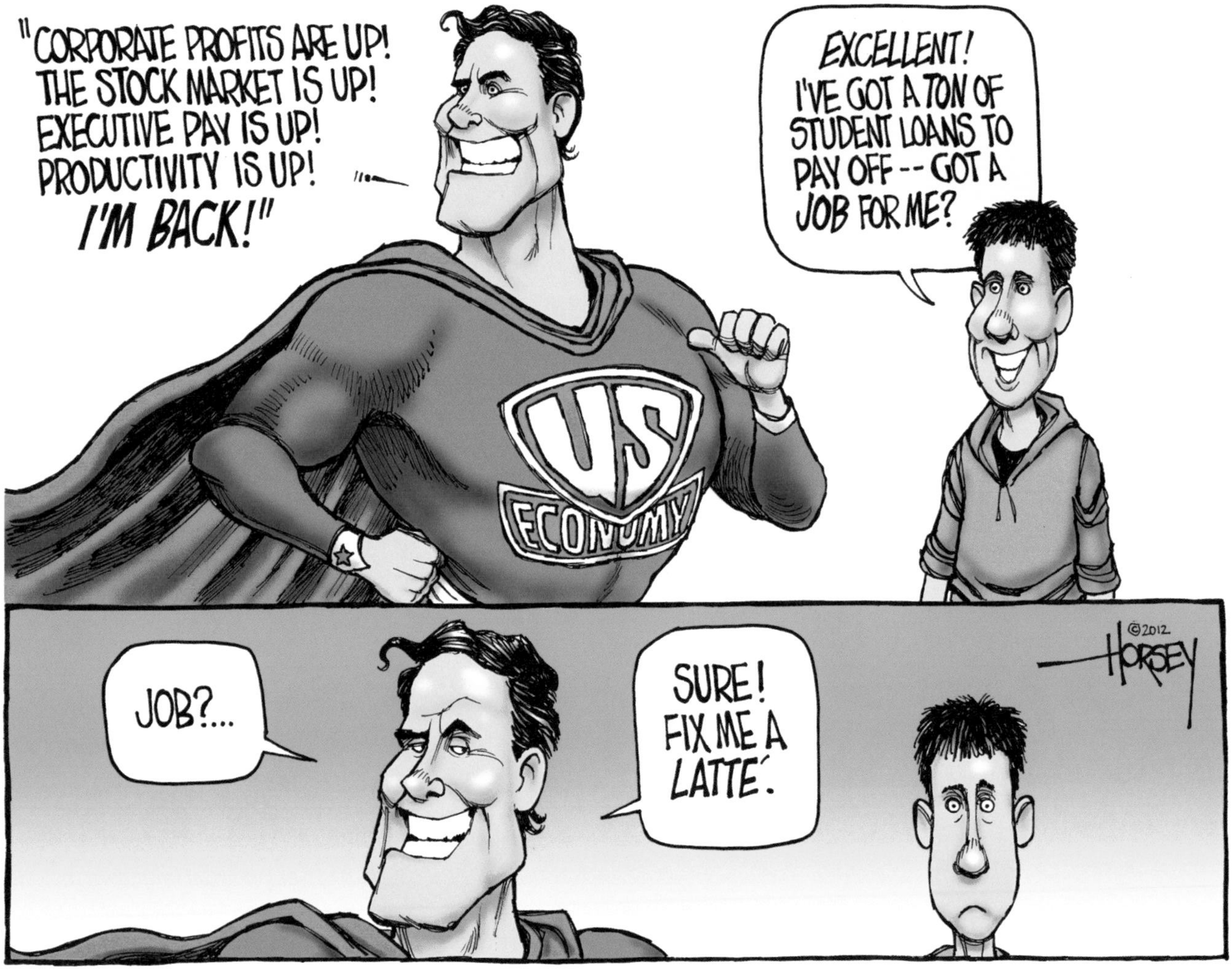
"CORPORATE PROFITS ARE UP! THE STOCK MARKET IS UP! EXECUTIVE PAY IS UP! PRODUCTIVITY IS UP! I'M BACK!"
EXCELLENT! I'VE GOT A TON OF STUDENT LOANS TO PAY OFF -- GOT A JOB FOR ME?
US
ECONOMY
JOB?...
SURE! FIX ME A LATTE'.
©2012
HORSEY

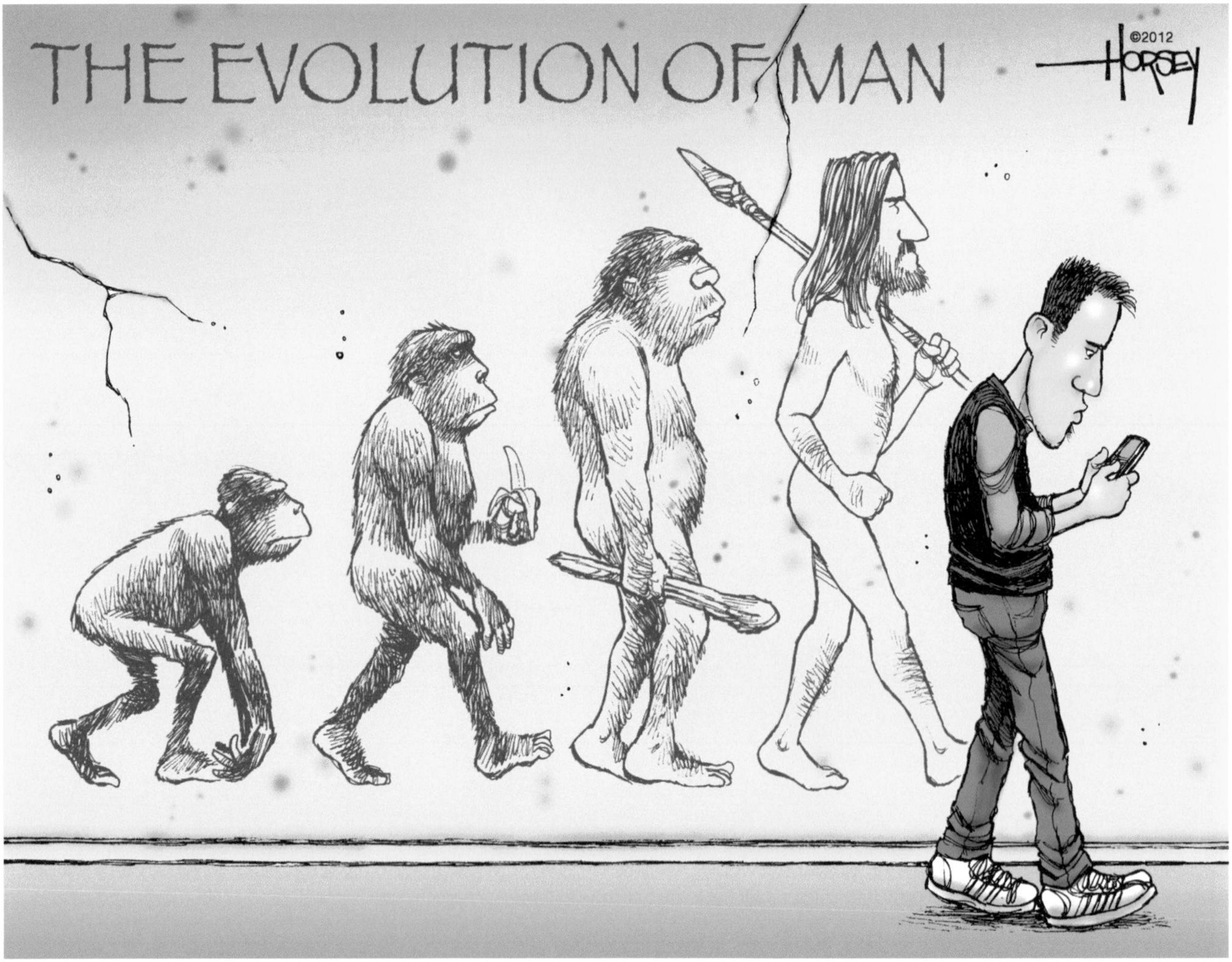
THE EVOLUTION OF MAN
©2012
HORSEY

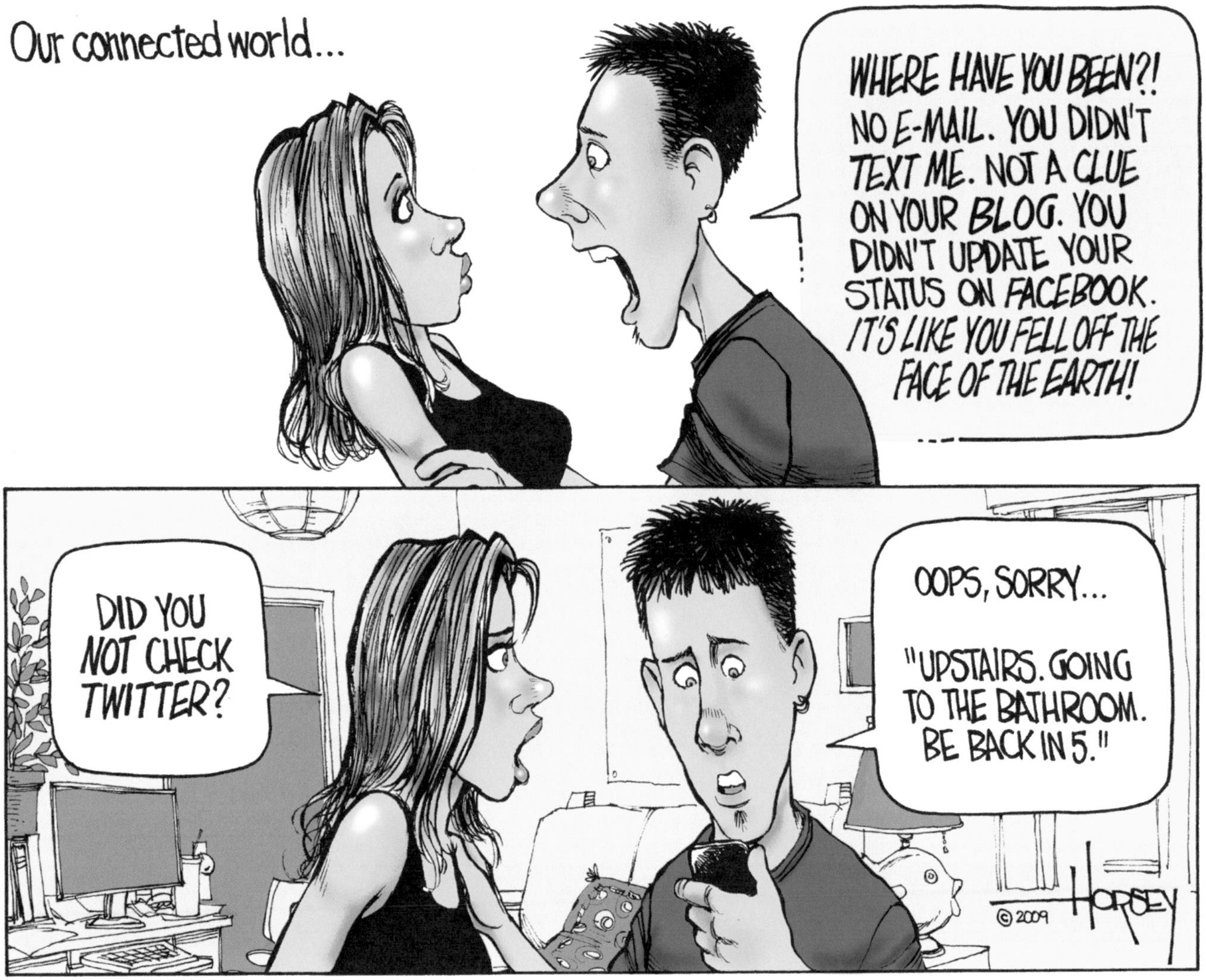
Our connected world...
WHERE HAVE YOU BEEN?! NO E-MAIL. YOU DIDN'T TEXT ME. NOT A CLUE ON YOUR BLOG. YOU DIDN'T UPDATE YOUR STATUS ON FACEBOOK. IT'S LIKE YOU FELL OFF THE FACE OF THE EARTH!
DID YOU NOT CHECK TWITTER?
OOPS, SORRY...
"UPSTAIRS. GOING TO THE BATHROOM. BE BACK IN 5."
© 2009 HORSEY

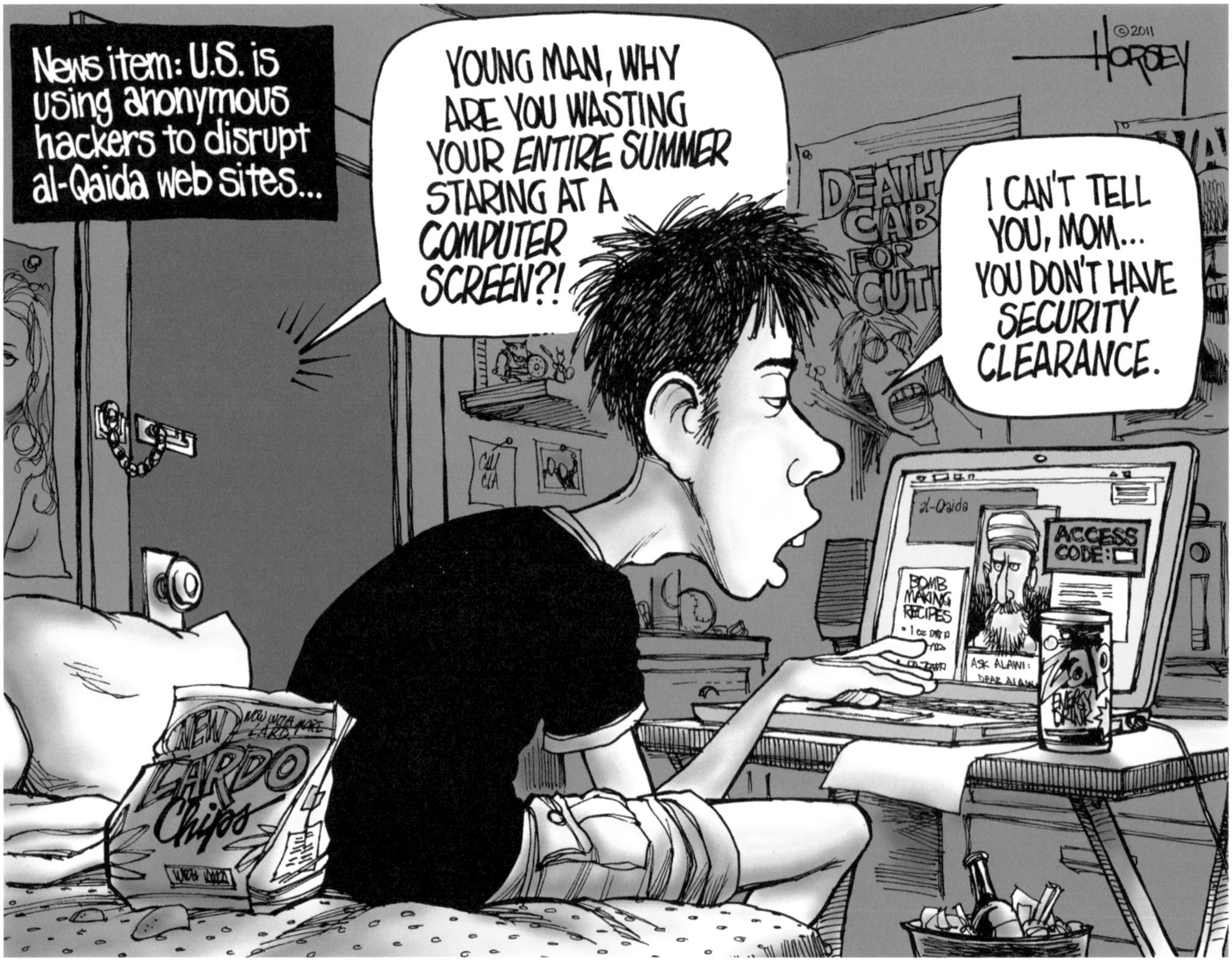
News item: U.S. is using anonymous hackers to disrupt al-Qaida web sites...
YOUNG MAN, WHY ARE YOU WASTING YOUR ENTIRE SUMMER STARING AT A COMPUTER SCREEN?!
I CAN'T TELL YOU, MOM... YOU DON'T HAVE SECURITY CLEARANCE.
©2011
HORSEY
al-Qaida
ACCESS CODE:
BOMB MAKING RECIPES
ASK ALAWI:
NEW
LARDO Chips
ENERGY DRINK

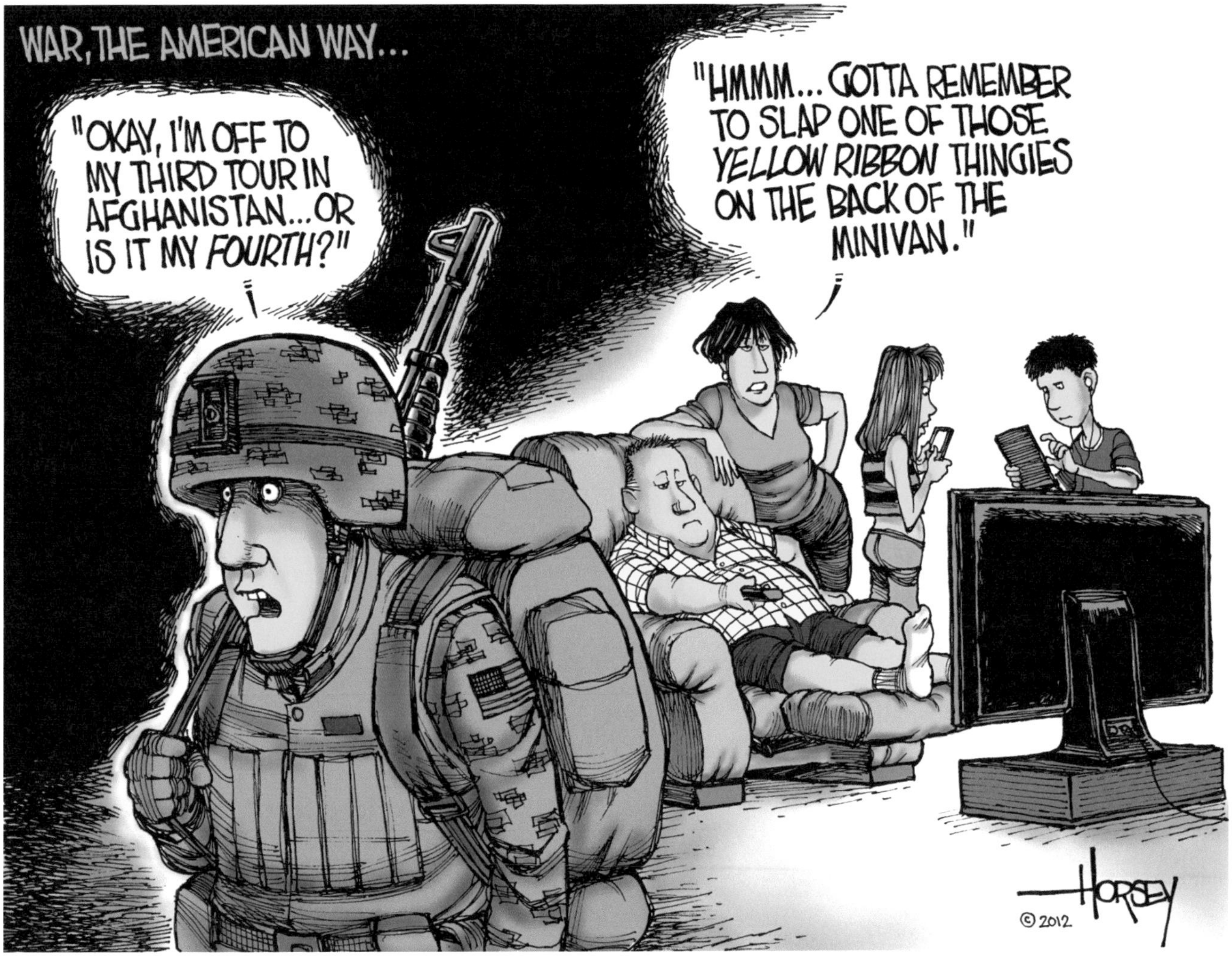
WAR, THE AMERICAN WAY...
"OKAY, I'M OFF TO MY THIRD TOUR IN AFGHANISTAN...OR IS IT MY FOURTH?"
"HMMM... GOTTA REMEMBER TO SLAP ONE OF THOSE YELLOW RIBBON THINGIES ON THE BACK OF THE MINIVAN."
HORSEY
© 2012

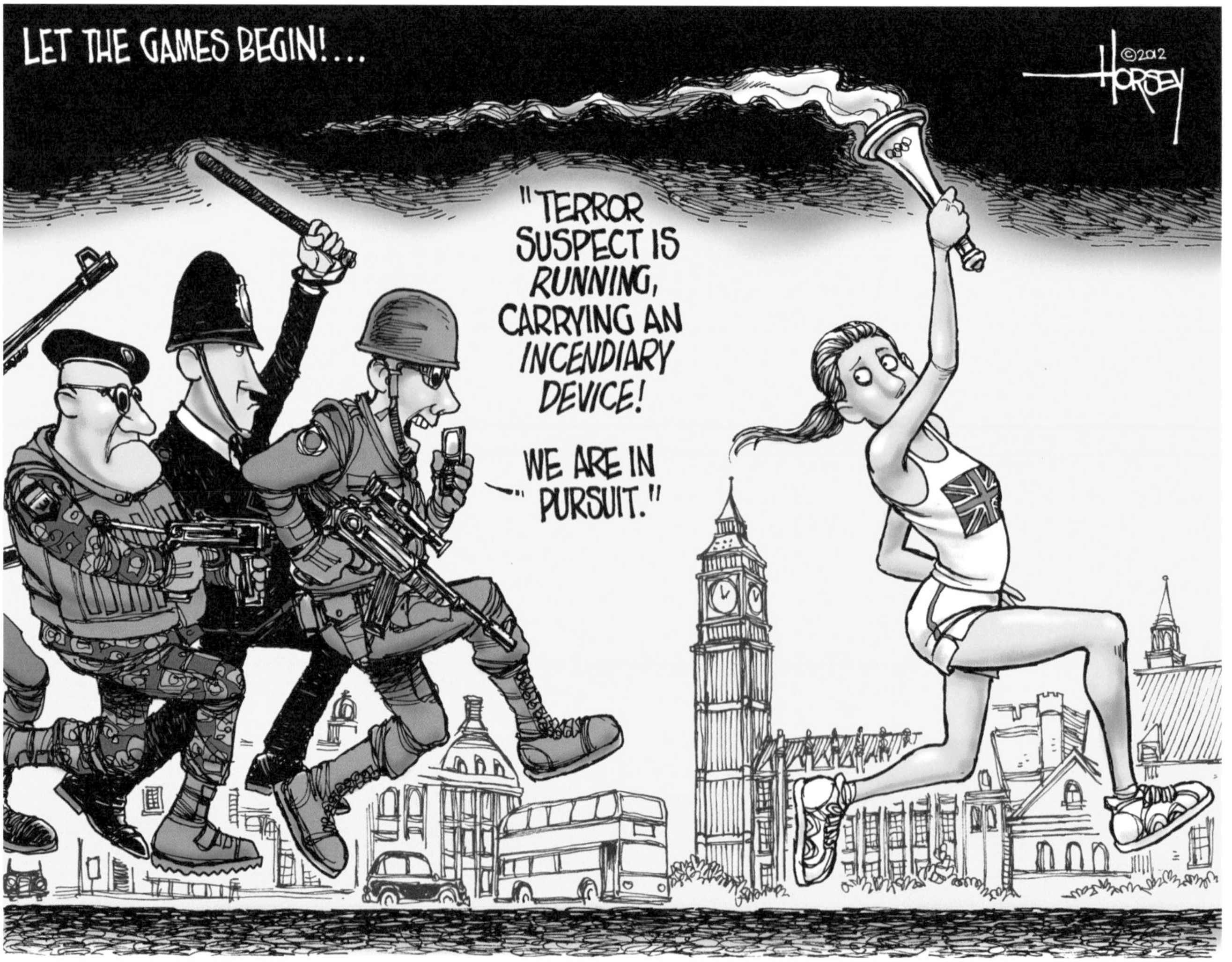
LET THE GAMES BEGIN!...
©2012 HORSEY
"TERROR SUSPECT IS RUNNING, CARRYING AN INCENDIARY DEVICE!
WE ARE IN PURSUIT."

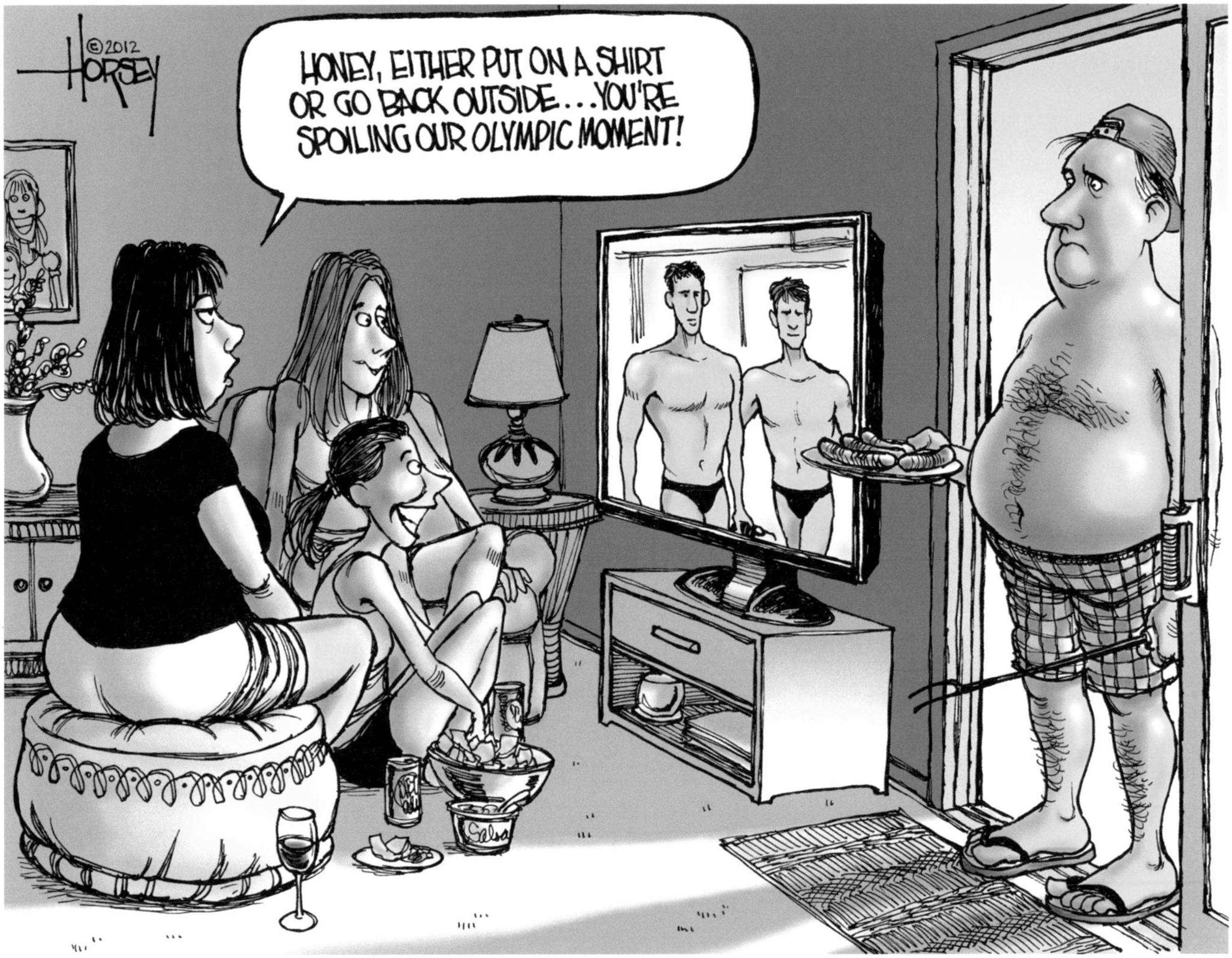
©2012
HORSEY
HONEY, EITHER PUT ON A SHIRT OR GO BACK OUTSIDE... YOU'RE SPOILING OUR OLYMPIC MOMENT!
Salsa

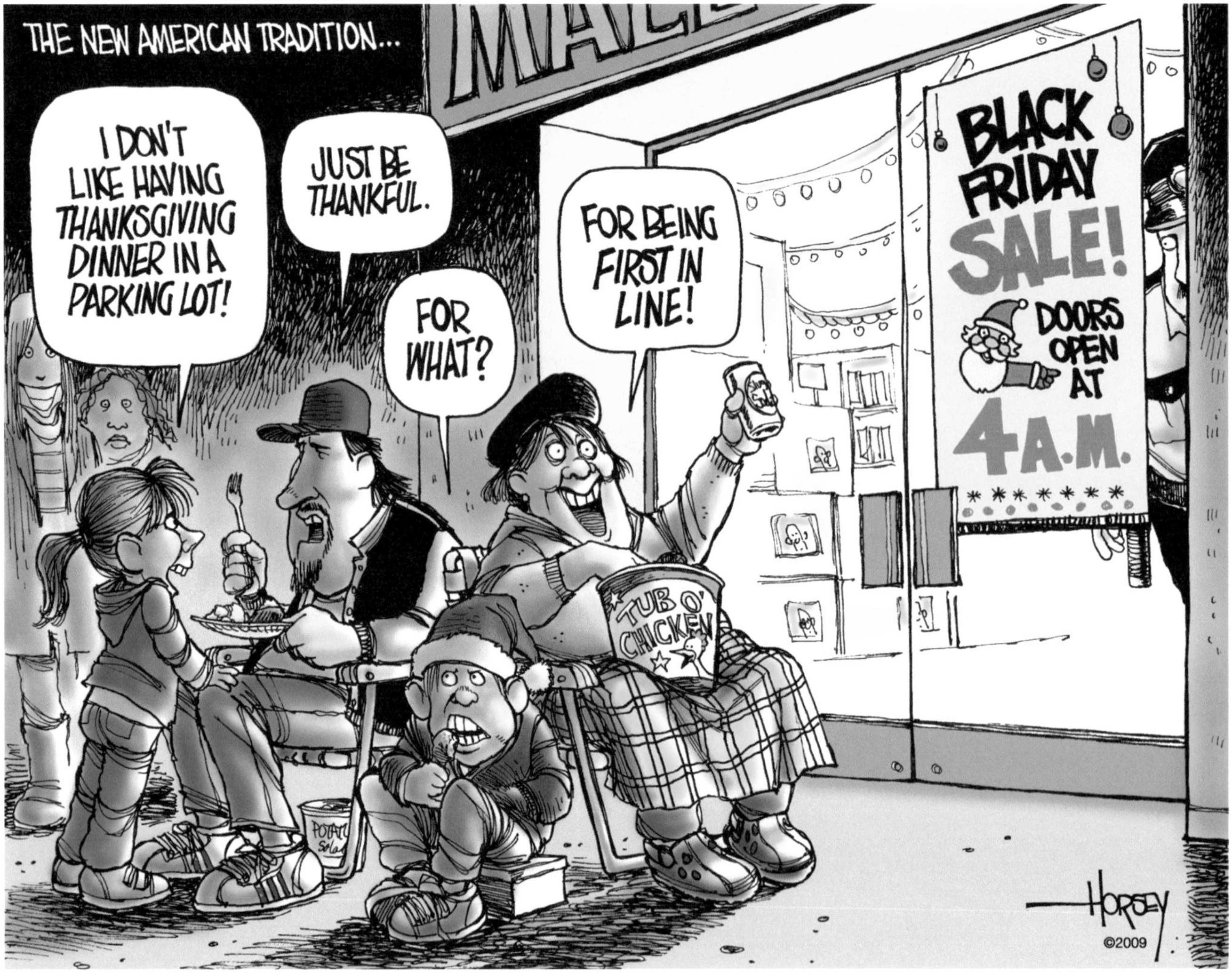
THE NEW AMERICAN TRADITION...
I DON'T LIKE HAVING THANKSGIVING DINNER IN A PARKING LOT!
JUST BE THANKFUL.
FOR WHAT?
FOR BEING FIRST IN LINE!
BLACK FRIDAY SALE!
DOORS OPEN AT
4 A.M.
TUB O' CHICKEN
HORSEY
©2009

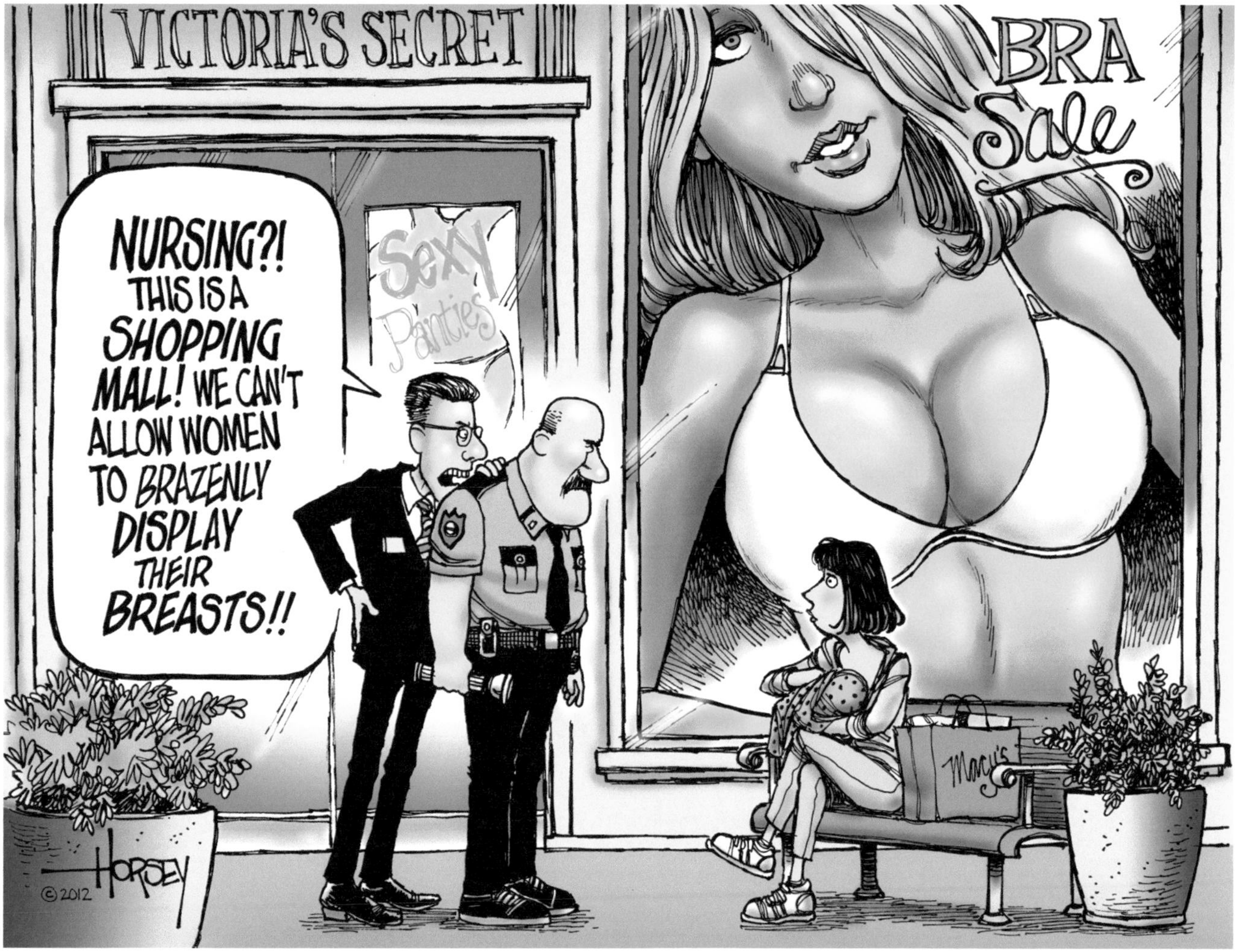
VICTORIA'S SECRET
BRA Sale
Sexy Panties
NURSING?! THIS IS A SHOPPING MALL! WE CAN'T ALLOW WOMEN TO BRAZENLY DISPLAY THEIR BREASTS!!
Macy's
HORSEY
©2012

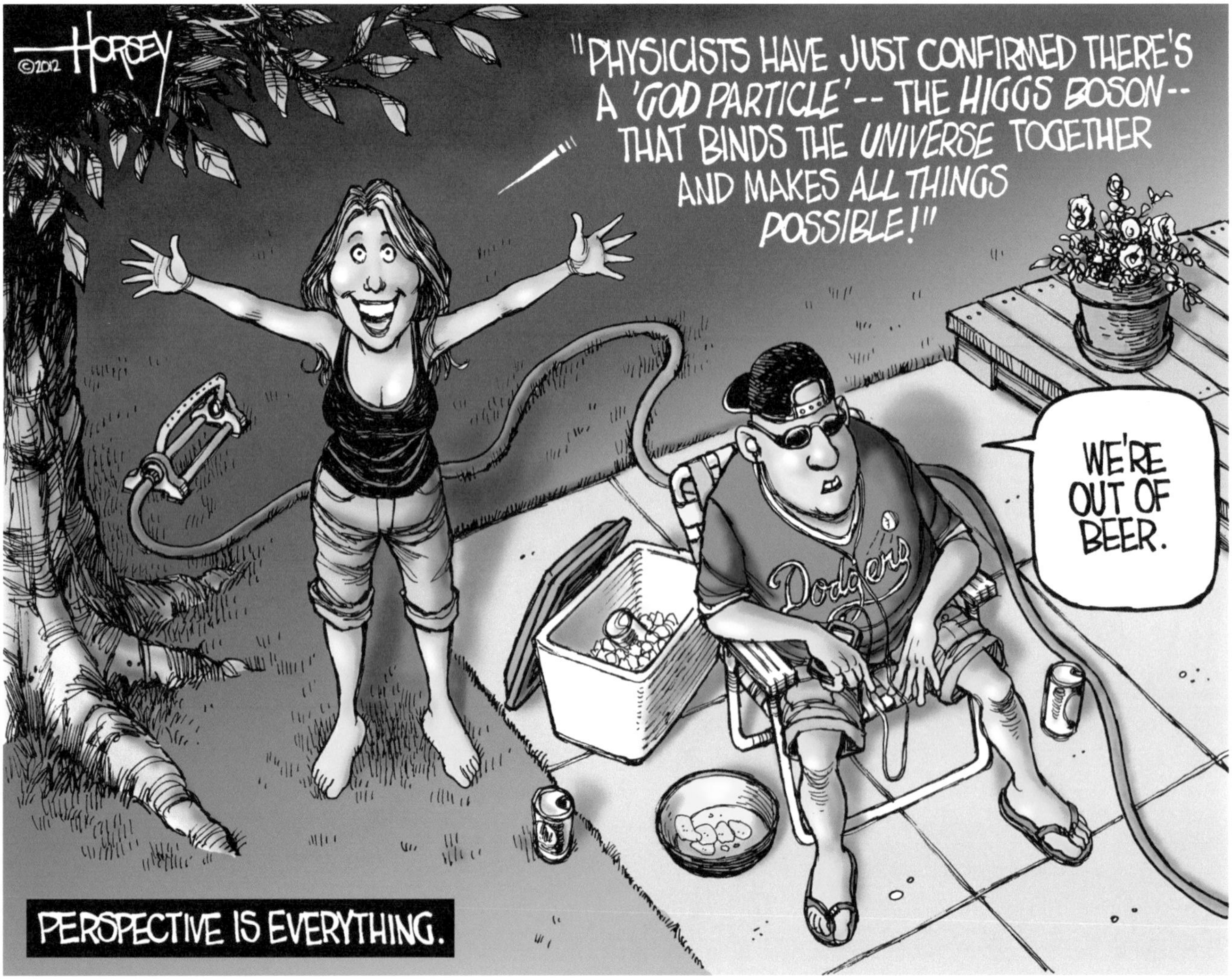
©2012 HORSEY
"PHYSICISTS HAVE JUST CONFIRMED THERE'S A 'GOD PARTICLE'-- THE HIGGS BOSON-- THAT BINDS THE UNIVERSE TOGETHER AND MAKES ALL THINGS POSSIBLE!"
WE'RE OUT OF BEER.
Dodgers
PERSPECTIVE IS EVERYTHING.

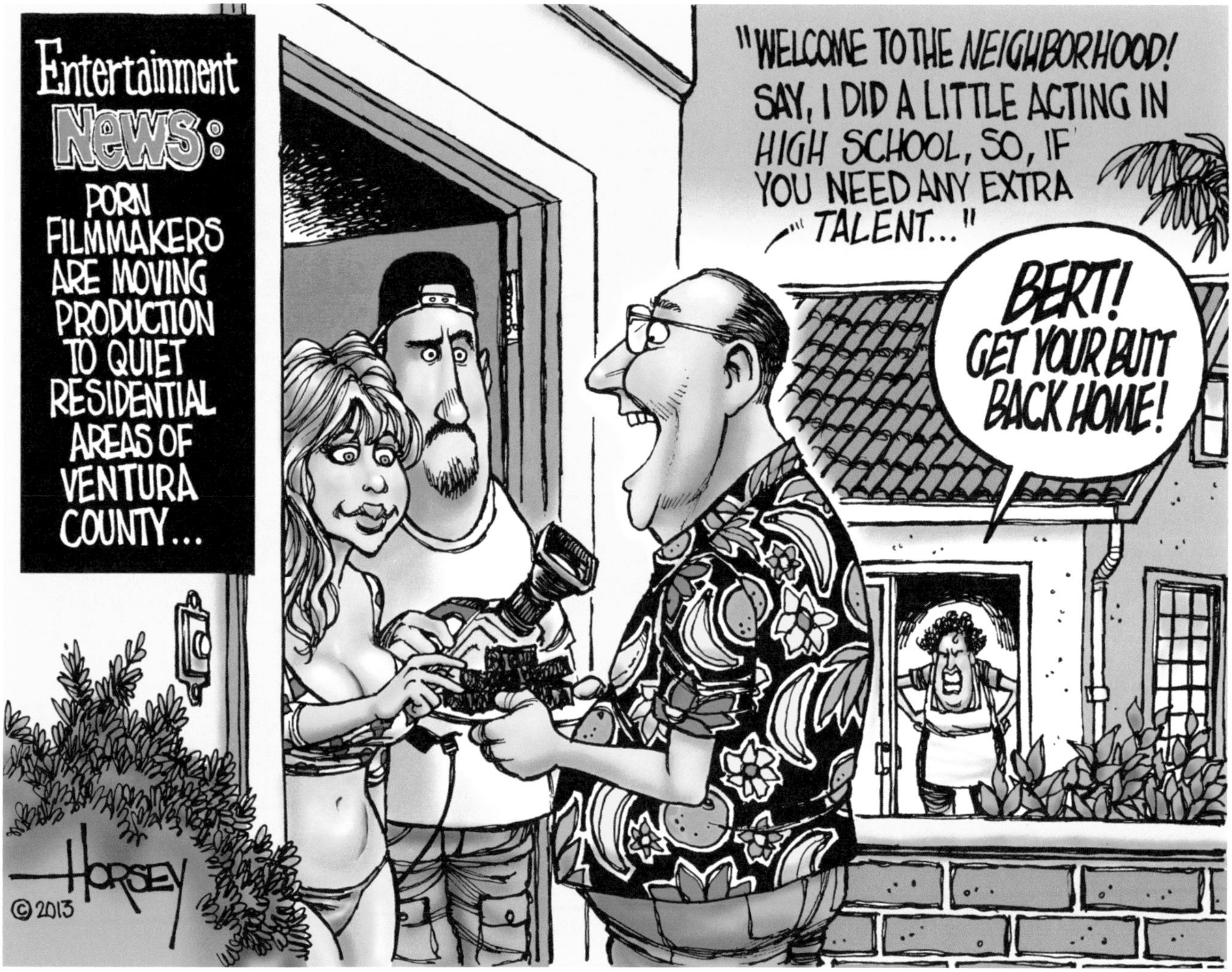
Entertainment News:
PORN FILMMAKERS ARE MOVING PRODUCTION TO QUIET RESIDENTIAL AREAS OF VENTURA COUNTY...
"WELCOME TO THE NEIGHBORHOOD! SAY, I DID A LITTLE ACTING IN HIGH SCHOOL, SO, IF YOU NEED ANY EXTRA "TALENT..."
BERT! GET YOUR BUTT BACK HOME!
HORSEY
©2013

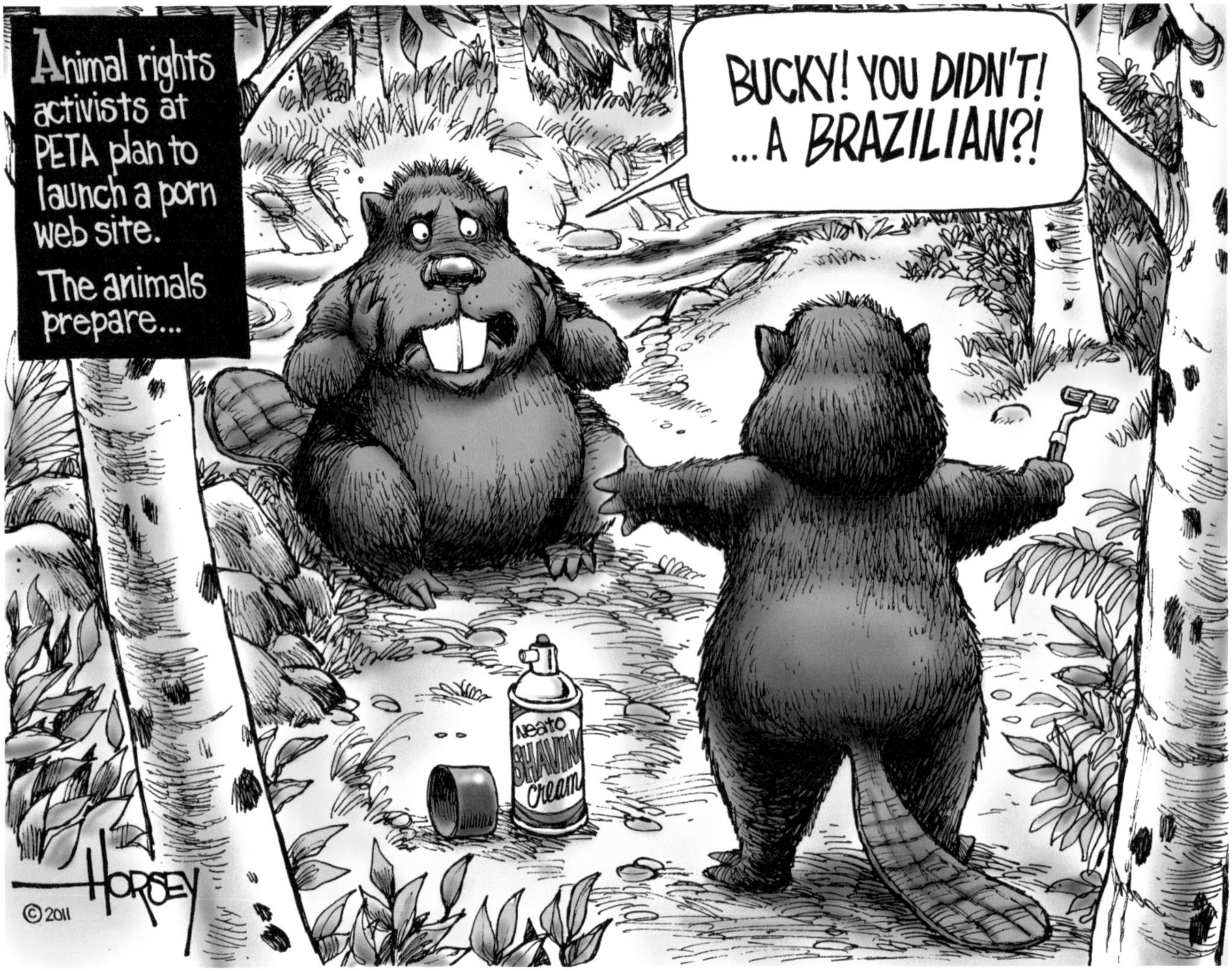
Animal rights activists at PETA plan to launch a porn web site.
The animals prepare...
BUCKY! YOU DIDN'T! ...A BRAZILIAN?!
Neato SHAVING Cream
HORSEY
© 2011

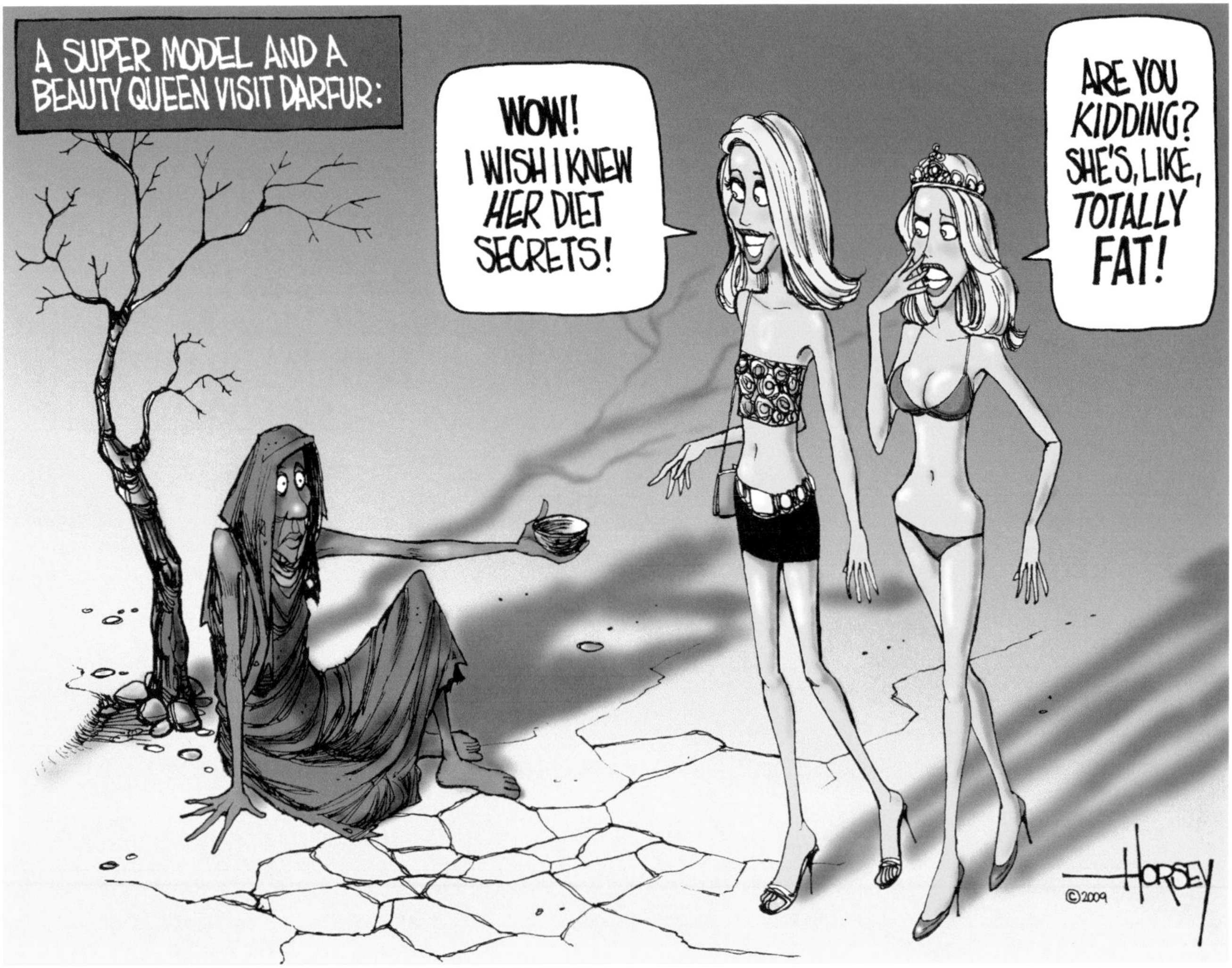
A SUPER MODEL AND A BEAUTY QUEEN VISIT DARFUR:
WOW! I WISH I KNEW HER DIET SECRETS!
ARE YOU KIDDING? SHE'S, LIKE, TOTALLY FAT!
HORSEY
©2009

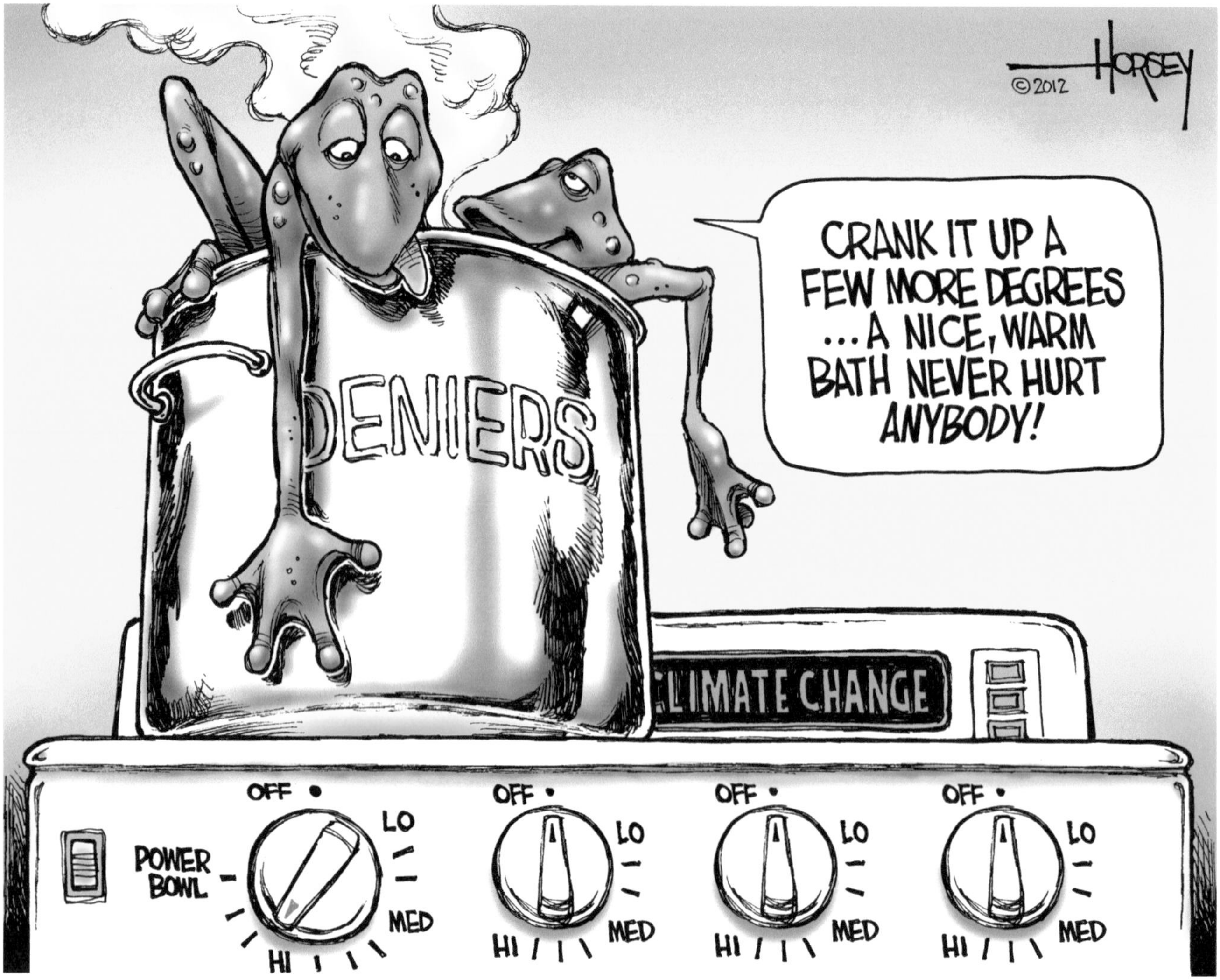
HORSEY
©2012
CRANK IT UP A FEW MORE DEGREES ...A NICE, WARM BATH NEVER HURT ANYBODY!
DENIERS
CLIMATE CHANGE
OFF
LO
MED
HI
POWER BOWL

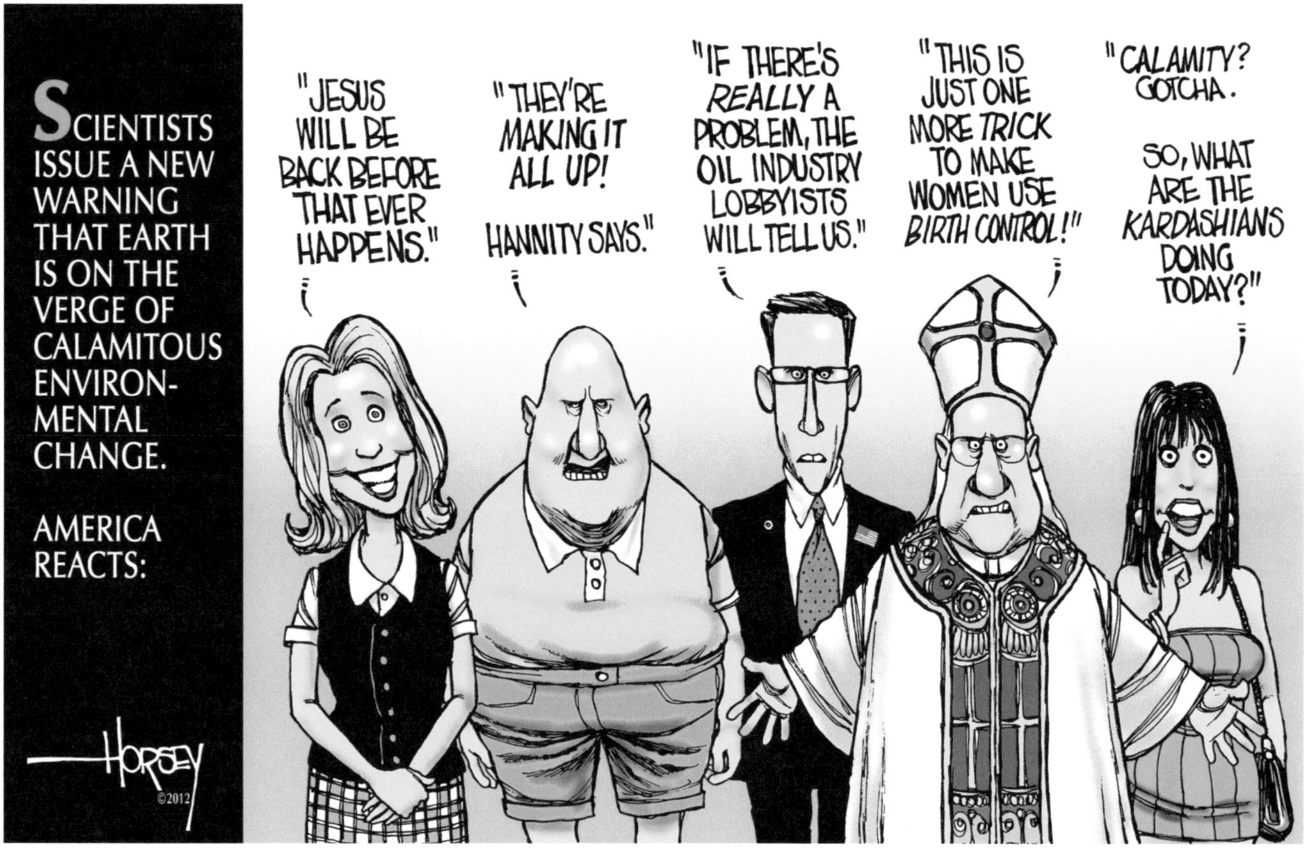
SCIENTISTS ISSUE A NEW WARNING THAT EARTH IS ON THE VERGE OF CALAMITOUS ENVIRON-MENTAL CHANGE.
AMERICA REACTS:
"JESUS WILL BE BACK BEFORE THAT EVER HAPPENS."
"THEY'RE MAKING IT ALL UP! HANNITY SAYS."
"IF THERE'S REALLY A PROBLEM, THE OIL INDUSTRY LOBBYISTS WILL TELL US."
"THIS IS JUST ONE MORE TRICK TO MAKE WOMEN USE BIRTH CONTROL!"
"CALAMITY? GOTCHA. SO, WHAT ARE THE KARDASHIANS DOING TODAY?"
HORSEY ©2012

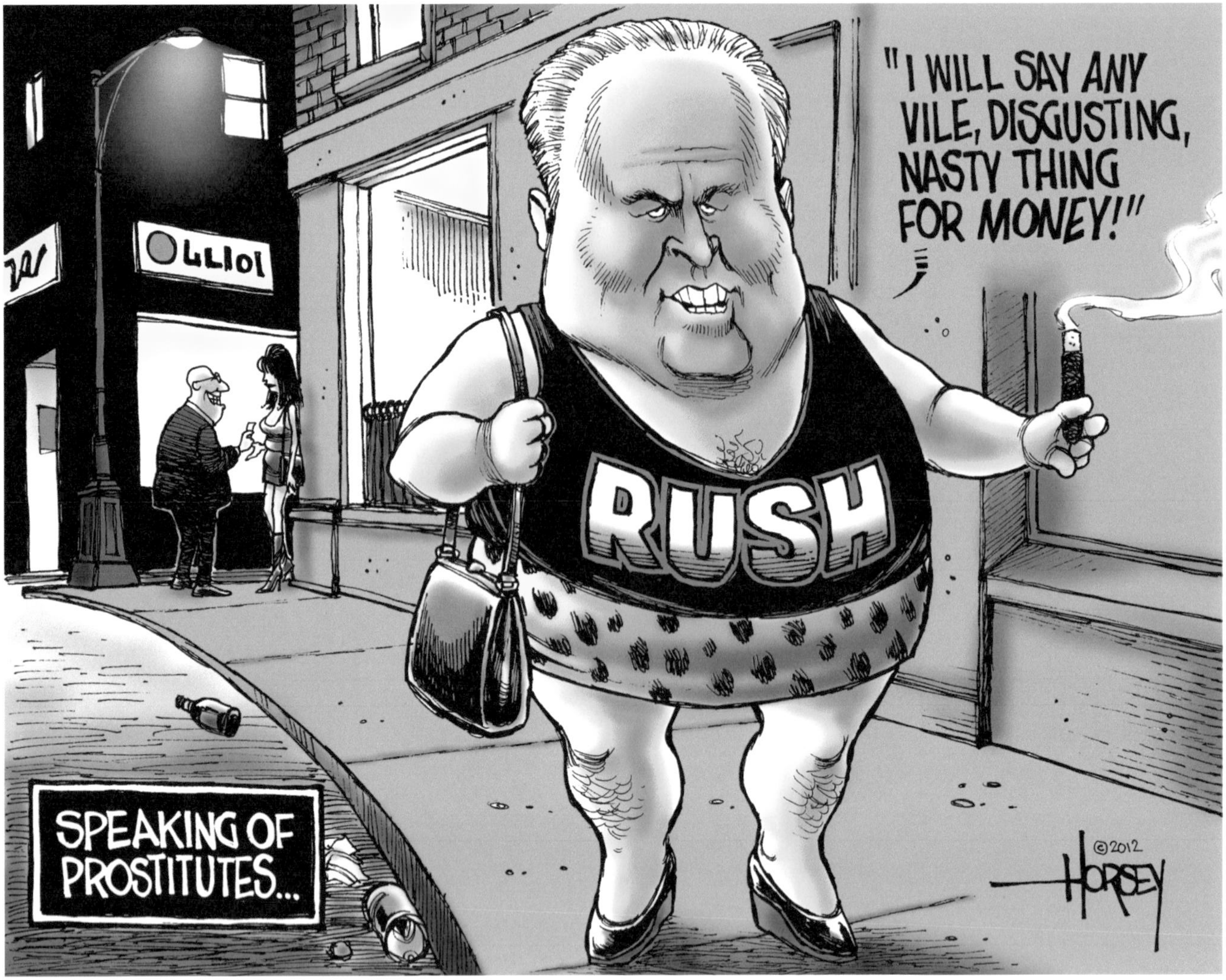
"I WILL SAY ANY VILE, DISGUSTING, NASTY THING FOR MONEY!"
RUSH
SPEAKING OF PROSTITUTES...
©2012
HORSEY

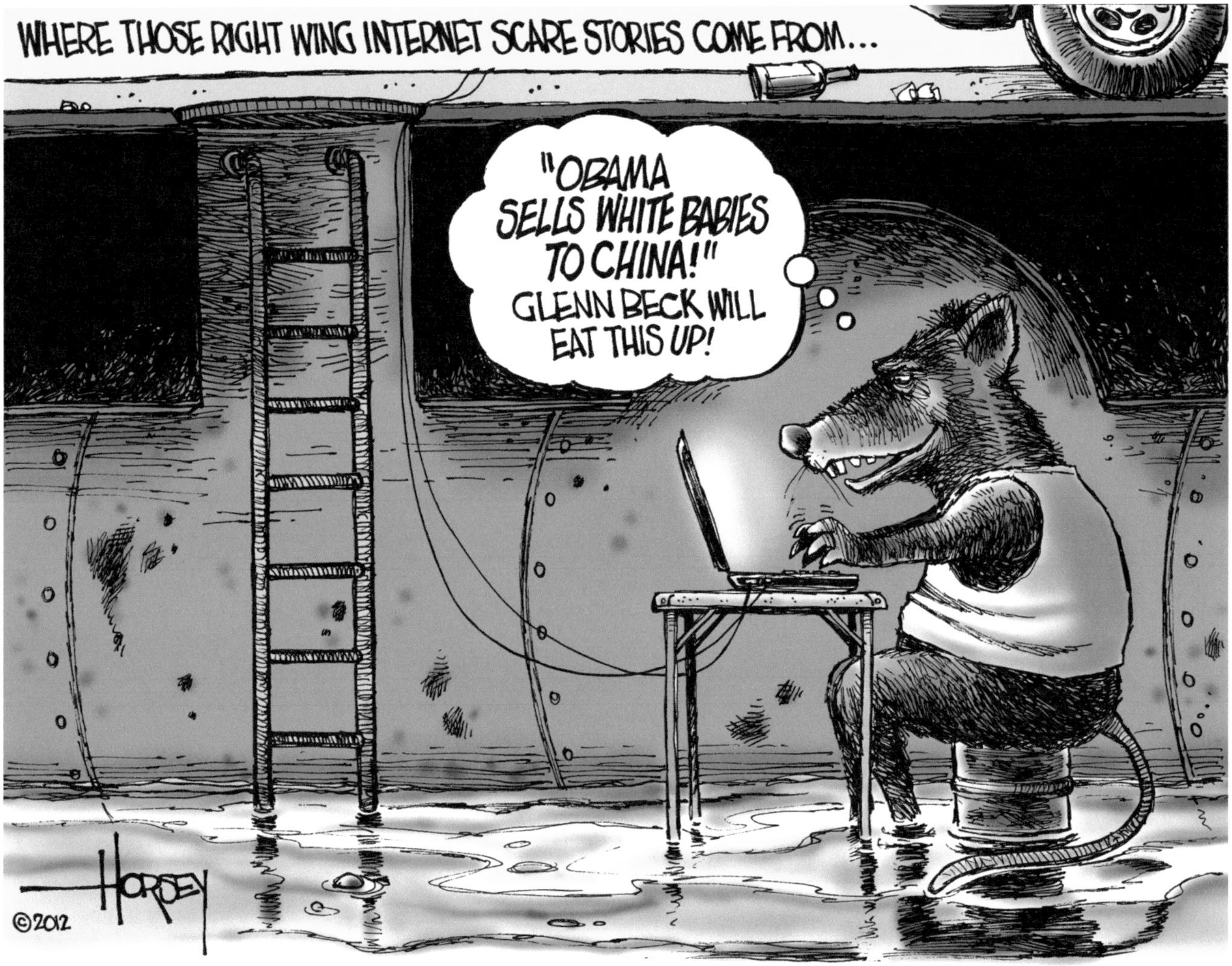
WHERE THOSE RIGHT WING INTERNET SCARE STORIES COME FROM...
"OBAMA SELLS WHITE BABIES TO CHINA!" GLENN BECK WILL EAT THIS UP!
HORSEY
©2012

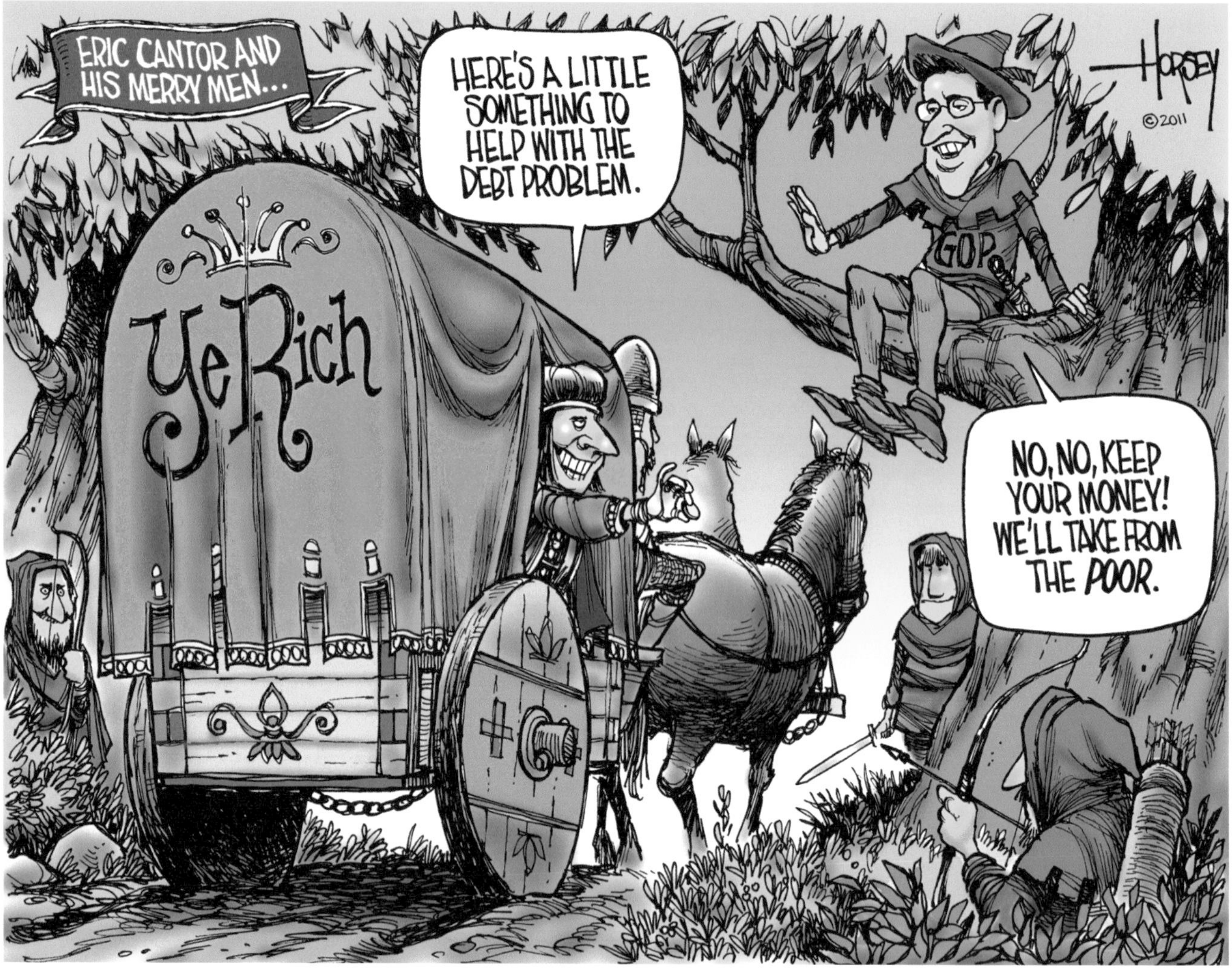
ERIC CANTOR AND HIS MERRY MEN...
HERE'S A LITTLE SOMETHING TO HELP WITH THE DEBT PROBLEM.
HORSEY ©2011
GOP
Ye Rich
NO, NO, KEEP YOUR MONEY! WE'LL TAKE FROM THE *POOR*.

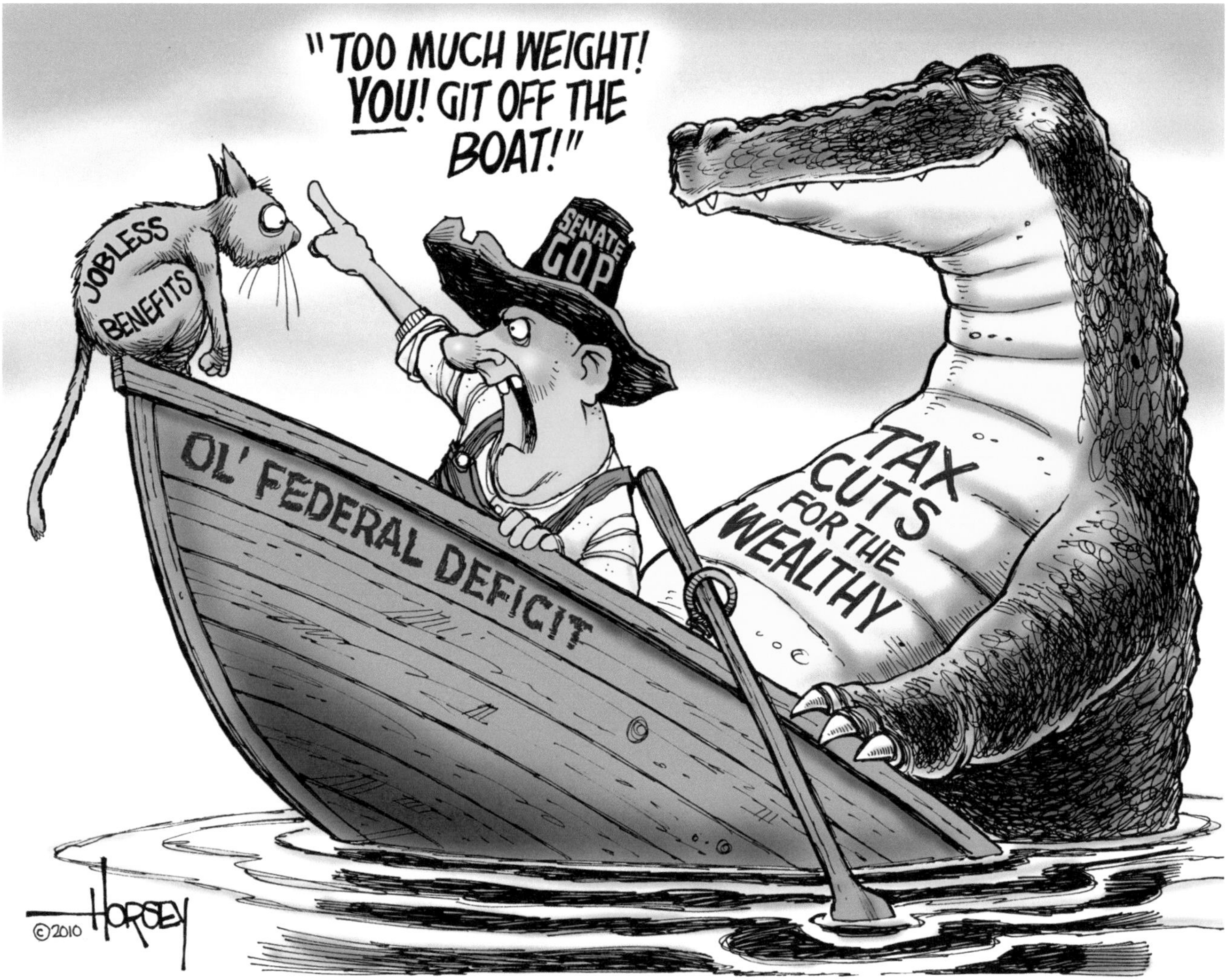
"TOO MUCH WEIGHT! YOU! GIT OFF THE BOAT!"
JOBLESS BENEFITS
SENATE GOP
TAX CUTS FOR THE WEALTHY
OL' FEDERAL DEFICIT
©2010 HORSEY

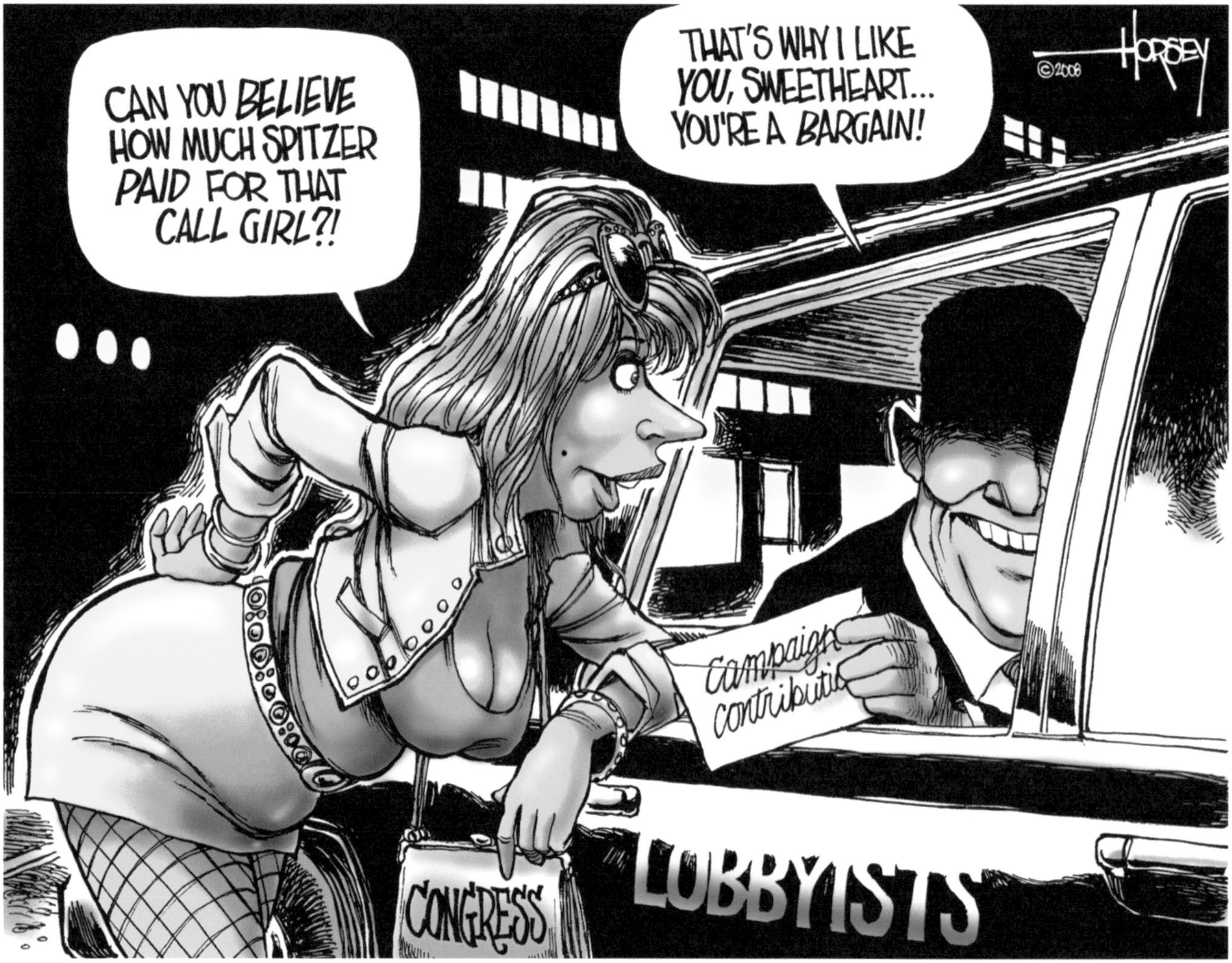
CAN YOU BELIEVE HOW MUCH SPITZER PAID FOR THAT CALL GIRL?!
...
THAT'S WHY I LIKE YOU, SWEETHEART... YOU'RE A BARGAIN!
©2008 HORSEY
Campaign contributi
CONGRESS
LOBBYISTS

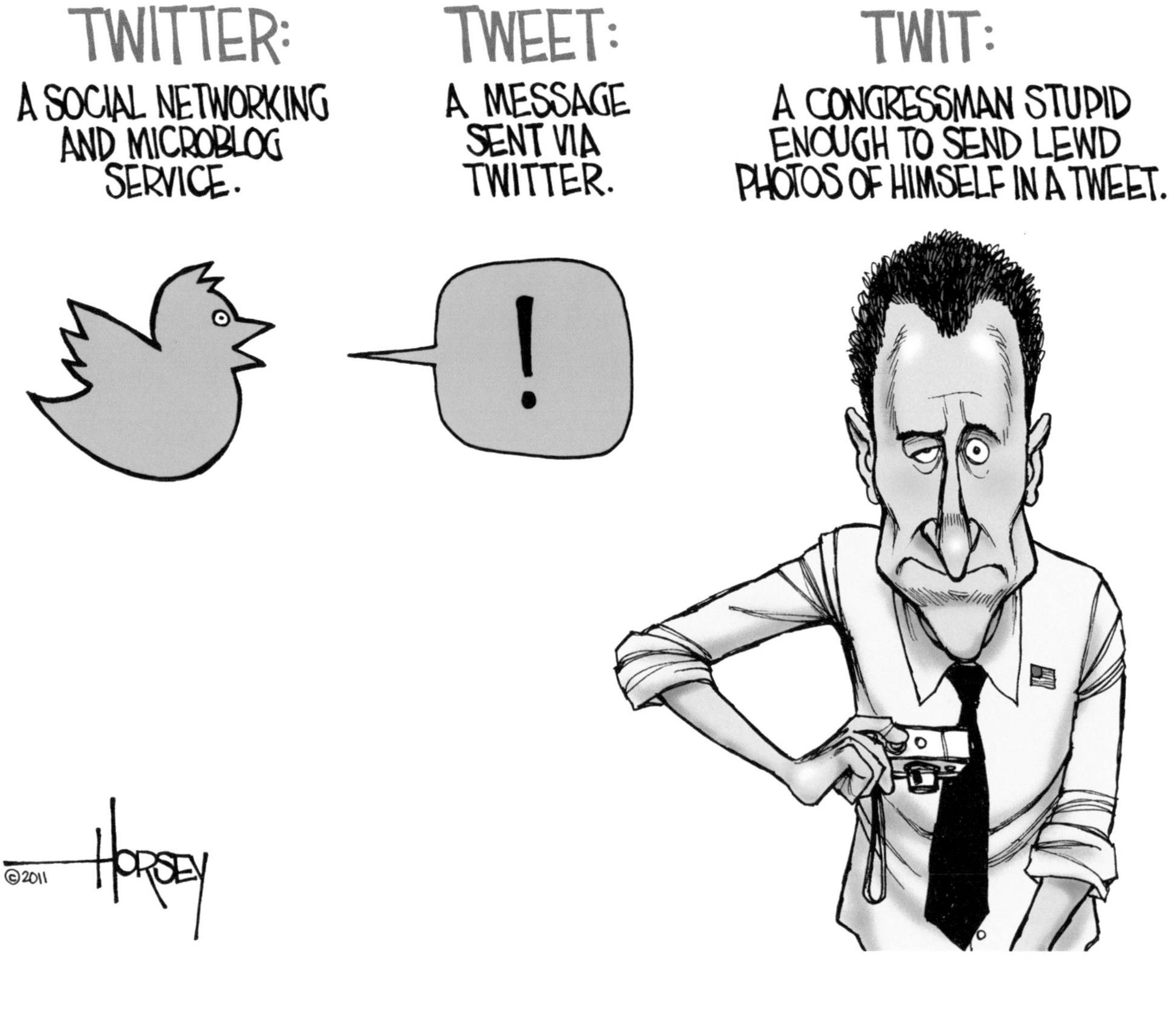
TWITTER:
A SOCIAL NETWORKING AND MICROBLOG SERVICE.
TWEET:
A MESSAGE SENT VIA TWITTER.
TWIT:
A CONGRESSMAN STUPID ENOUGH TO SEND LEWD PHOTOS OF HIMSELF IN A TWEET.
!
©2011 HORSEY

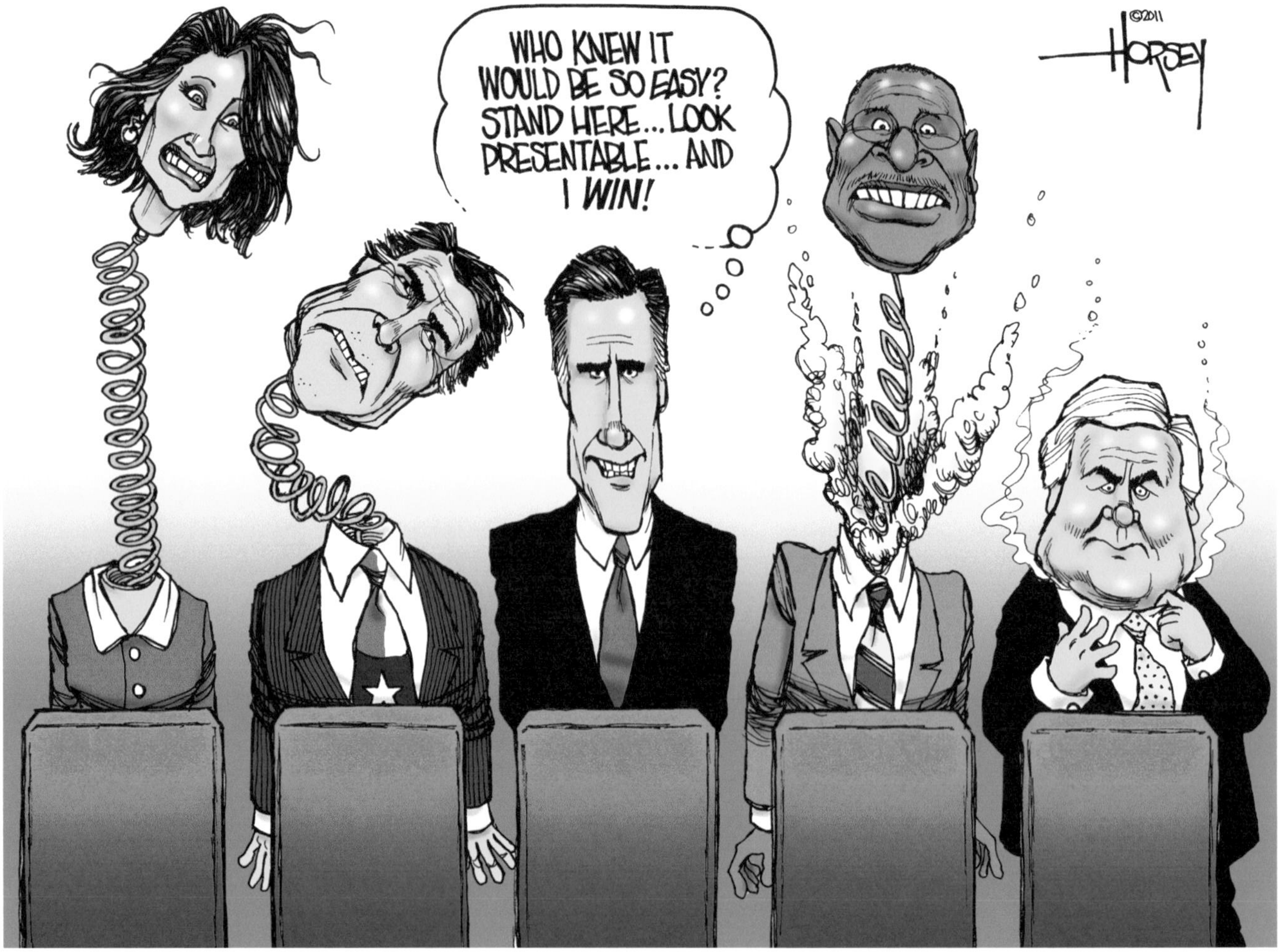
WHO KNEW IT WOULD BE SO EASY? STAND HERE... LOOK PRESENTABLE... AND I WIN!
©2011
HORSEY

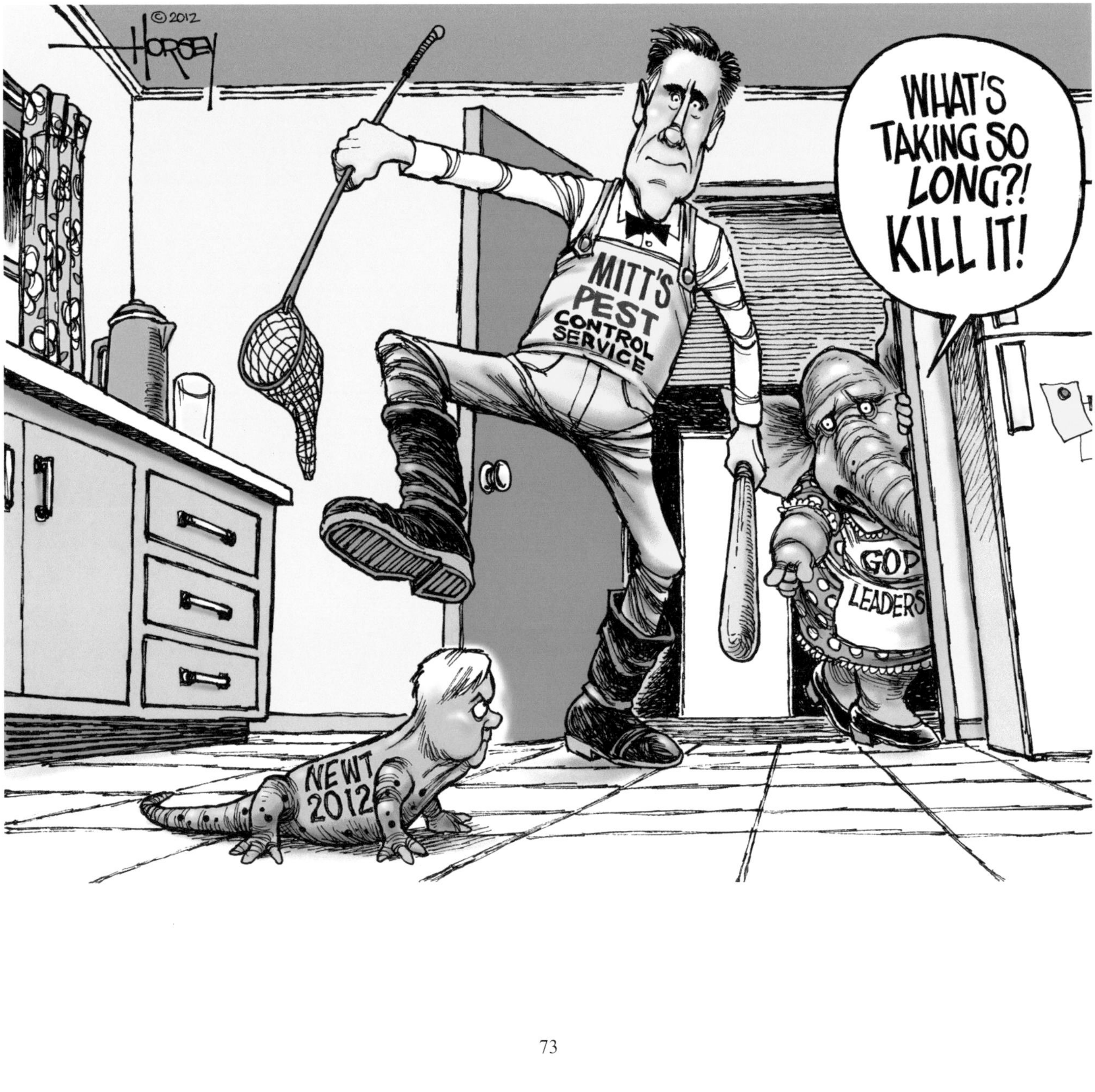
©2012
HORSEY
WHAT'S TAKING SO LONG?! KILL IT!
MITT'S PEST CONTROL SERVICE
GOP LEADERS
NEWT 2012

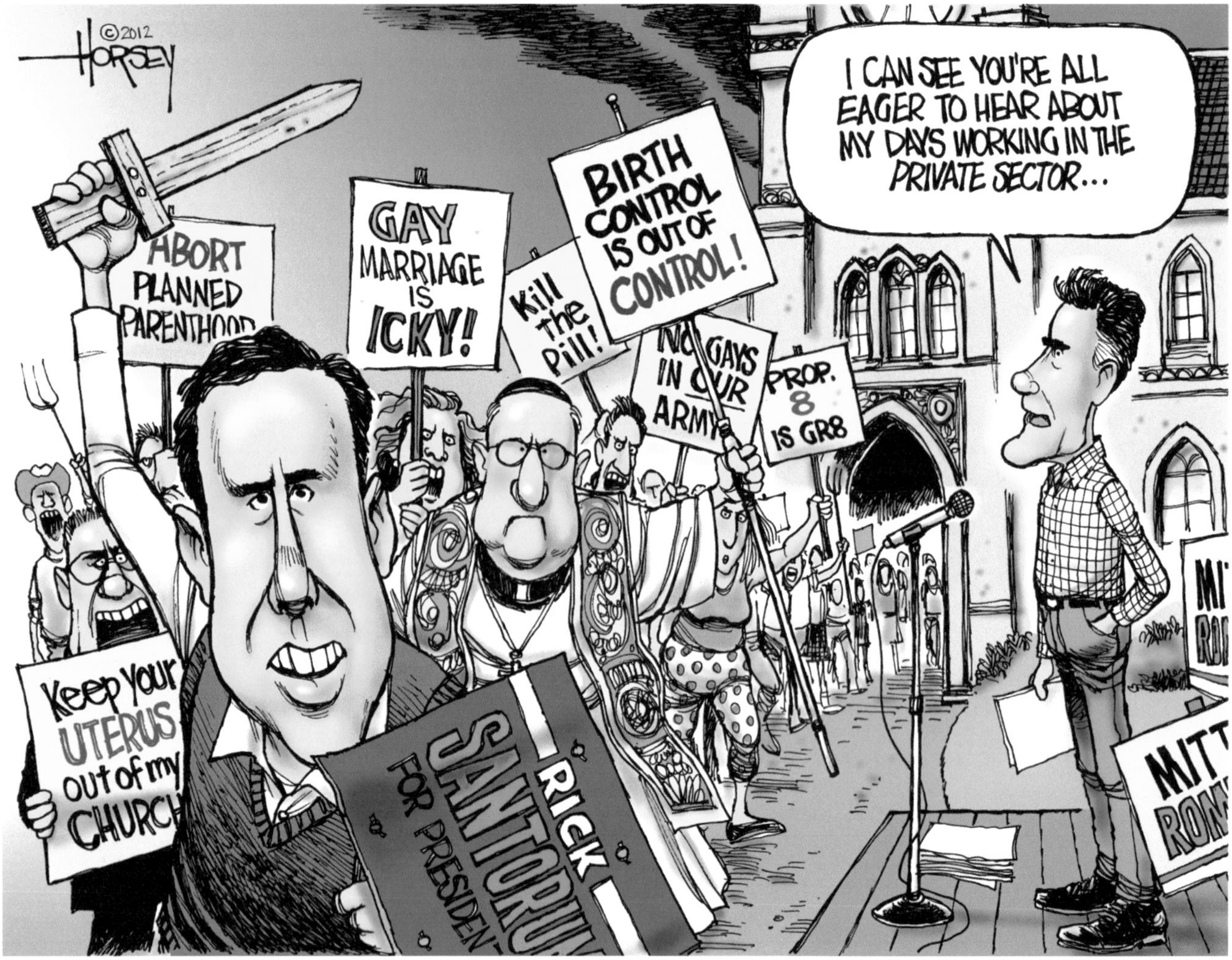
©2012 HORSEY
I CAN SEE YOU'RE ALL EAGER TO HEAR ABOUT MY DAYS WORKING IN THE PRIVATE SECTOR...
GAY MARRIAGE IS ICKY!
BIRTH CONTROL IS OUT OF CONTROL!
Kill the Pill!
NO GAYS IN OUR ARMY
PROP. 8 IS GR8
Keep your UTERUS out of my CHURCH
RICK SANTORUM FOR PRESIDENT

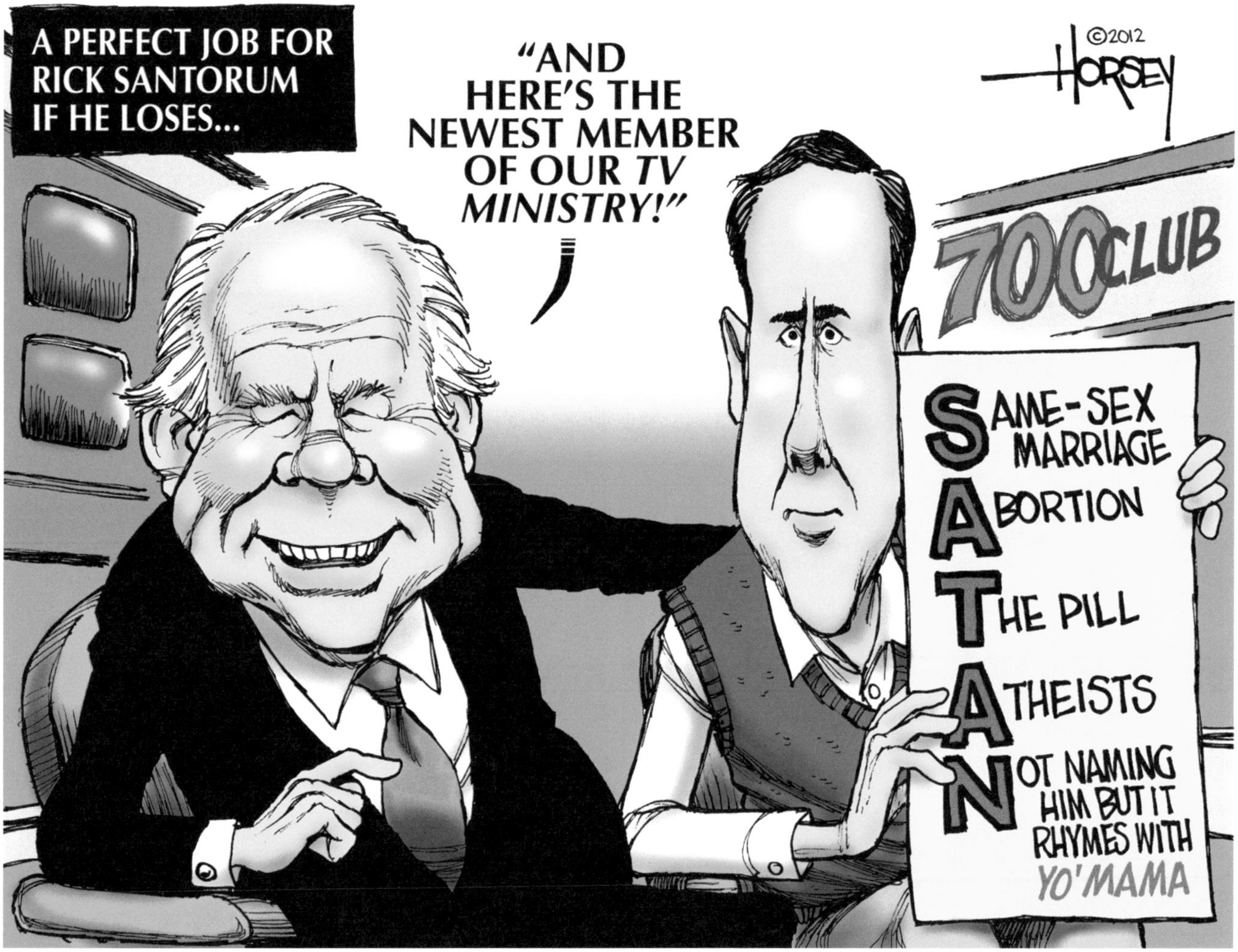
A PERFECT JOB FOR RICK SANTORUM IF HE LOSES...
"AND HERE'S THE NEWEST MEMBER OF OUR *TV MINISTRY!*"
©2012 HORSEY
700 CLUB
SAME-SEX MARRIAGE
ABORTION
THE PILL
ATHEISTS
NOT NAMING HIM BUT IT RHYMES WITH YO'MAMA

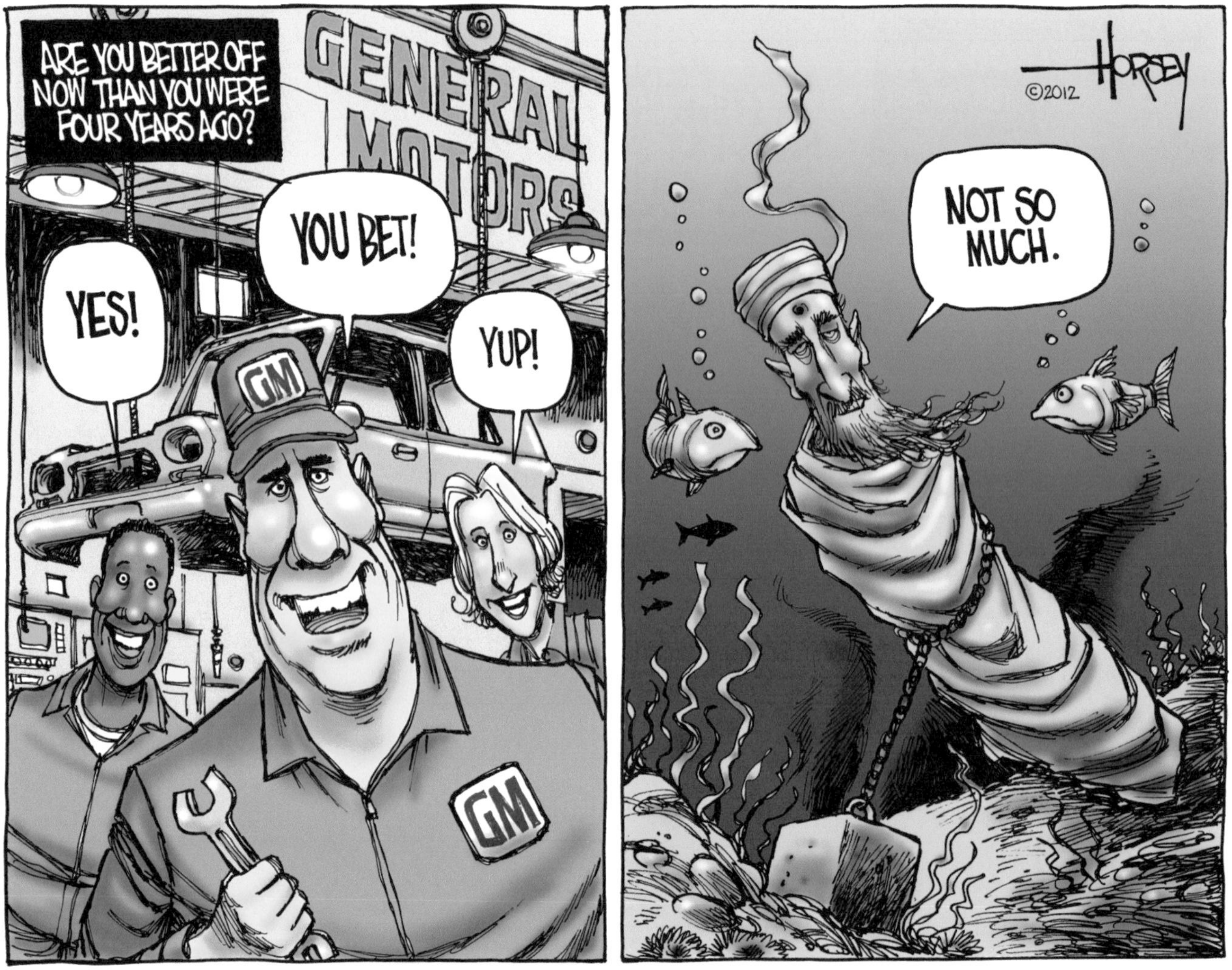
ARE YOU BETTER OFF NOW THAN YOU WERE FOUR YEARS AGO?
GENERAL MOTORS
YES!
YOU BET!
YUP!
GM
GM
HORSEY ©2012
NOT SO MUCH.

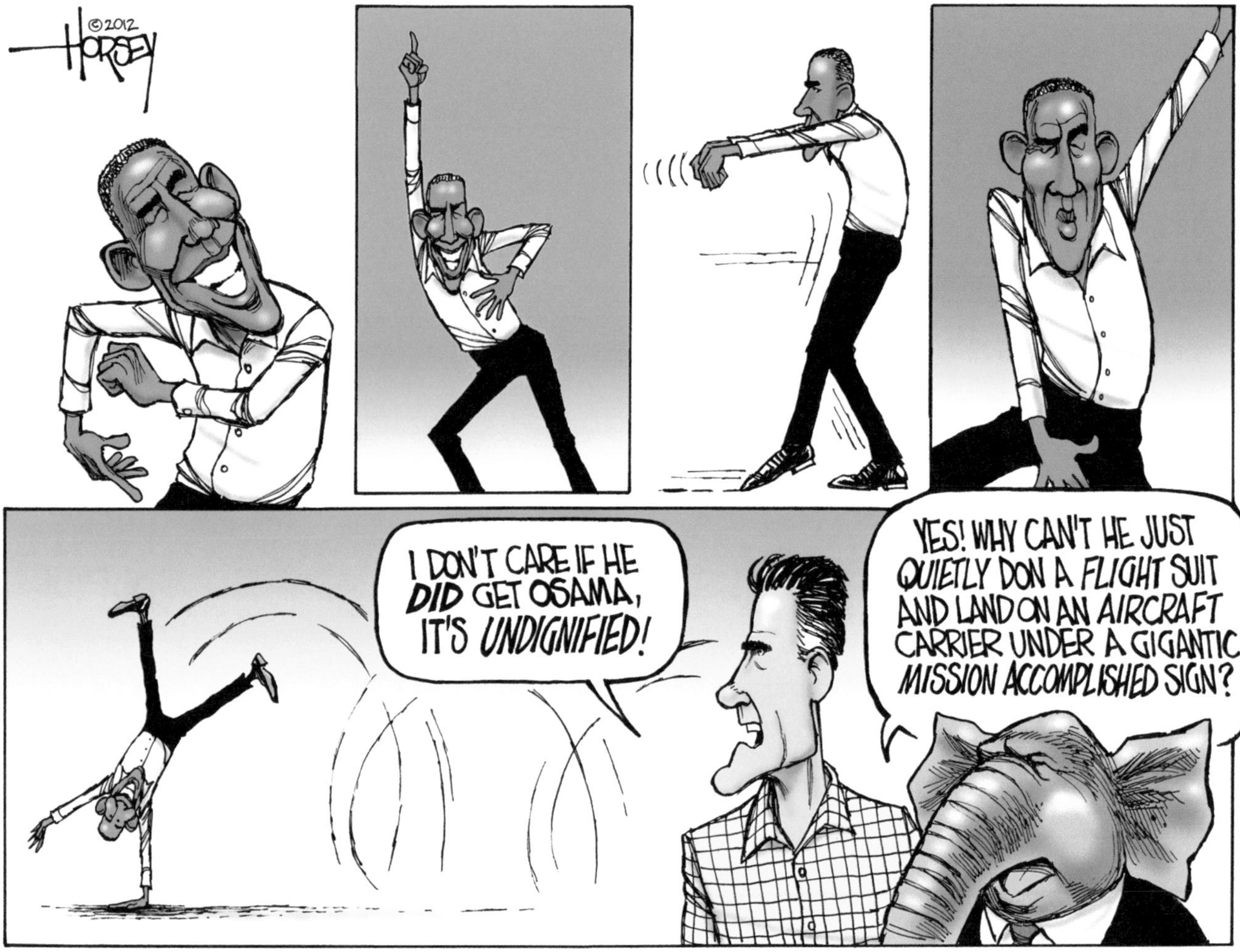

©2012 HORSEY
I DON'T CARE IF HE DID GET OSAMA, IT'S UNDIGNIFIED!
YES! WHY CAN'T HE JUST QUIETLY DON A FLIGHT SUIT AND LAND ON AN AIRCRAFT CARRIER UNDER A GIGANTIC MISSION ACCOMPLISHED SIGN?

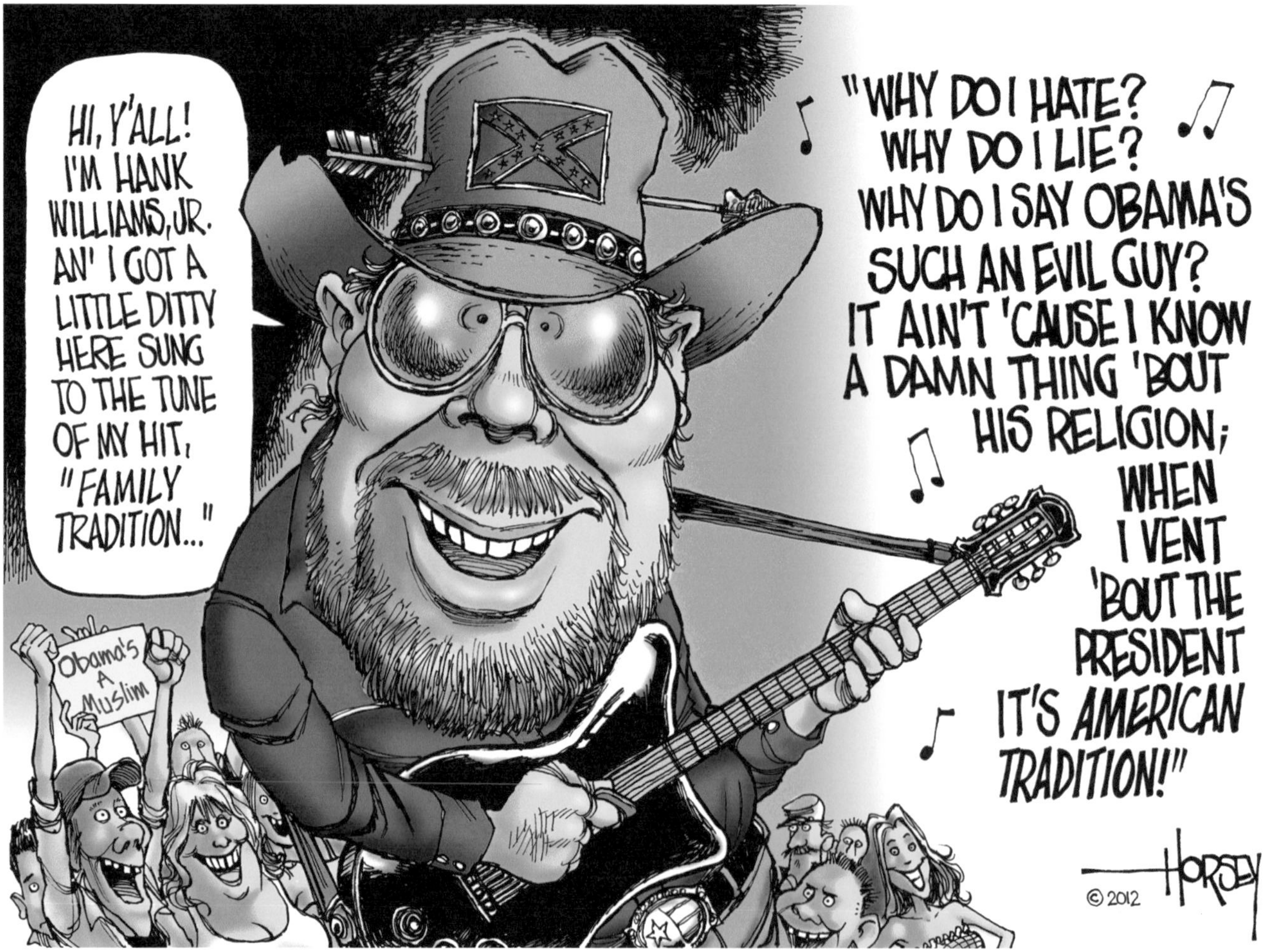
HI, Y'ALL! I'M HANK WILLIAMS, JR. AN' I GOT A LITTLE DITTY HERE SUNG TO THE TUNE OF MY HIT, "FAMILY TRADITION..."
Obama's A Muslim
"WHY DO I HATE? WHY DO I LIE? WHY DO I SAY OBAMA'S SUCH AN EVIL GUY? IT AIN'T 'CAUSE I KNOW A DAMN THING 'BOUT HIS RELIGION; WHEN I VENT 'BOUT THE PRESIDENT IT'S *AMERICAN TRADITION!*"
HORSEY
© 2012

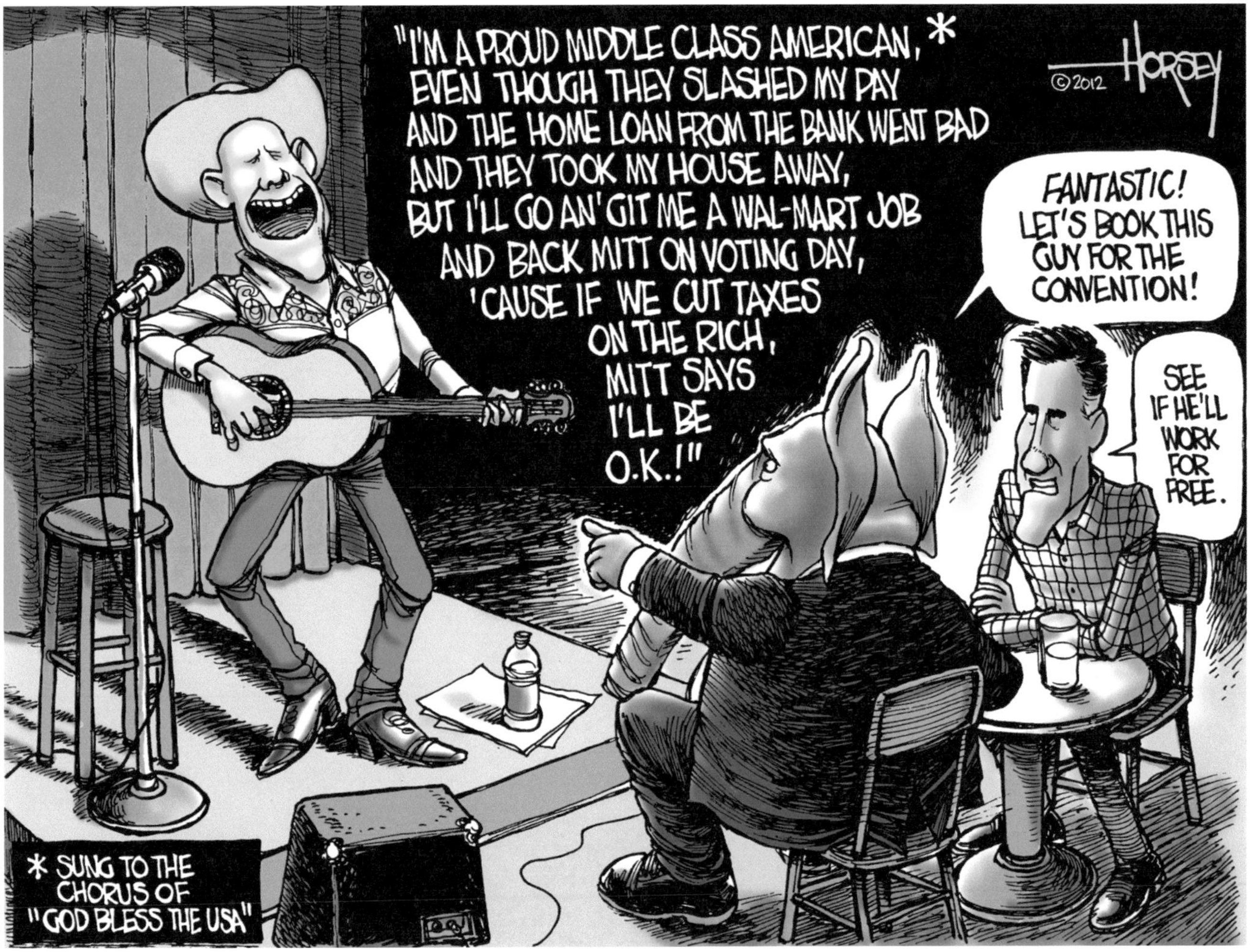
"I'M A PROUD MIDDLE CLASS AMERICAN,*
EVEN THOUGH THEY SLASHED MY PAY
AND THE HOME LOAN FROM THE BANK WENT BAD
AND THEY TOOK MY HOUSE AWAY,
BUT I'LL GO AN' GIT ME A WAL-MART JOB
AND BACK MITT ON VOTING DAY,
'CAUSE IF WE CUT TAXES
ON THE RICH,
MITT SAYS
I'LL BE
O.K.!"
©2012 HORSEY
FANTASTIC! LET'S BOOK THIS GUY FOR THE CONVENTION!
SEE IF HE'LL WORK FOR FREE.
* SUNG TO THE CHORUS OF "GOD BLESS THE USA"

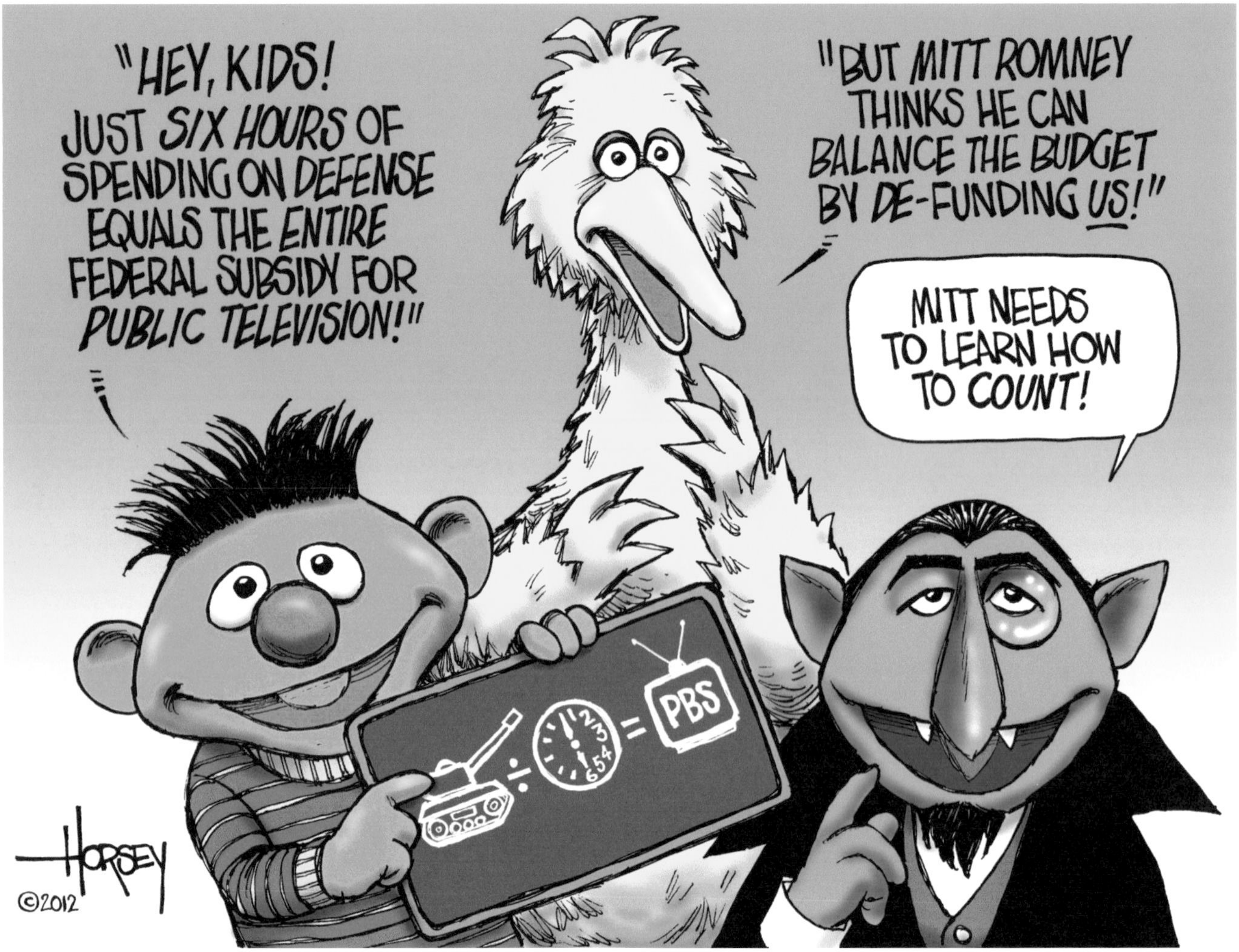
"HEY, KIDS! JUST SIX HOURS OF SPENDING ON DEFENSE EQUALS THE ENTIRE FEDERAL SUBSIDY FOR PUBLIC TELEVISION!"
"BUT MITT ROMNEY THINKS HE CAN BALANCE THE BUDGET BY DE-FUNDING US!"
MITT NEEDS TO LEARN HOW TO COUNT!
PBS
HORSEY
©2012

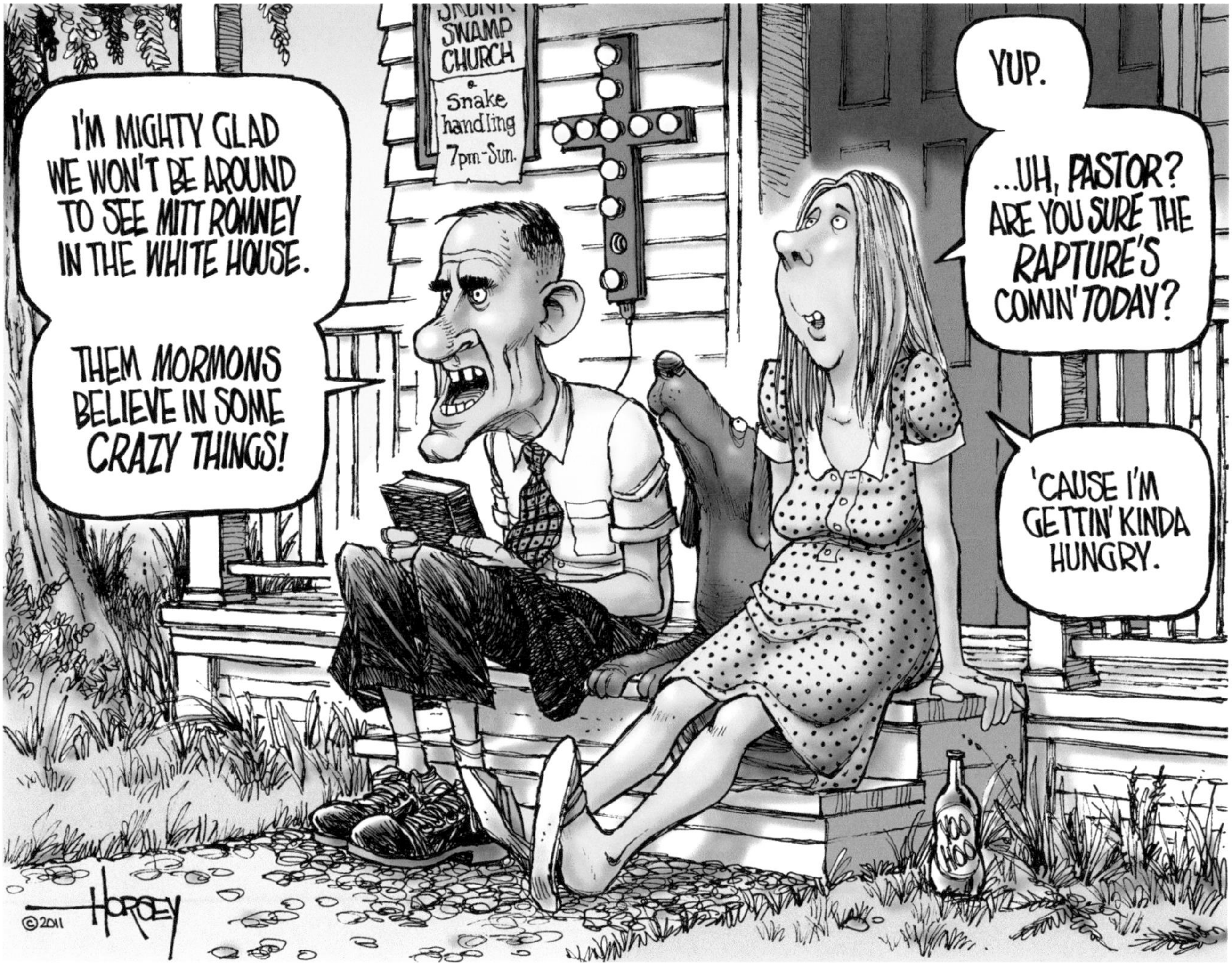
SWAMP CHURCH
Snake handling 7pm-Sun.
I'M MIGHTY GLAD WE WON'T BE AROUND TO SEE MITT ROMNEY IN THE WHITE HOUSE.
THEM MORMONS BELIEVE IN SOME CRAZY THINGS!
YUP.
...UH, PASTOR? ARE YOU SURE THE RAPTURE'S COMIN' TODAY?
'CAUSE I'M GETTIN' KINDA HUNGRY.
©2011 HORSEY

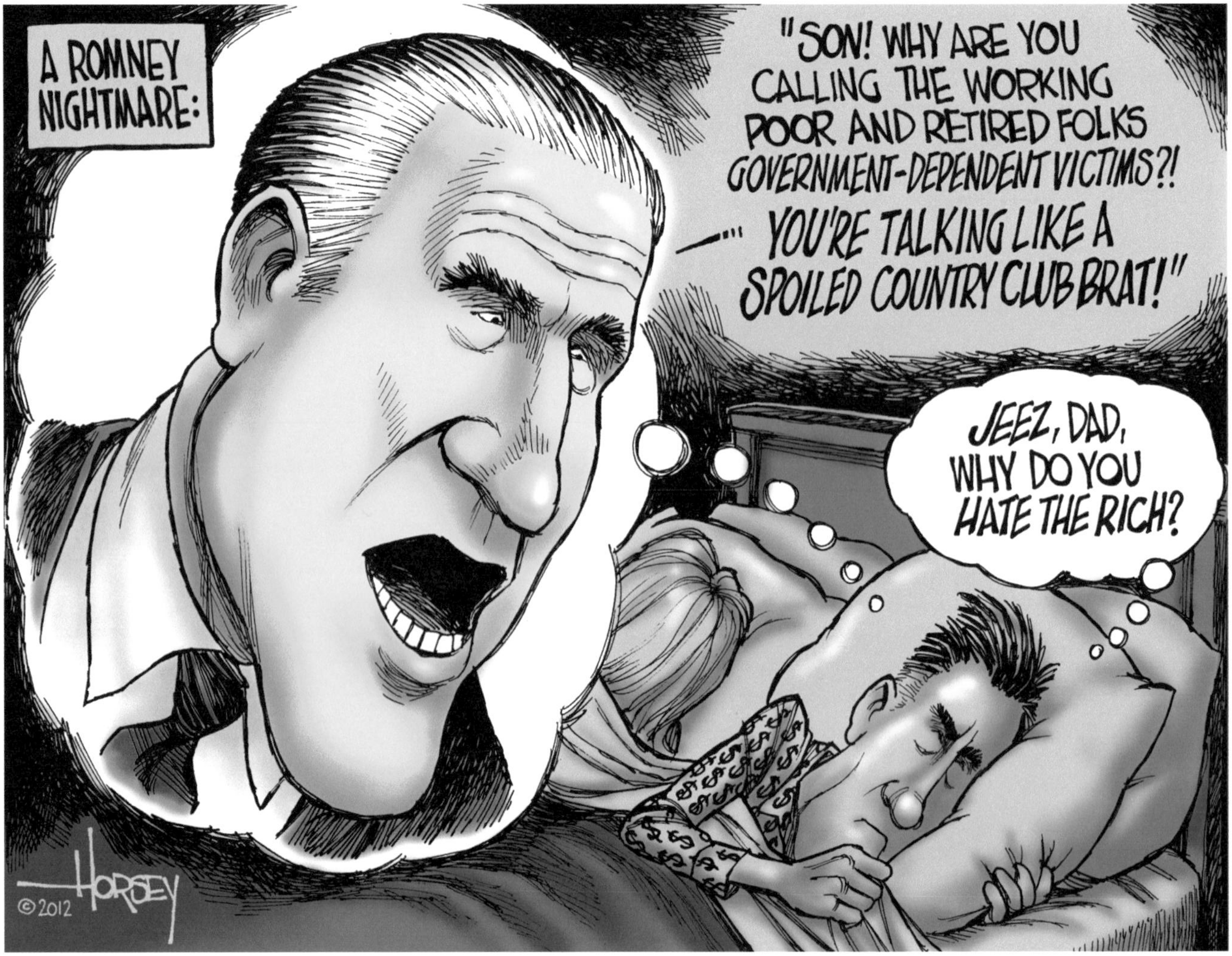
A ROMNEY NIGHTMARE:
"SON! WHY ARE YOU CALLING THE WORKING POOR AND RETIRED FOLKS GOVERNMENT-DEPENDENT VICTIMS?!
YOU'RE TALKING LIKE A SPOILED COUNTRY CLUB BRAT!"
JEEZ, DAD, WHY DO YOU HATE THE RICH?
HORSEY
©2012

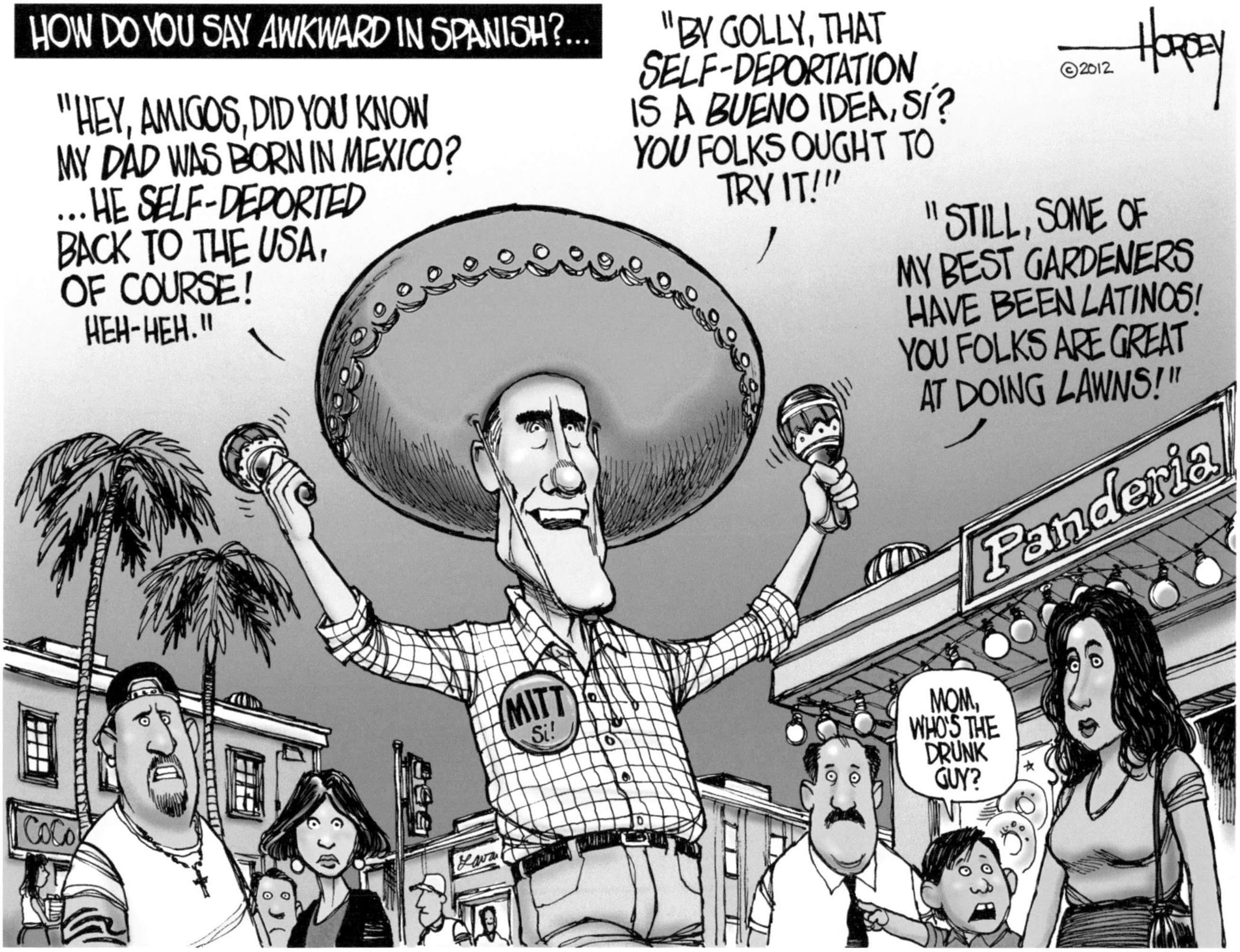
HOW DO YOU SAY AWKWARD IN SPANISH?...
"HEY, AMIGOS, DID YOU KNOW MY DAD WAS BORN IN MEXICO? ...HE SELF-DEPORTED BACK TO THE USA, OF COURSE! HEH-HEH."
"BY GOLLY, THAT SELF-DEPORTATION IS A BUENO IDEA, SÍ? YOU FOLKS OUGHT TO TRY IT!"
"STILL, SOME OF MY BEST GARDENERS HAVE BEEN LATINOS! YOU FOLKS ARE GREAT AT DOING LAWNS!"
©2012 HORSEY
MITT SÍ!
Panderia
CoCo
MOM, WHO'S THE DRUNK GUY?

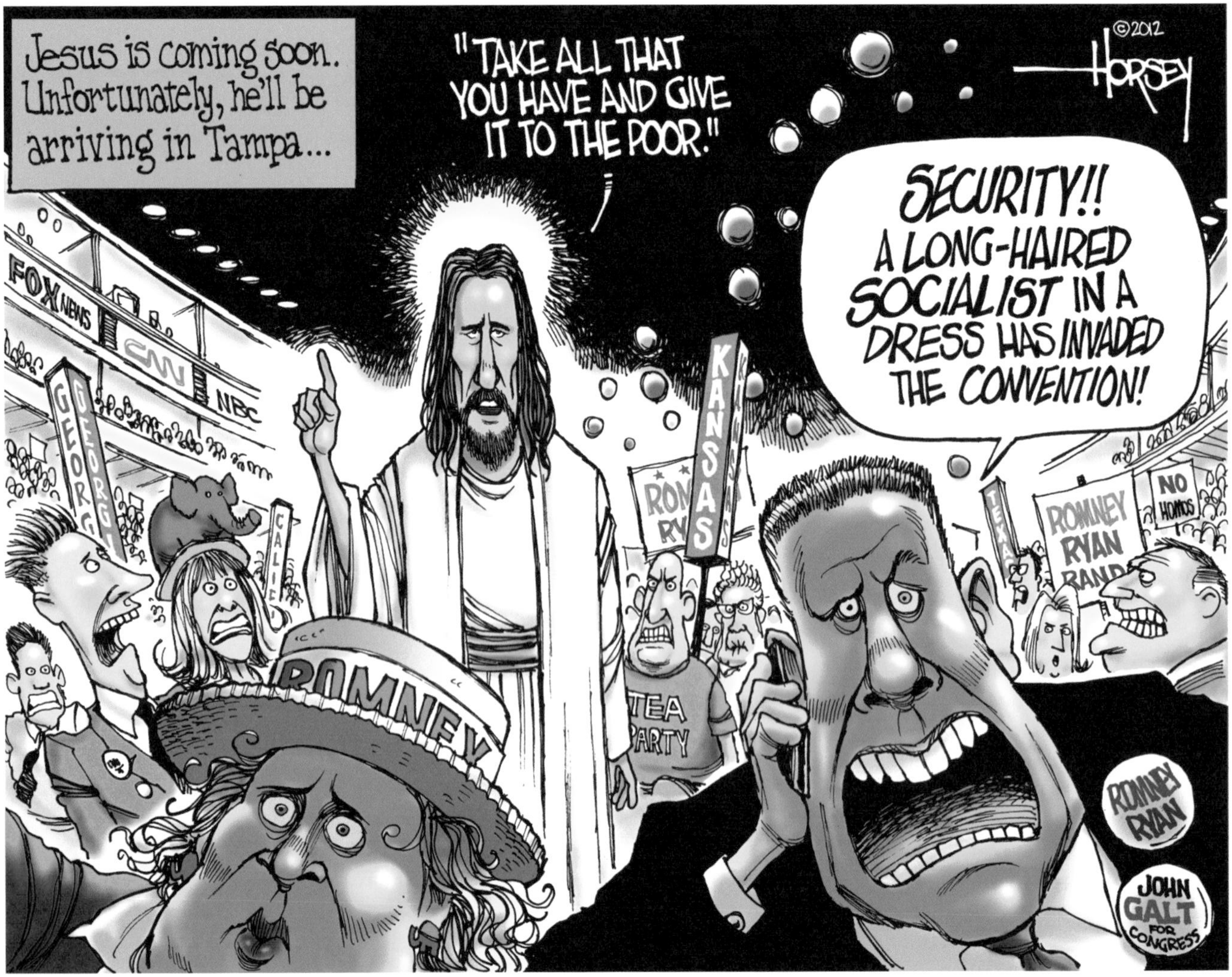
Jesus is coming soon. Unfortunately, he'll be arriving in Tampa...
"TAKE ALL THAT YOU HAVE AND GIVE IT TO THE POOR."
SECURITY!! A LONG-HAIRED SOCIALIST IN A DRESS HAS INVADED THE CONVENTION!
©2012 HORSEY
FOX NEWS
CNN
NBC
GEORGIA
KANSAS
ROMNEY
TEA PARTY
ROMNEY RYAN RAND
NO HOMOS
TEXAS
ROMNEY RYAN
JOHN GALT FOR CONGRESS

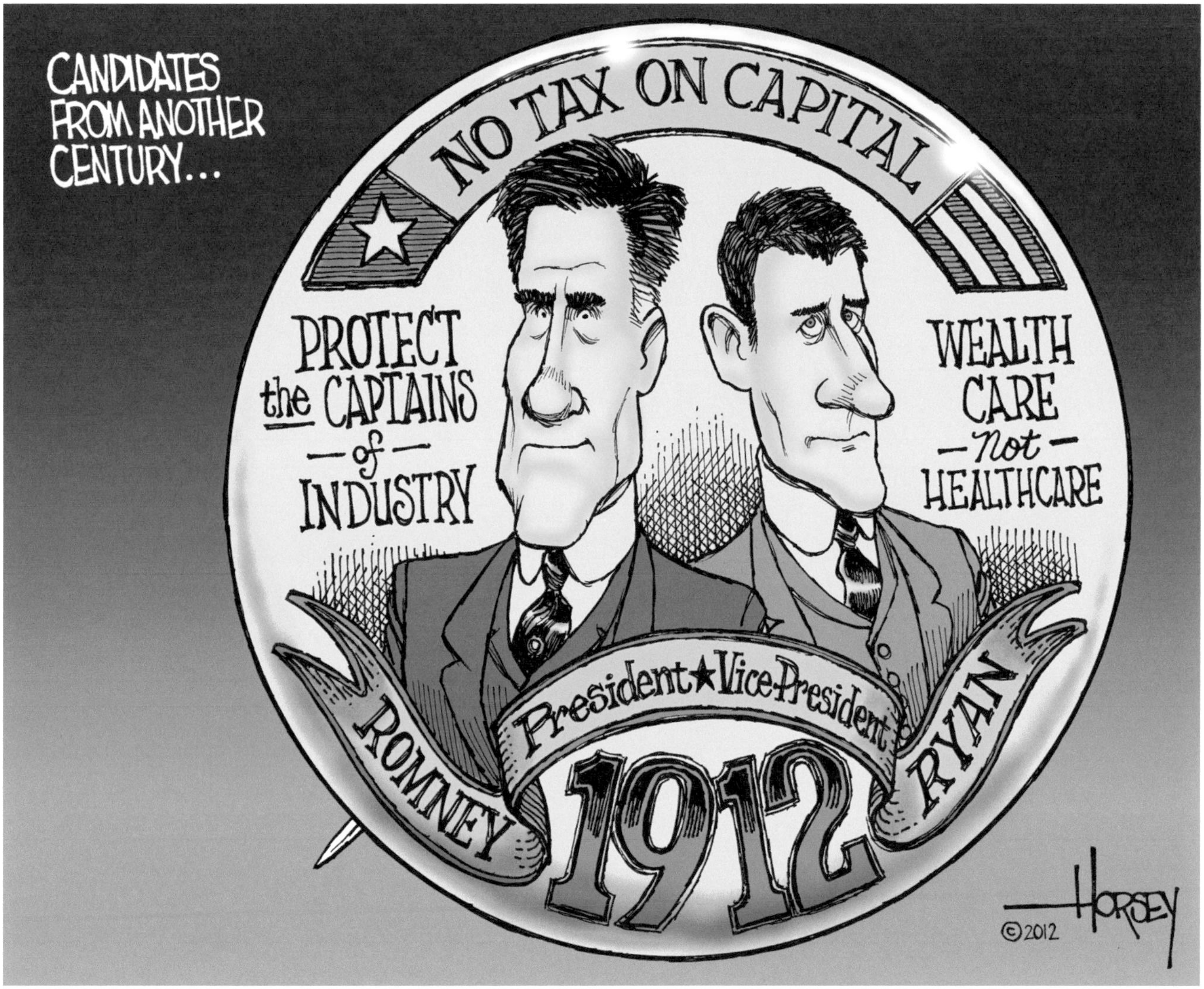
CANDIDATES FROM ANOTHER CENTURY...
NO TAX ON CAPITAL
PROTECT the CAPTAINS of INDUSTRY
WEALTH CARE not HEALTHCARE
President★Vice President
ROMNEY
RYAN
1912
HORSEY
©2012

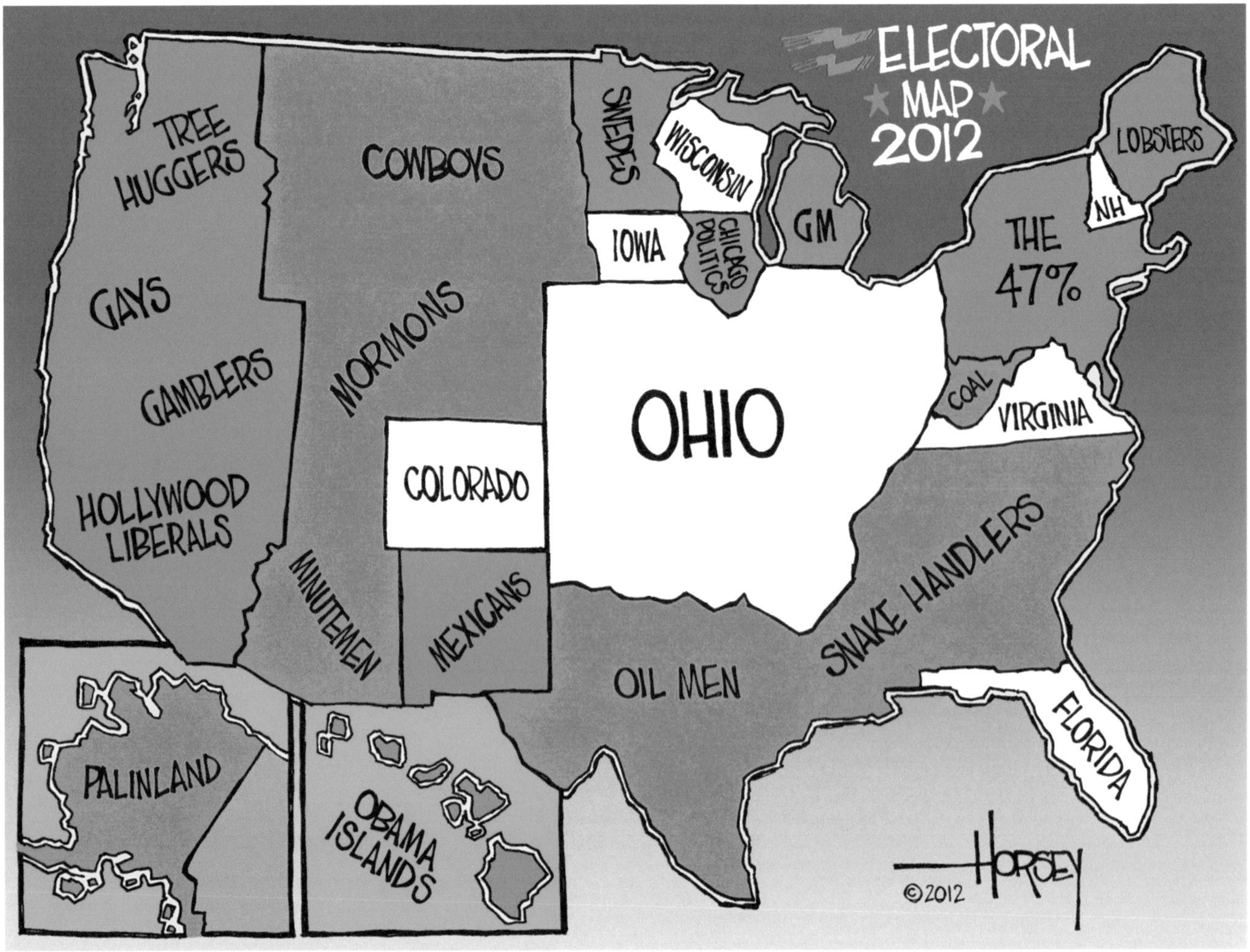
ELECTORAL MAP 2012
TREE HUGGERS
COWBOYS
SWEDES
WISCONSIN
LOBSTERS
NH
GAYS
GAMBLERS
HOLLYWOOD LIBERALS
MORMONS
IOWA
CHICAGO POLITICS
GM
THE 47%
OHIO
COAL
VIRGINIA
COLORADO
MINUTEMEN
MEXICANS
OIL MEN
SNAKE HANDLERS
FLORIDA
PALINLAND
OBAMA ISLANDS
HORSEY
©2012

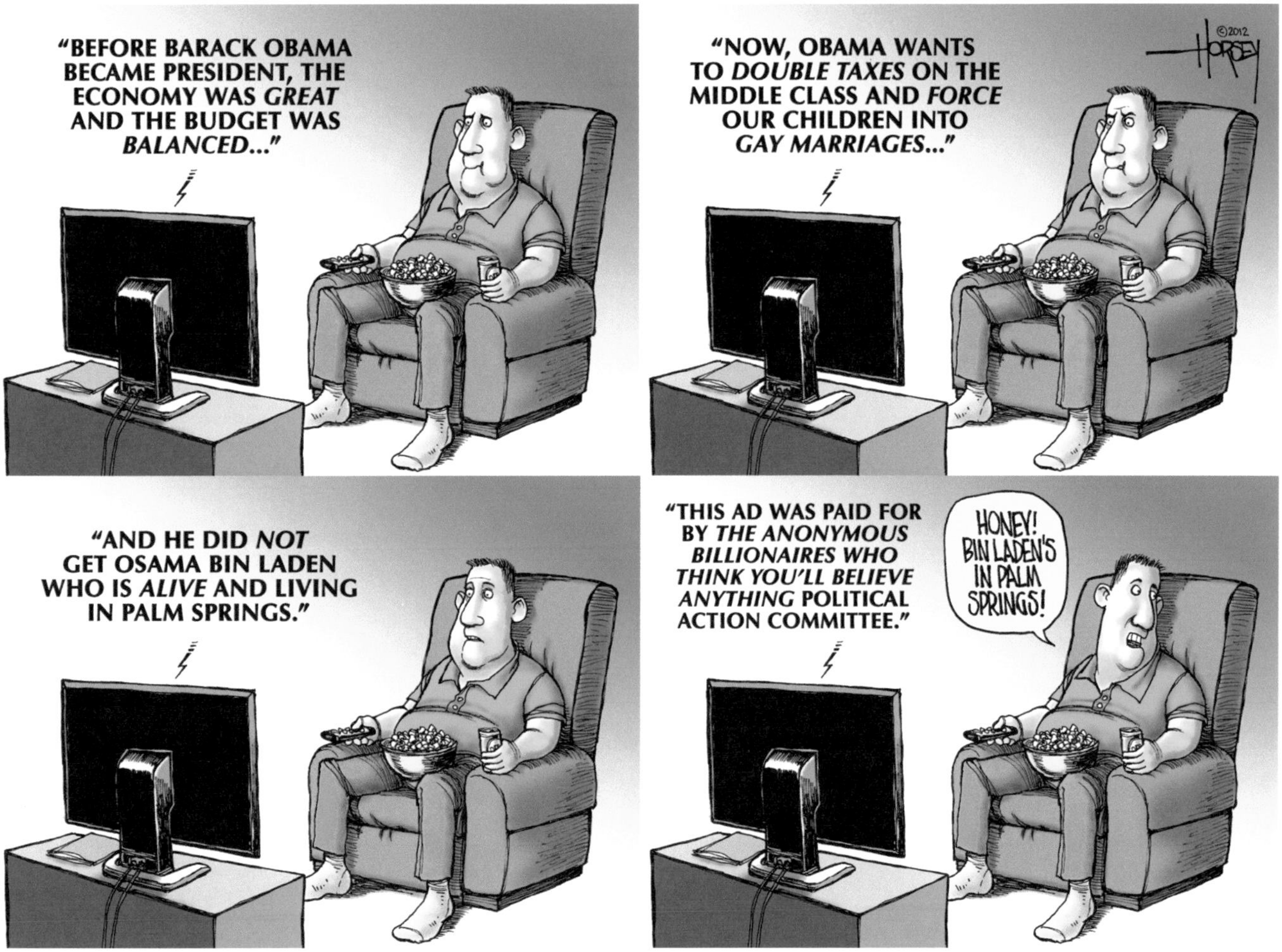
"BEFORE BARACK OBAMA BECAME PRESIDENT, THE ECONOMY WAS *GREAT* AND THE BUDGET WAS *BALANCED...*"
©2012 HORSEY
"NOW, OBAMA WANTS TO *DOUBLE TAXES* ON THE MIDDLE CLASS AND *FORCE* OUR CHILDREN INTO *GAY MARRIAGES...*"
"AND HE DID *NOT* GET OSAMA BIN LADEN WHO IS *ALIVE* AND LIVING IN PALM SPRINGS."
"THIS AD WAS PAID FOR BY *THE ANONYMOUS BILLIONAIRES WHO THINK YOU'LL BELIEVE ANYTHING* POLITICAL ACTION COMMITTEE."
HONEY! BIN LADEN'S IN PALM SPRINGS!

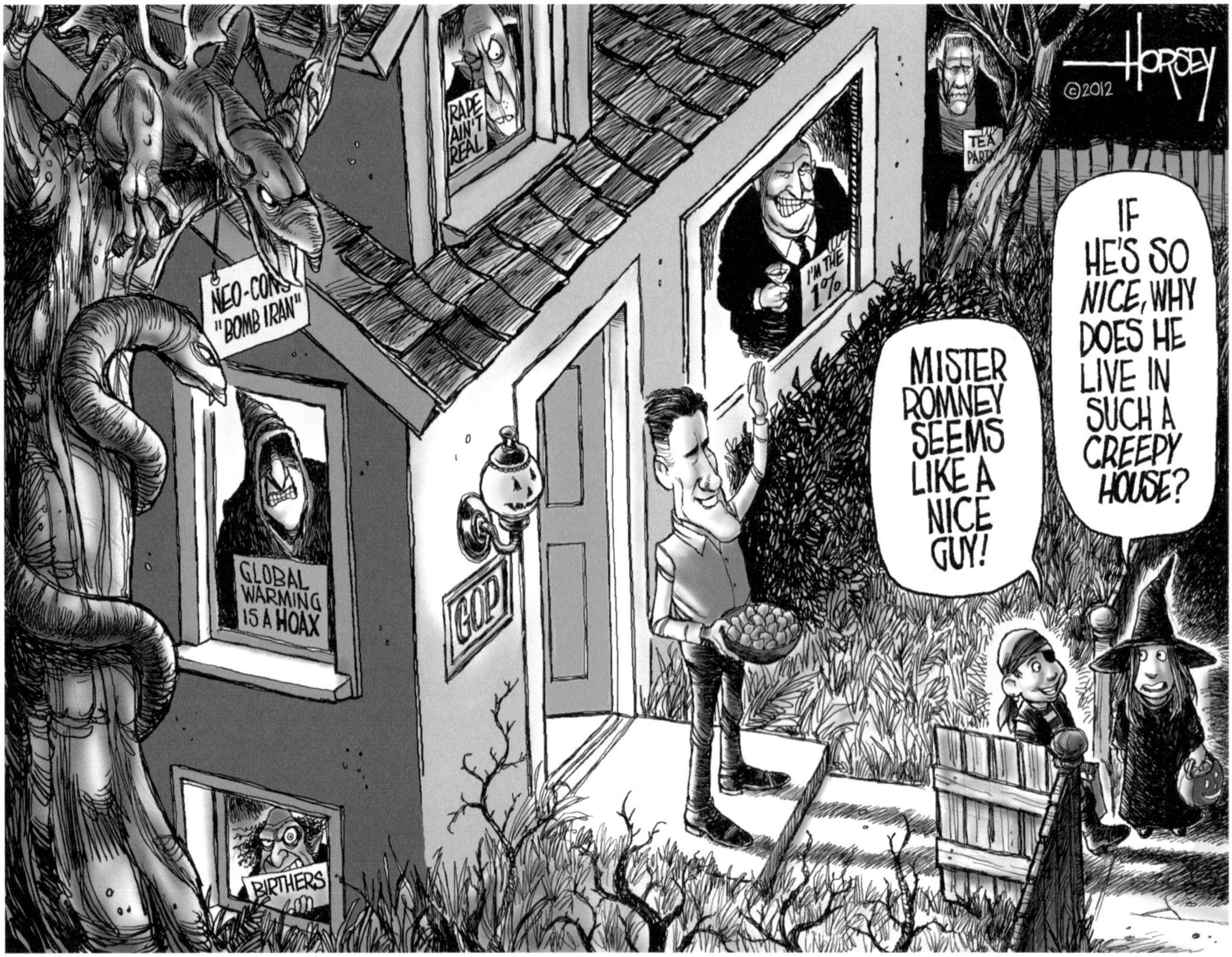
HORSEY
©2012
RAPE AIN'T REAL
TEA PARTY
NEO-CONS "BOMB IRAN"
I'M THE 1%
GLOBAL WARMING IS A HOAX
GOP
BIRTHERS
MISTER ROMNEY SEEMS LIKE A NICE GUY!
IF HE'S SO NICE, WHY DOES HE LIVE IN SUCH A CREEPY HOUSE?

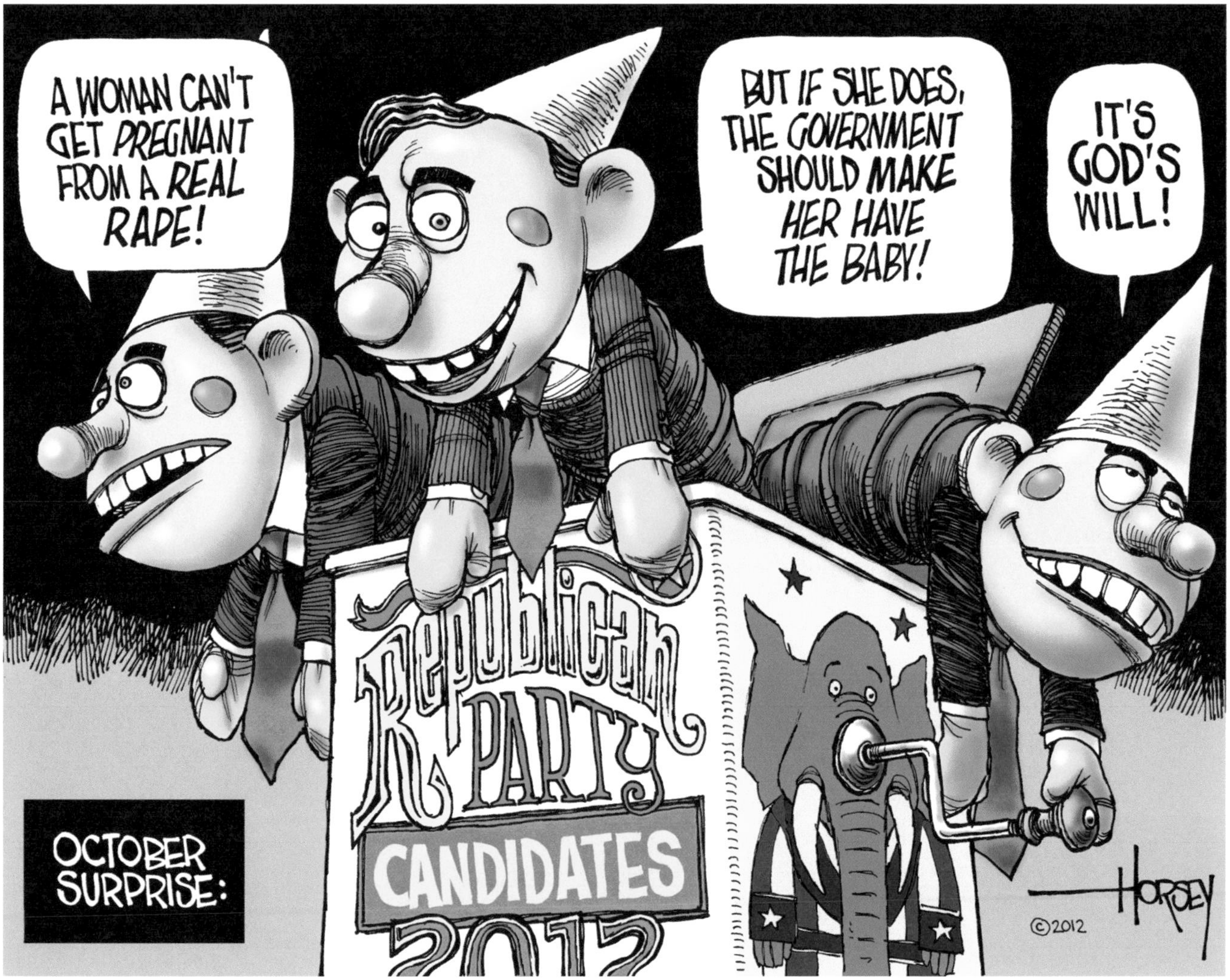
A WOMAN CAN'T GET PREGNANT FROM A REAL RAPE!
BUT IF SHE DOES, THE GOVERNMENT SHOULD MAKE HER HAVE THE BABY!
IT'S GOD'S WILL!
OCTOBER SURPRISE:
Republican PARTY
CANDIDATES
2012
HORSEY
©2012

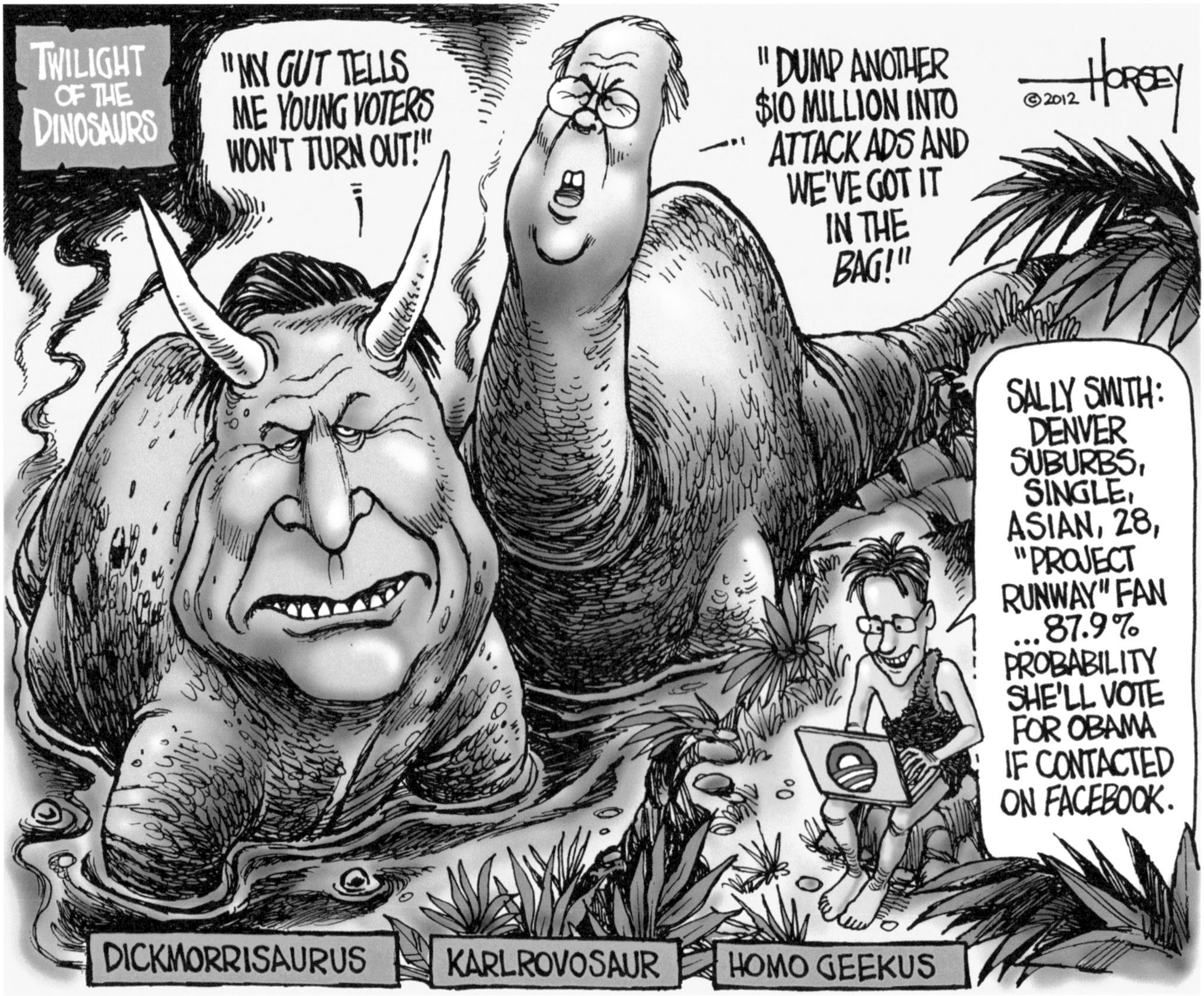
TWILIGHT OF THE DINOSAURS
"MY GUT TELLS ME YOUNG VOTERS WON'T TURN OUT!"
"DUMP ANOTHER $10 MILLION INTO ATTACK ADS AND WE'VE GOT IT IN THE BAG!"
HORSEY ©2012
SALLY SMITH: DENVER SUBURBS, SINGLE, ASIAN, 28, "PROJECT RUNWAY" FAN ...87.9% PROBABILITY SHE'LL VOTE FOR OBAMA IF CONTACTED ON FACEBOOK.
DICKMORRISAURUS
KARLROVOSAUR
HOMO GEEKUS

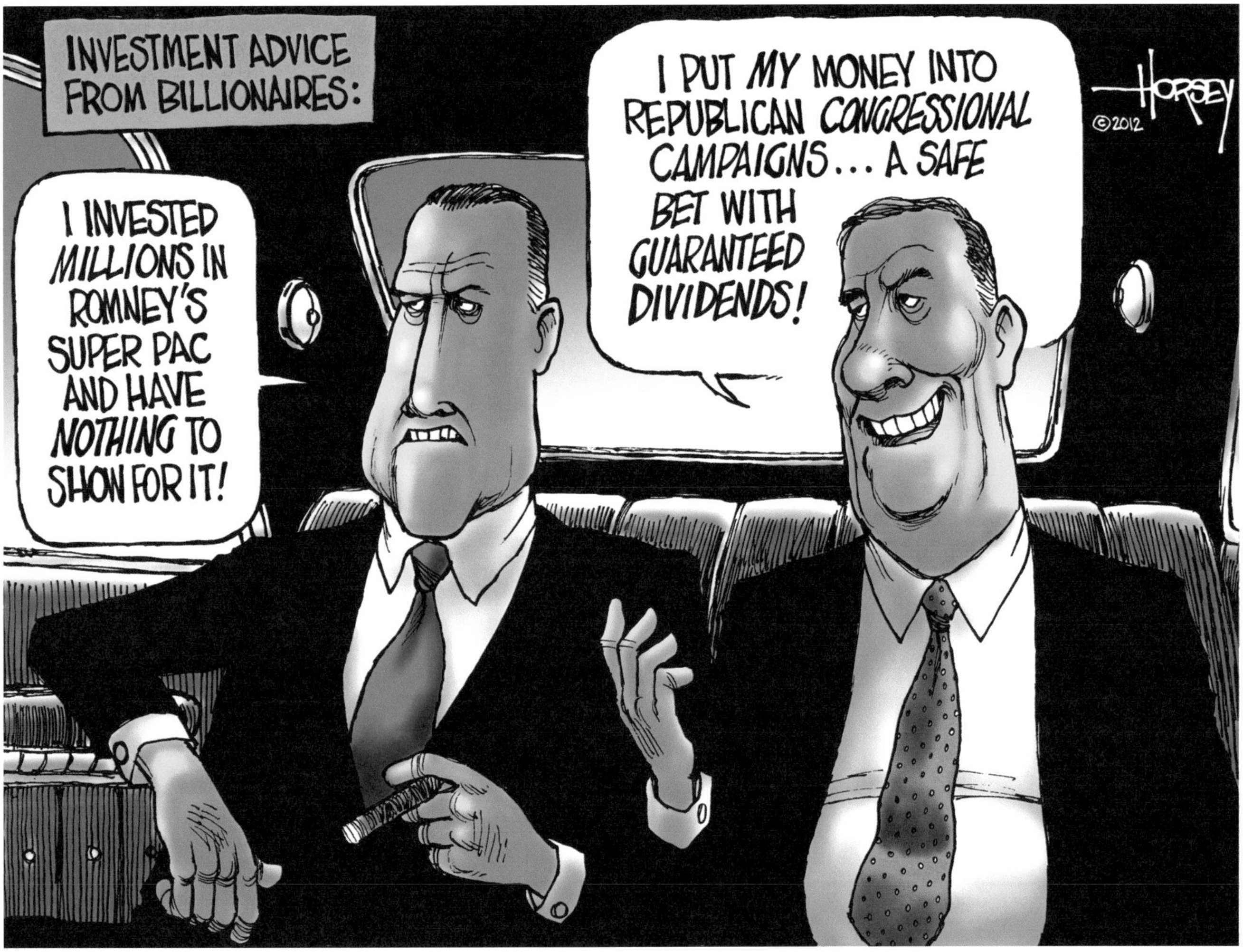
INVESTMENT ADVICE FROM BILLIONAIRES:
I INVESTED MILLIONS IN ROMNEY'S SUPER PAC AND HAVE NOTHING TO SHOW FOR IT!
I PUT MY MONEY INTO REPUBLICAN CONGRESSIONAL CAMPAIGNS... A SAFE BET WITH GUARANTEED DIVIDENDS!
HORSEY
©2012

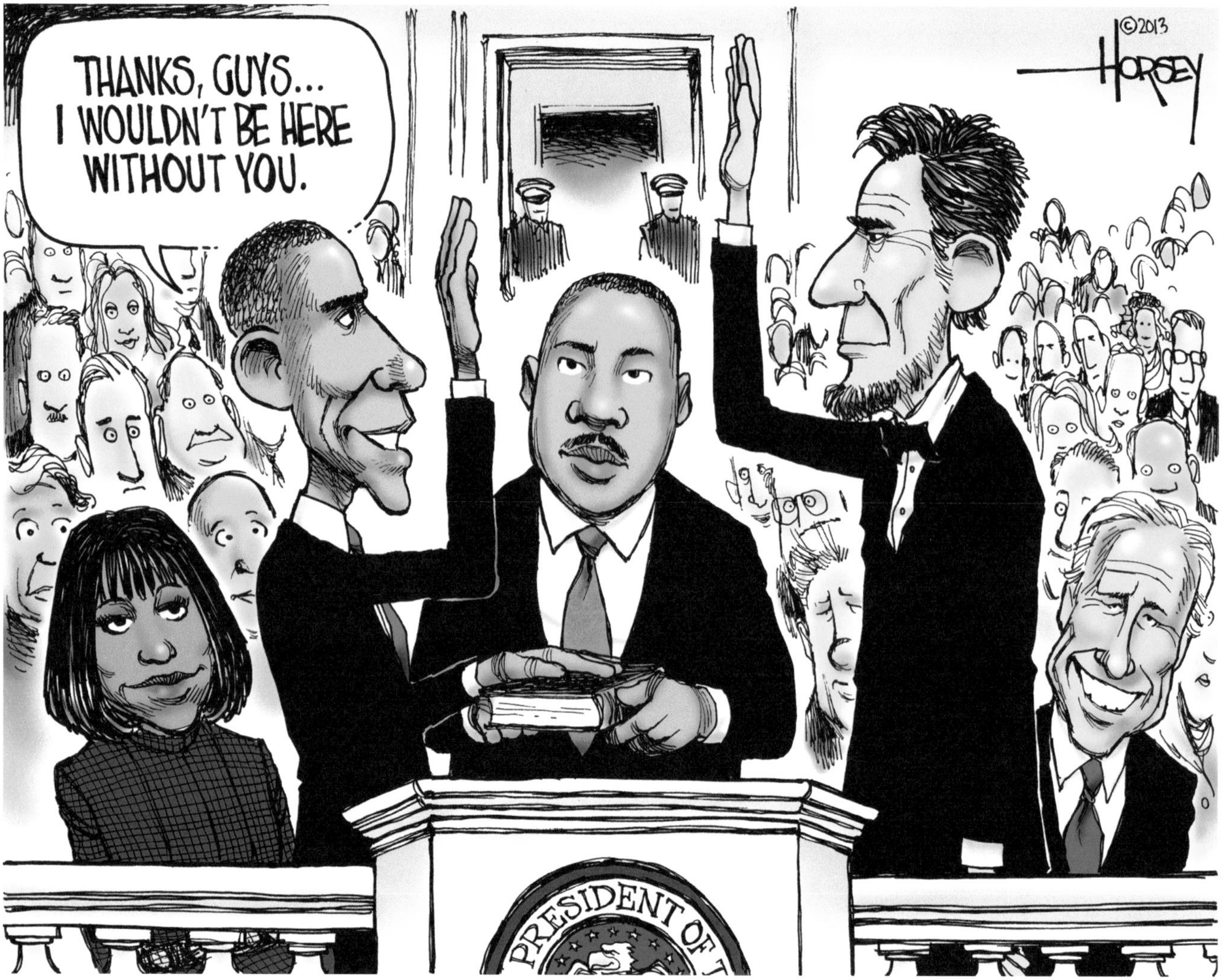
THANKS, GUYS...
I WOULDN'T BE HERE
WITHOUT YOU.
©2013
HORSEY
PRESIDENT OF T

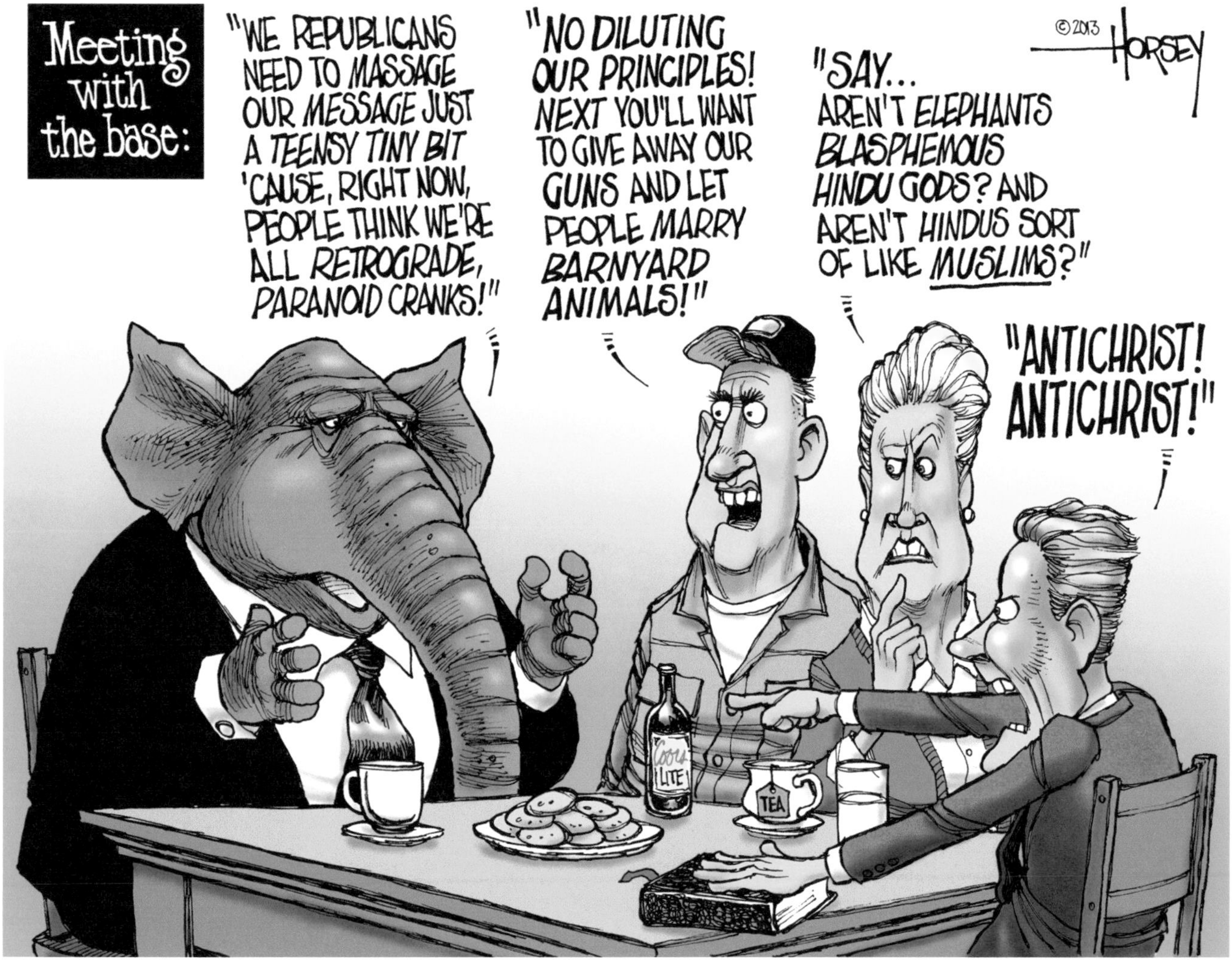
Meeting with the base:
"WE REPUBLICANS NEED TO MASSAGE OUR MESSAGE JUST A TEENSY TINY BIT 'CAUSE, RIGHT NOW, PEOPLE THINK WE'RE ALL RETROGRADE, PARANOID CRANKS!"
"NO DILUTING OUR PRINCIPLES! NEXT YOU'LL WANT TO GIVE AWAY OUR GUNS AND LET PEOPLE MARRY BARNYARD ANIMALS!"
"SAY... AREN'T ELEPHANTS BLASPHEMOUS HINDU GODS? AND AREN'T HINDUS SORT OF LIKE MUSLIMS?"
"ANTICHRIST! ANTICHRIST!"
©2013 HORSEY
Coors LITE
TEA

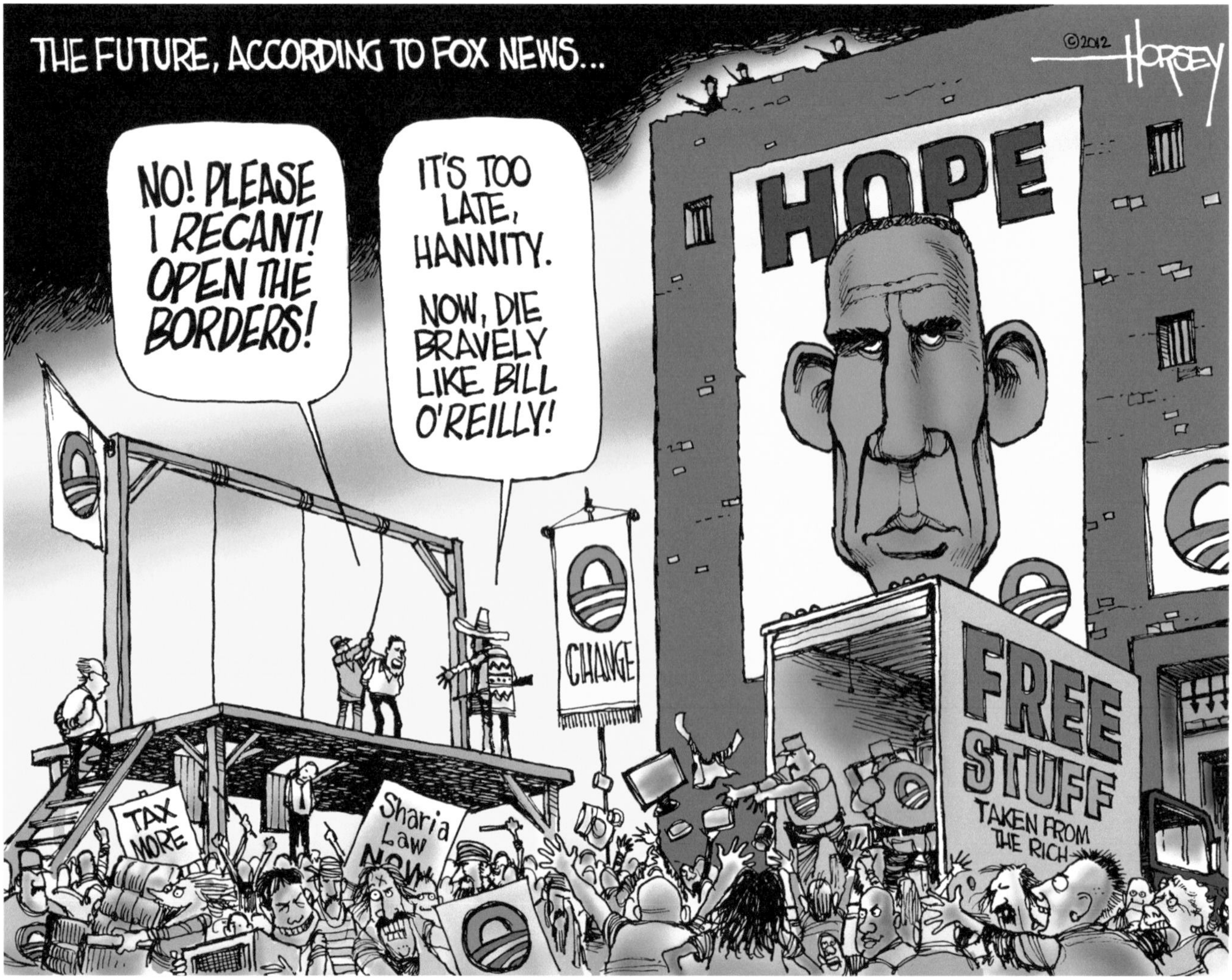
THE FUTURE, ACCORDING TO FOX NEWS...
©2012 HORSEY
NO! PLEASE I RECANT! OPEN THE BORDERS!
IT'S TOO LATE, HANNITY.
NOW, DIE BRAVELY LIKE BILL O'REILLY!
HOPE
CHANGE
FREE STUFF
TAKEN FROM THE RICH
TAX MORE
Sharia Law NOW

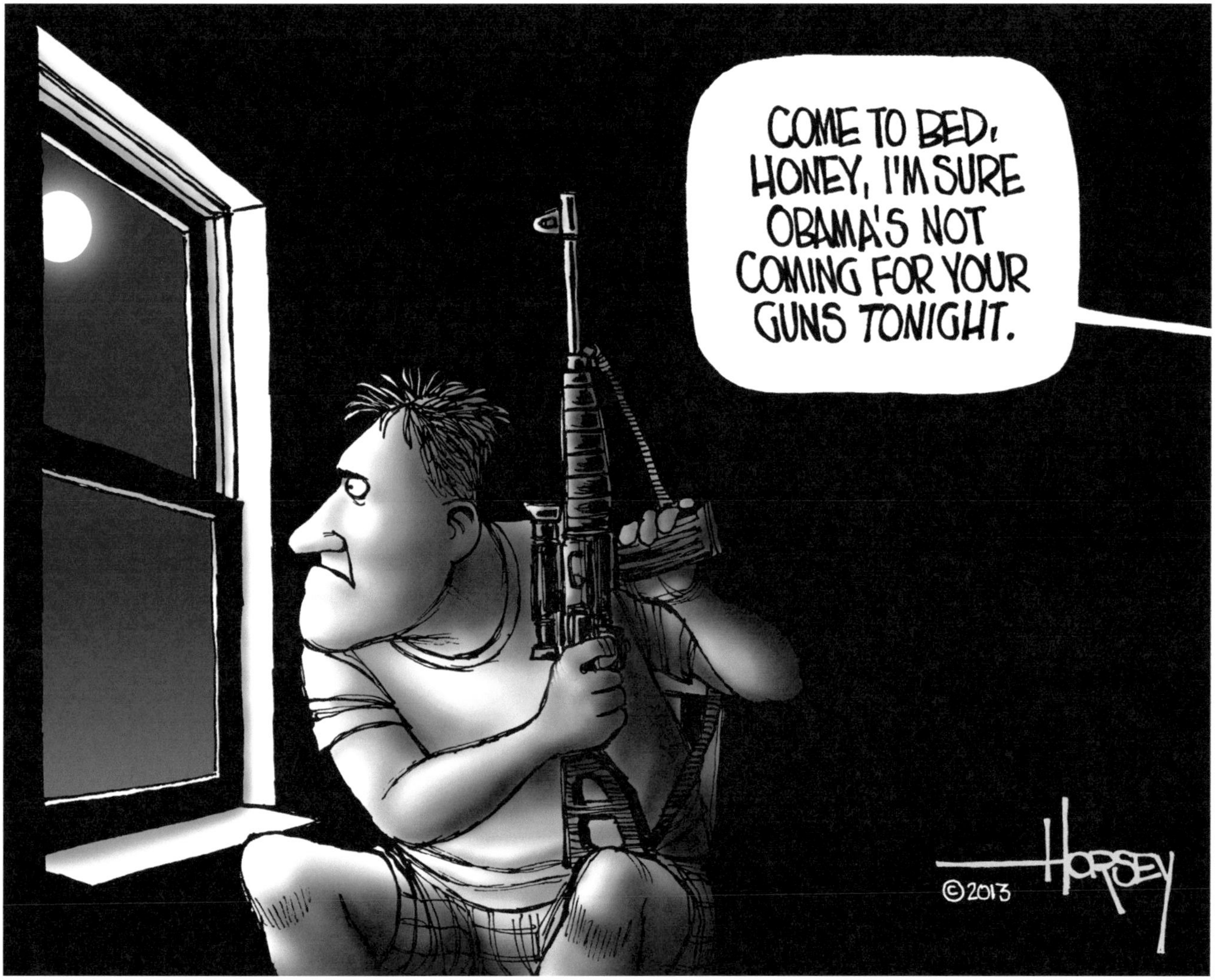
COME TO BED, HONEY, I'M SURE OBAMA'S NOT COMING FOR YOUR GUNS TONIGHT.
©2013
HORSEY

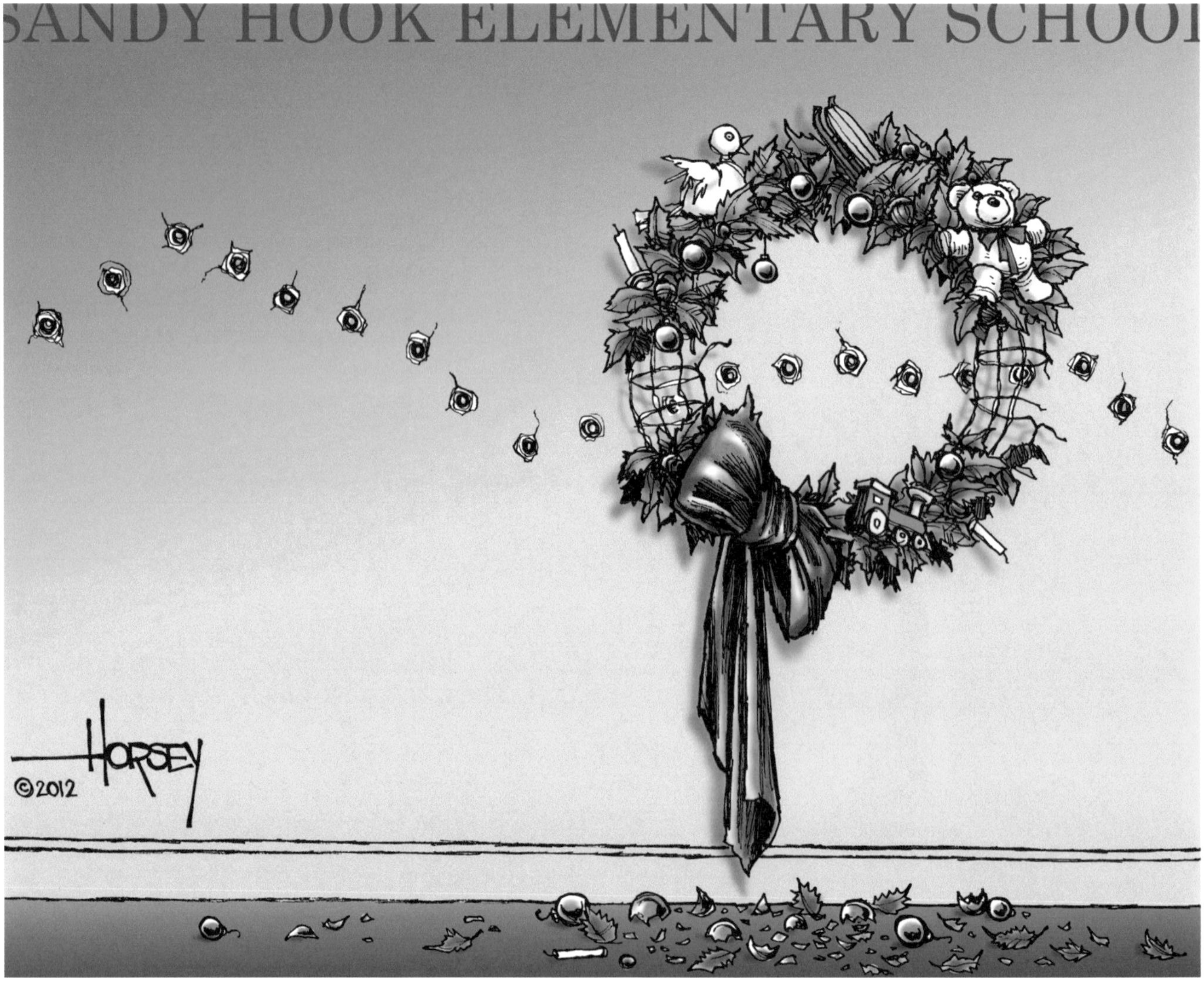
SANDY HOOK ELEMENTARY SCHOOL
HORSEY
©2012

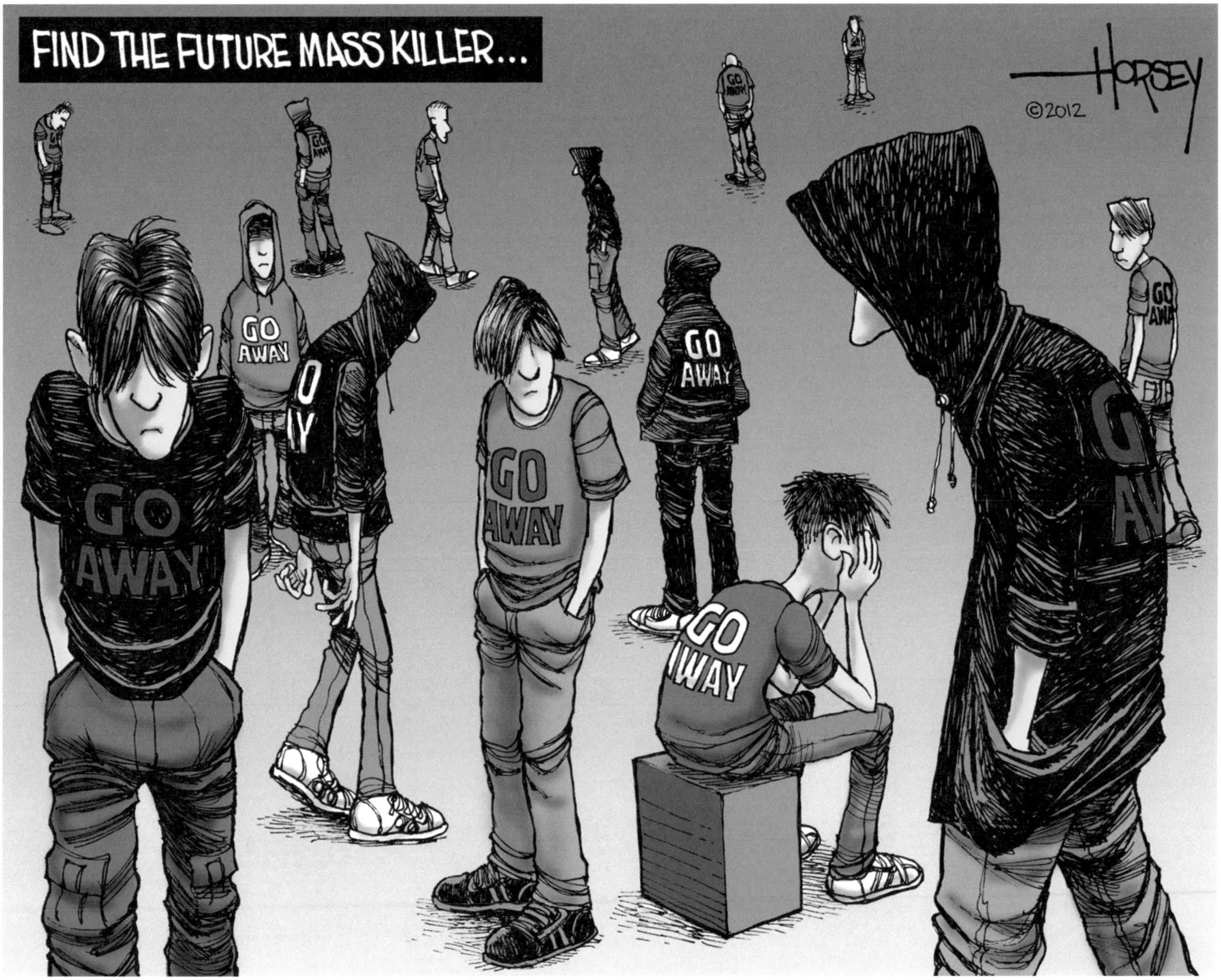

FIND THE FUTURE MASS KILLER...
HORSEY
©2012
GO AWAY
GO AWAY
GO AWAY
GO AWAY
GO AWAY
GO AWAY

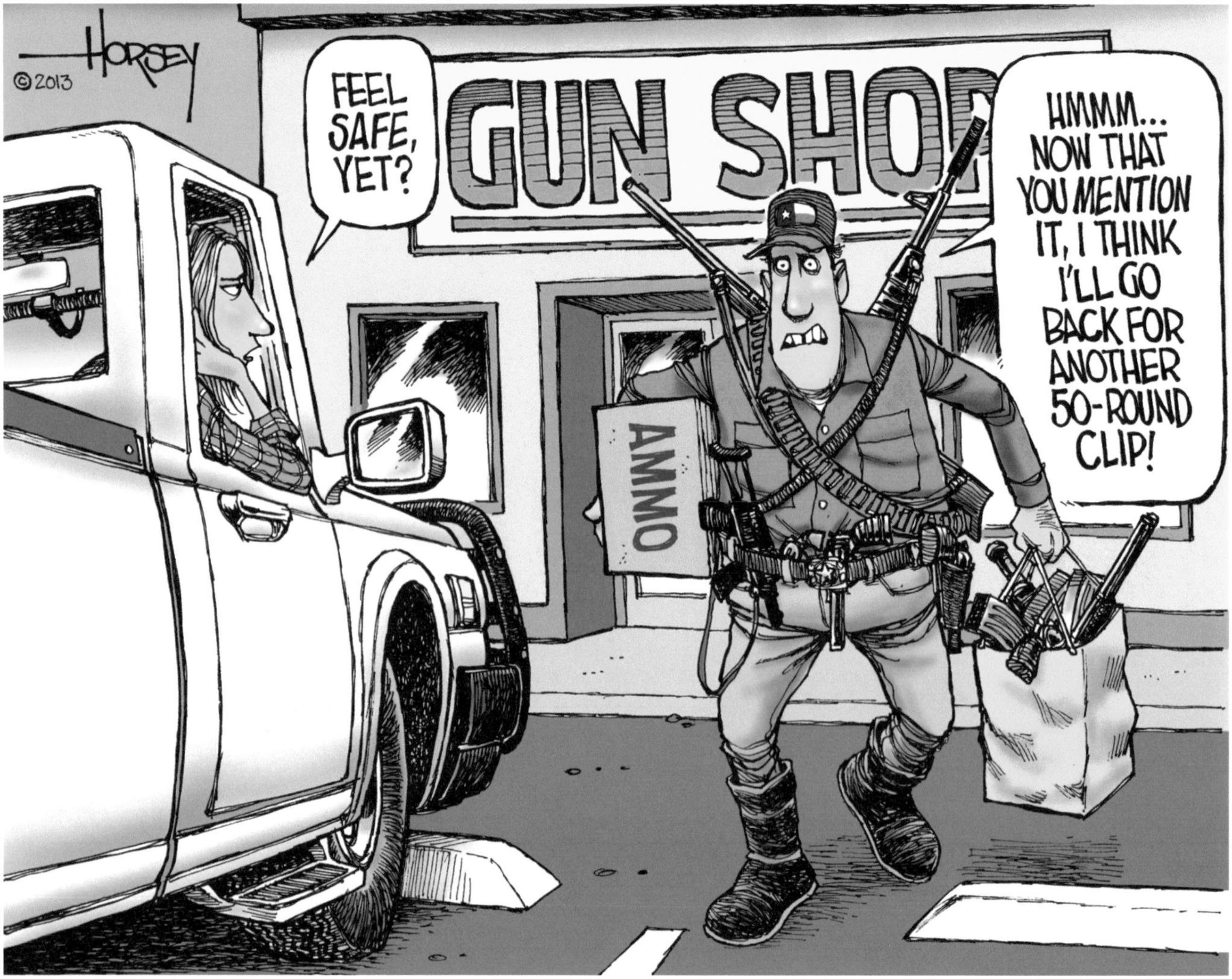
HORSEY
©2013
FEEL SAFE, YET?
GUN SHOP
HMMM... NOW THAT YOU MENTION IT, I THINK I'LL GO BACK FOR ANOTHER 50-ROUND CLIP!
AMMO

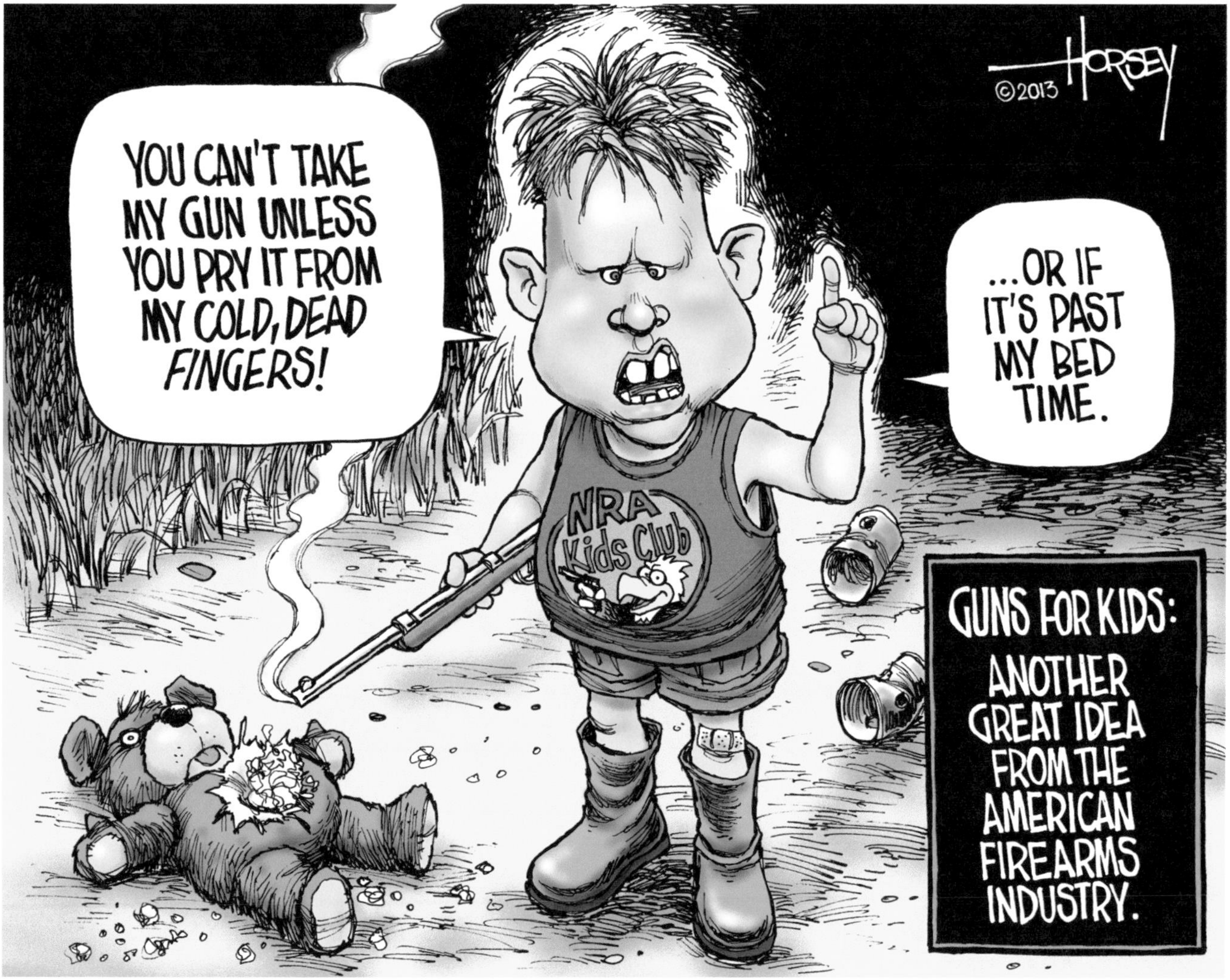
HORSEY
©2013
YOU CAN'T TAKE MY GUN UNLESS YOU PRY IT FROM MY COLD, DEAD FINGERS!
...OR IF IT'S PAST MY BED TIME.
NRA Kids Club
GUNS FOR KIDS:
ANOTHER GREAT IDEA FROM THE AMERICAN FIREARMS INDUSTRY.

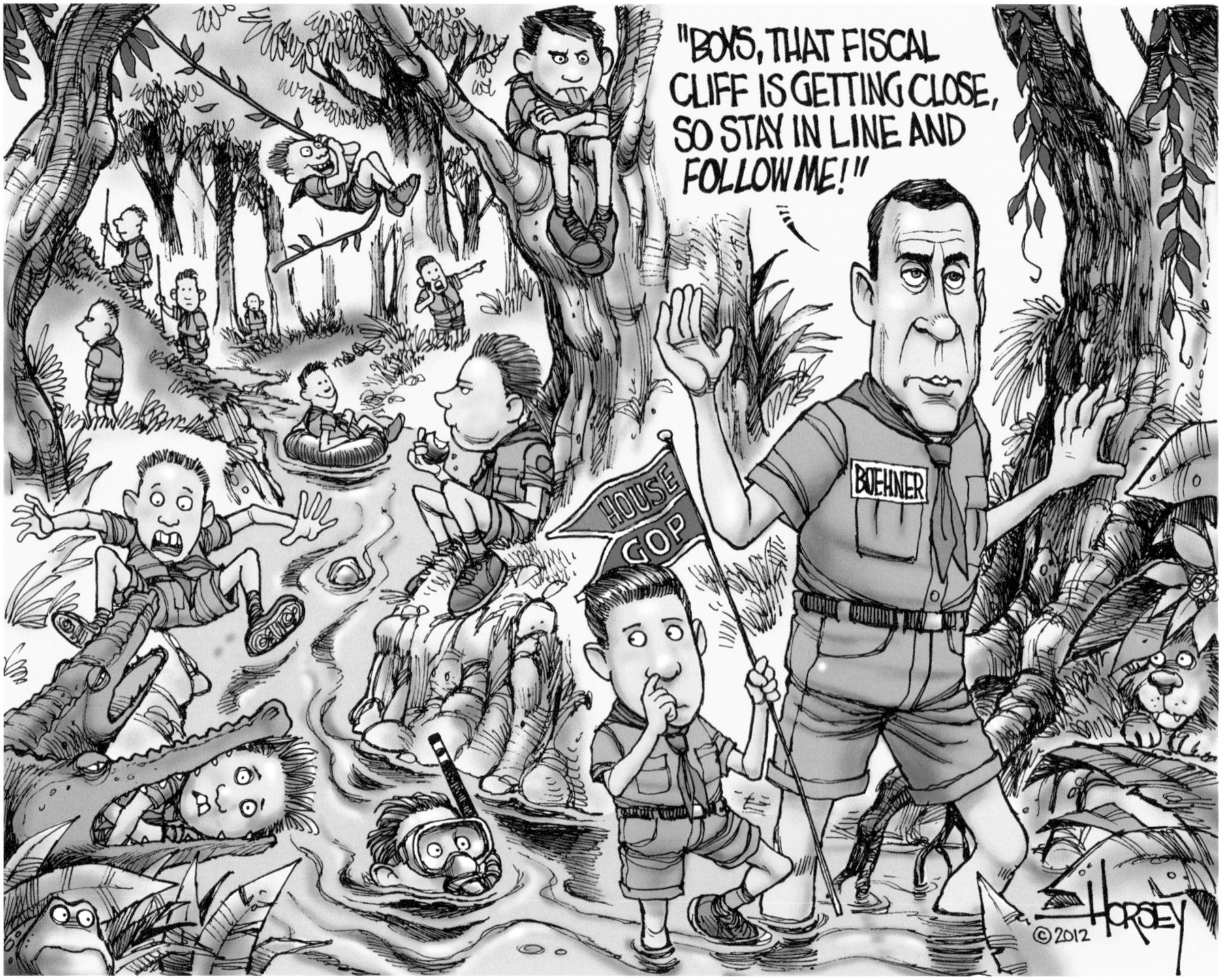
"BOYS, THAT FISCAL CLIFF IS GETTING CLOSE, SO STAY IN LINE AND FOLLOW ME!"
BOEHNER
HOUSE GOP
HORSEY
©2012

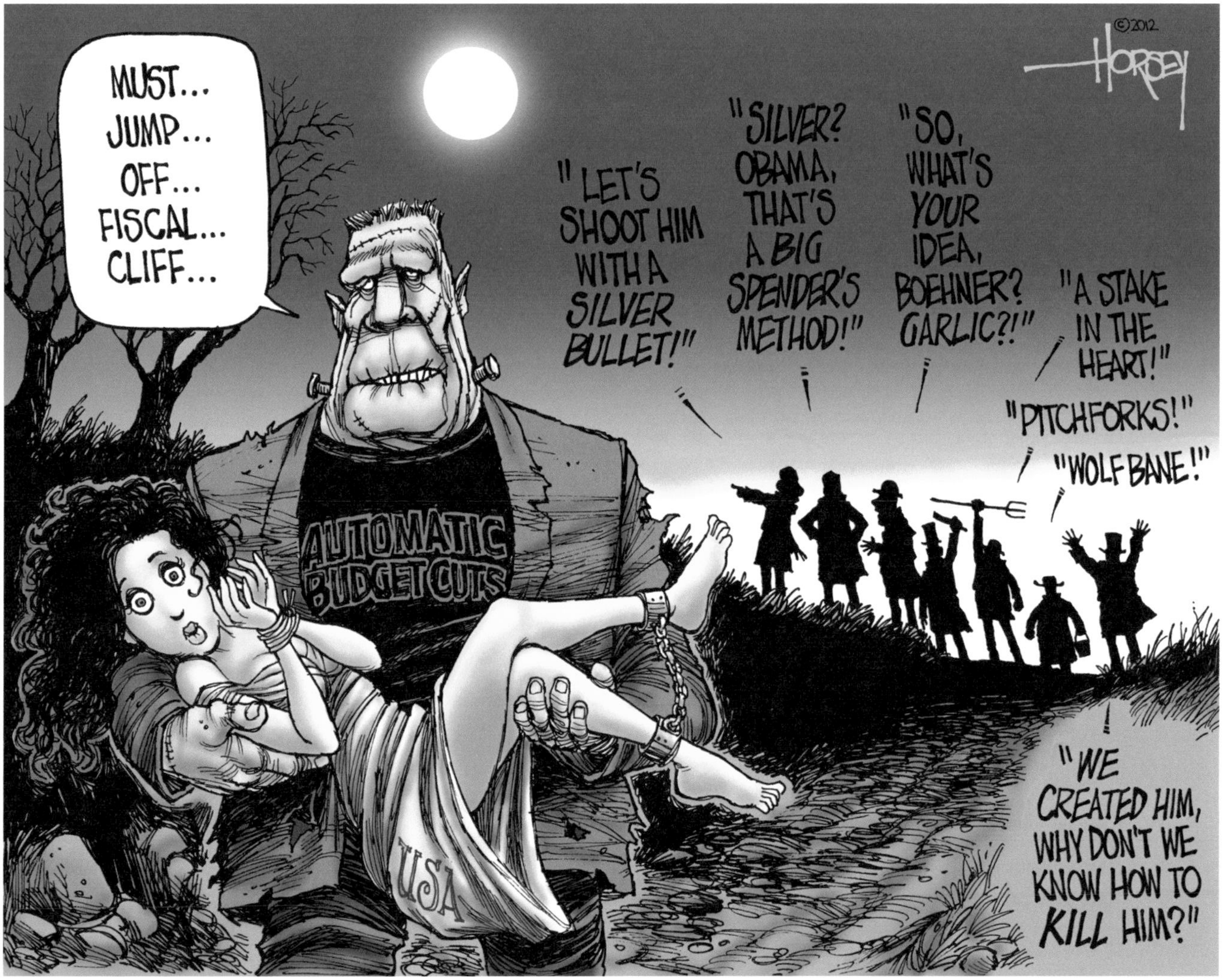
©2012
HORSEY
MUST... JUMP... OFF... FISCAL... CLIFF...
AUTOMATIC BUDGET CUTS
USA
"LET'S SHOOT HIM WITH A SILVER BULLET!"
"SILVER? OBAMA, THAT'S A BIG SPENDER'S METHOD!"
"SO, WHAT'S YOUR IDEA, BOEHNER? GARLIC?!"
"A STAKE IN THE HEART!"
"PITCHFORKS!"
"WOLFBANE!"
"WE CREATED HIM, WHY DON'T WE KNOW HOW TO KILL HIM?"

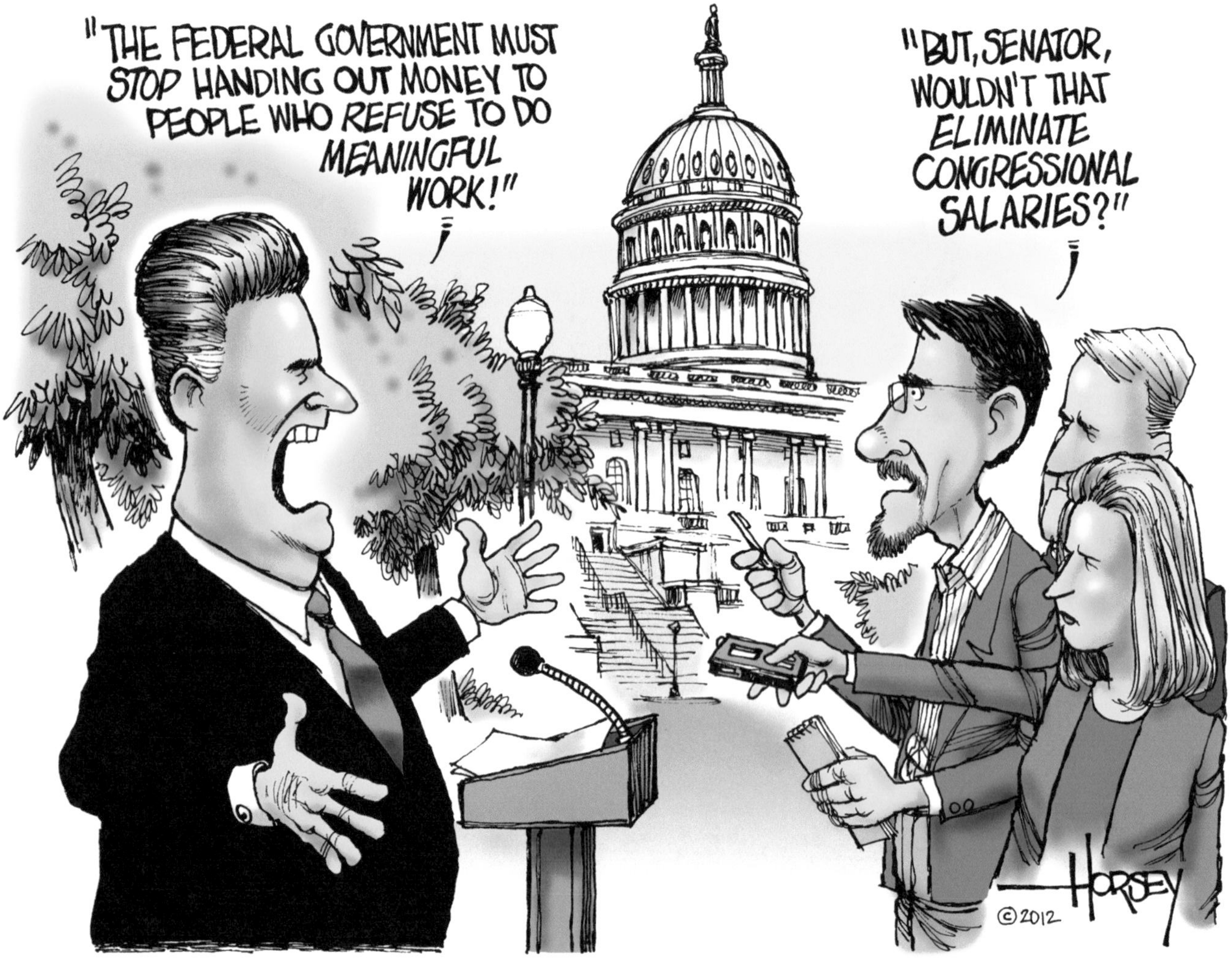
"THE FEDERAL GOVERNMENT MUST STOP HANDING OUT MONEY TO PEOPLE WHO *REFUSE* TO DO *MEANINGFUL* WORK!"
"BUT, SENATOR, WOULDN'T THAT *ELIMINATE* CONGRESSIONAL SALARIES?"
HORSEY
©2012

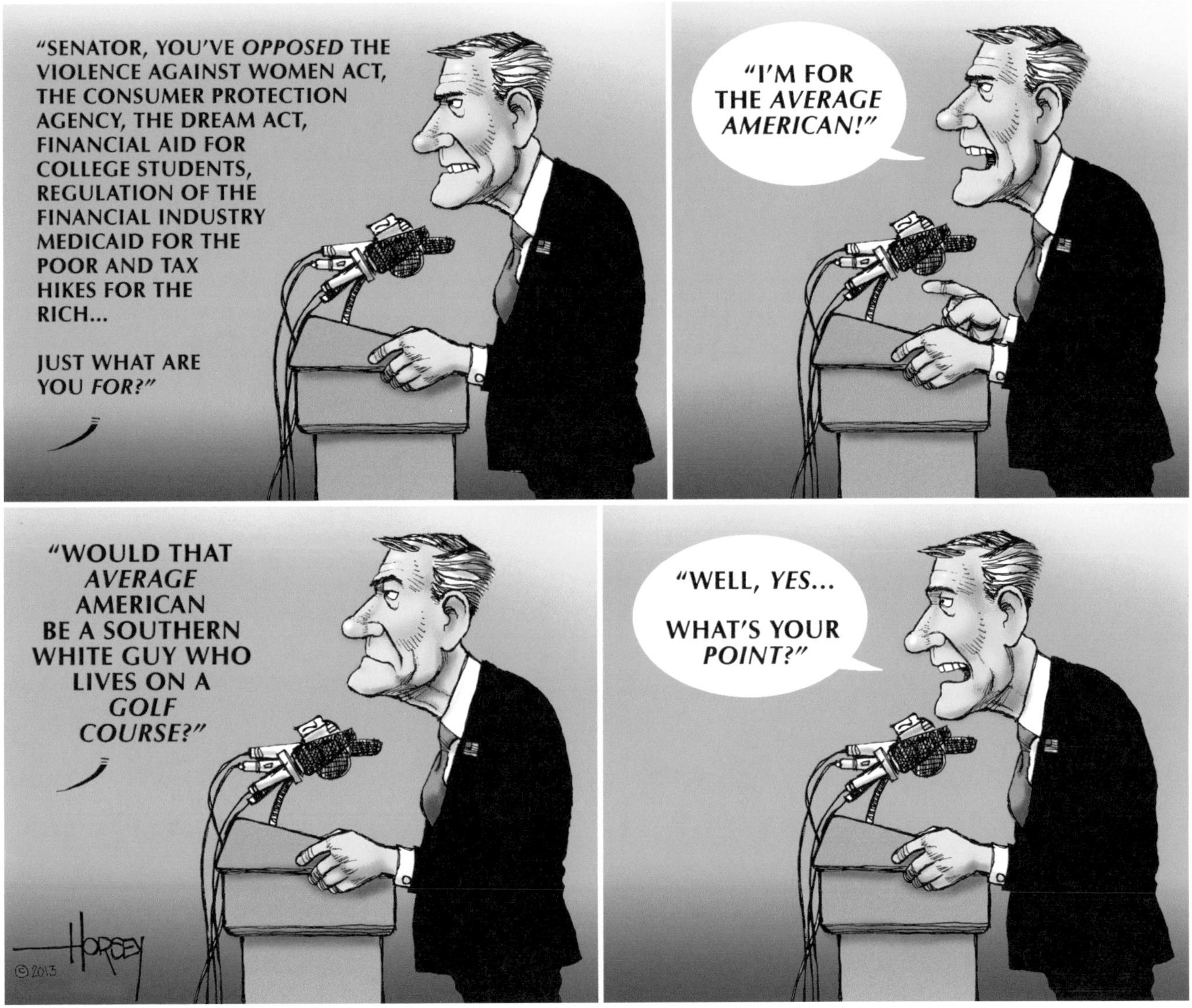
"SENATOR, YOU'VE OPPOSED THE VIOLENCE AGAINST WOMEN ACT, THE CONSUMER PROTECTION AGENCY, THE DREAM ACT, FINANCIAL AID FOR COLLEGE STUDENTS, REGULATION OF THE FINANCIAL INDUSTRY MEDICAID FOR THE POOR AND TAX HIKES FOR THE RICH...
JUST WHAT ARE YOU FOR?"
"I'M FOR THE AVERAGE AMERICAN!"
"WOULD THAT AVERAGE AMERICAN BE A SOUTHERN WHITE GUY WHO LIVES ON A GOLF COURSE?"
HORSEY
©2013
"WELL, YES...
WHAT'S YOUR POINT?"

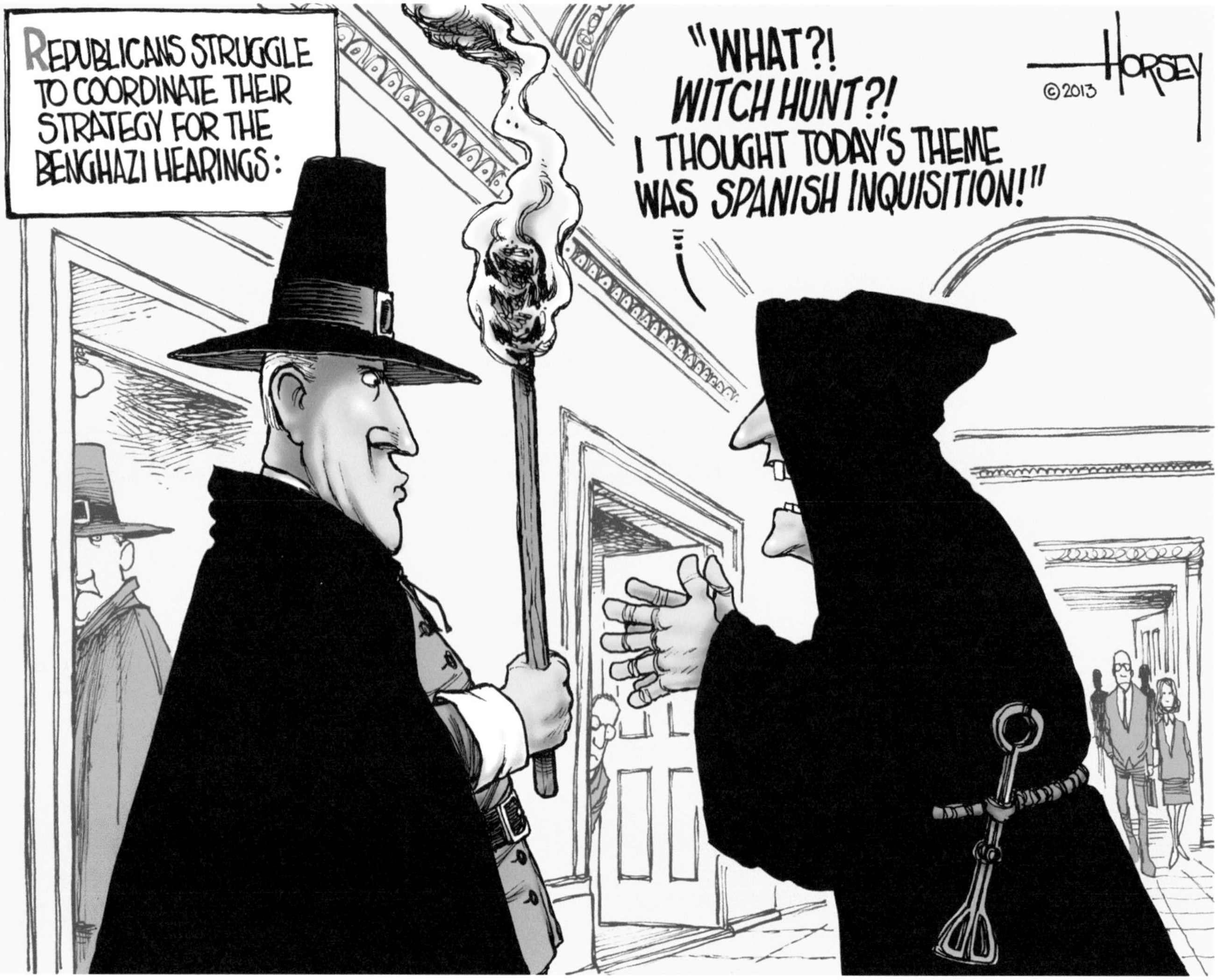
REPUBLICANS STRUGGLE TO COORDINATE THEIR STRATEGY FOR THE BENGHAZI HEARINGS:
"WHAT?! WITCH HUNT?! I THOUGHT TODAY'S THEME WAS SPANISH INQUISITION!"
HORSEY
©2013

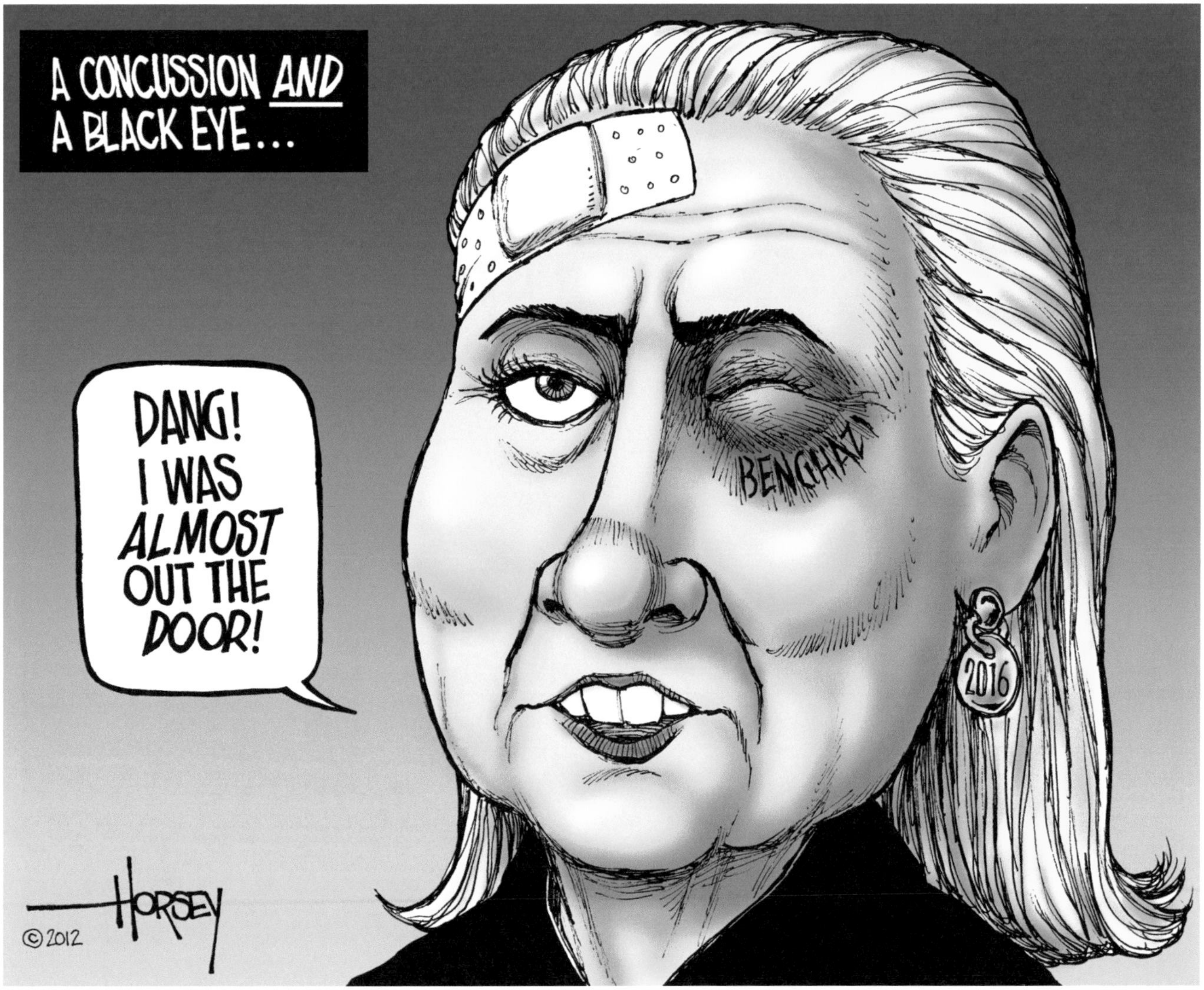
A CONCUSSION AND A BLACK EYE...
DANG! I WAS ALMOST OUT THE DOOR!
BENGHAZI
2016
HORSEY
©2012

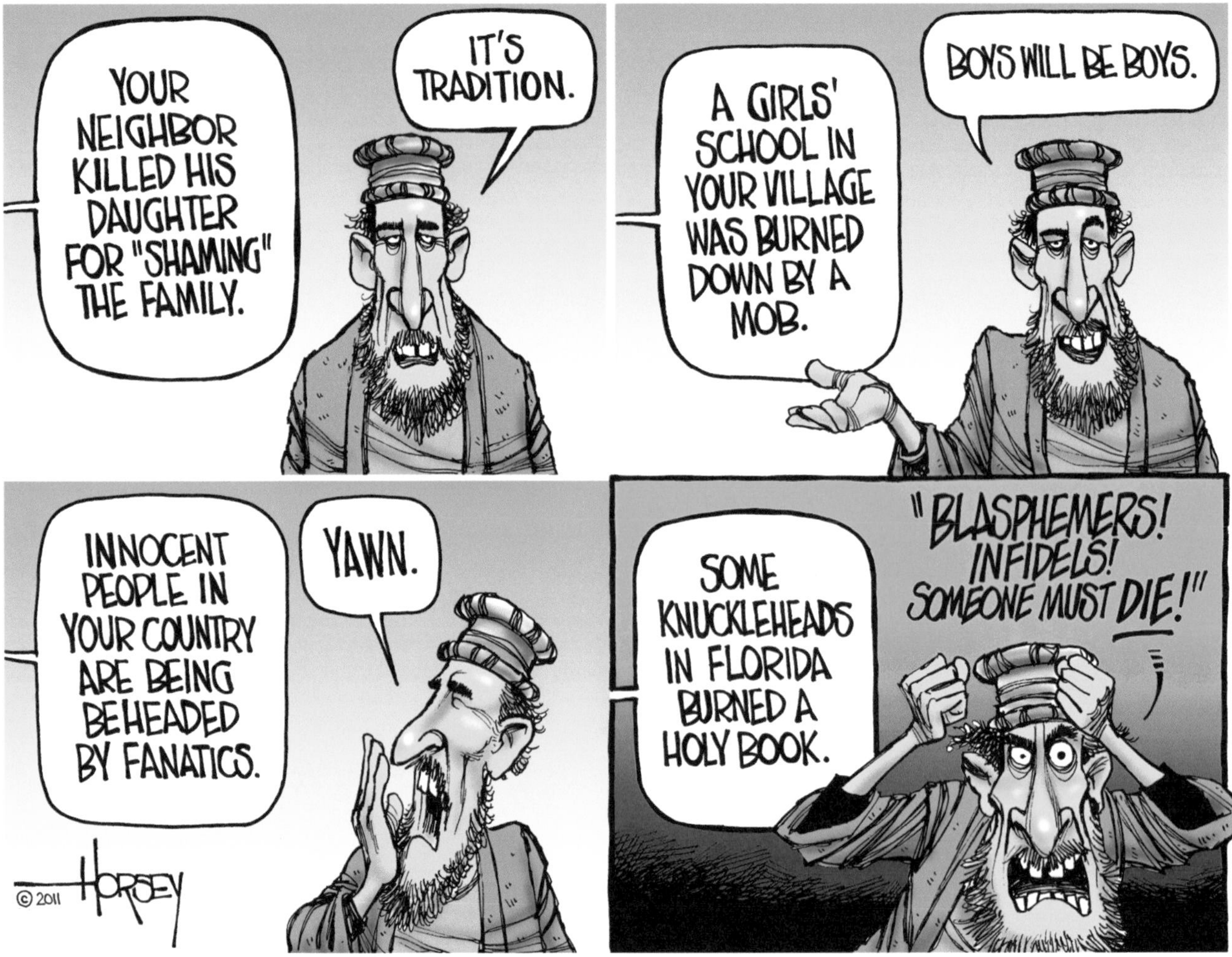
YOUR NEIGHBOR KILLED HIS DAUGHTER FOR "SHAMING" THE FAMILY.
IT'S TRADITION.
A GIRLS' SCHOOL IN YOUR VILLAGE WAS BURNED DOWN BY A MOB.
BOYS WILL BE BOYS.
INNOCENT PEOPLE IN YOUR COUNTRY ARE BEING BEHEADED BY FANATICS.
YAWN.
SOME KNUCKLEHEADS IN FLORIDA BURNED A HOLY BOOK.
"BLASPHEMERS! INFIDELS! SOMEONE MUST DIE!"
© 2011 HORSEY

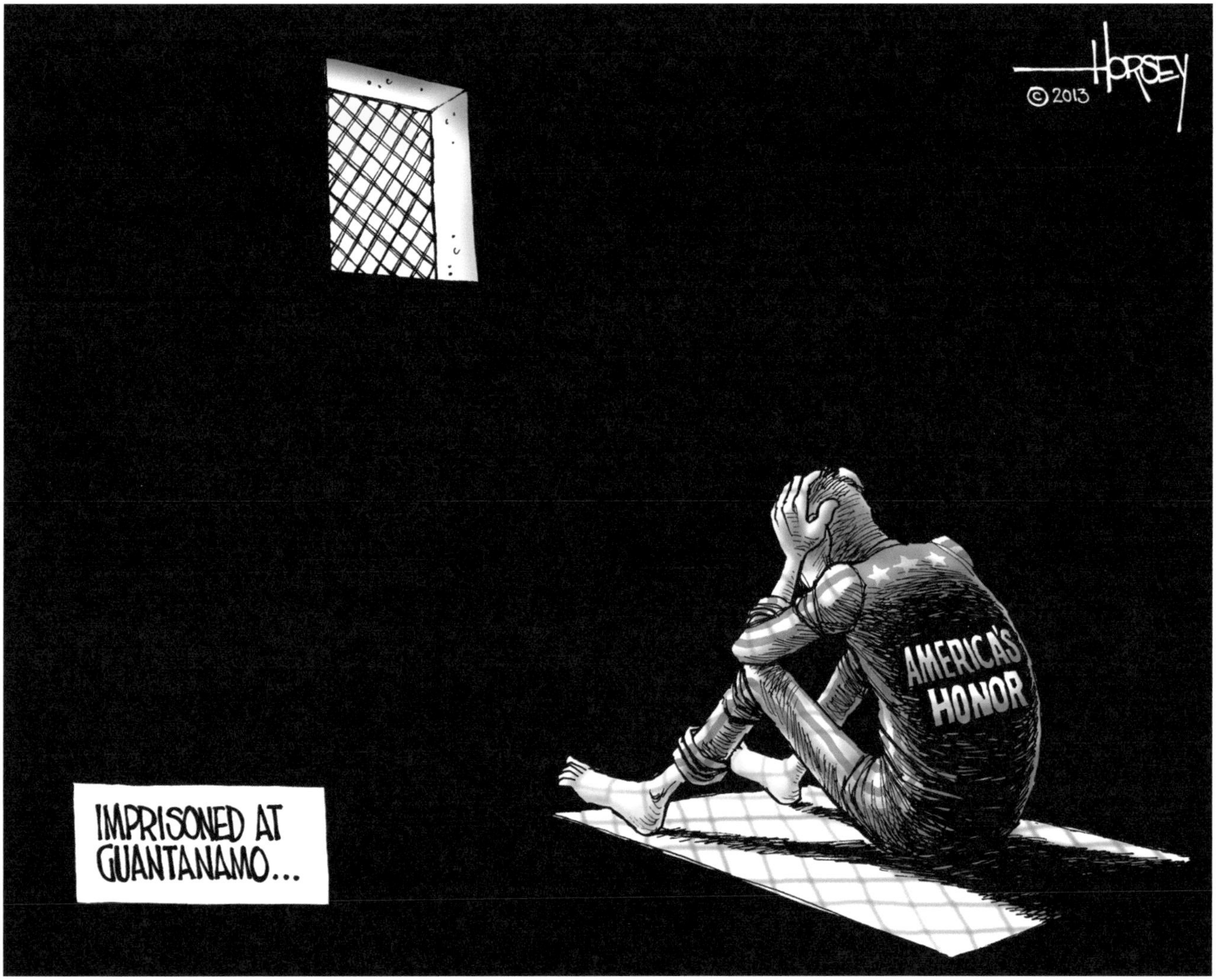
HORSEY
©2013
AMERICA'S HONOR
IMPRISONED AT GUANTANAMO...

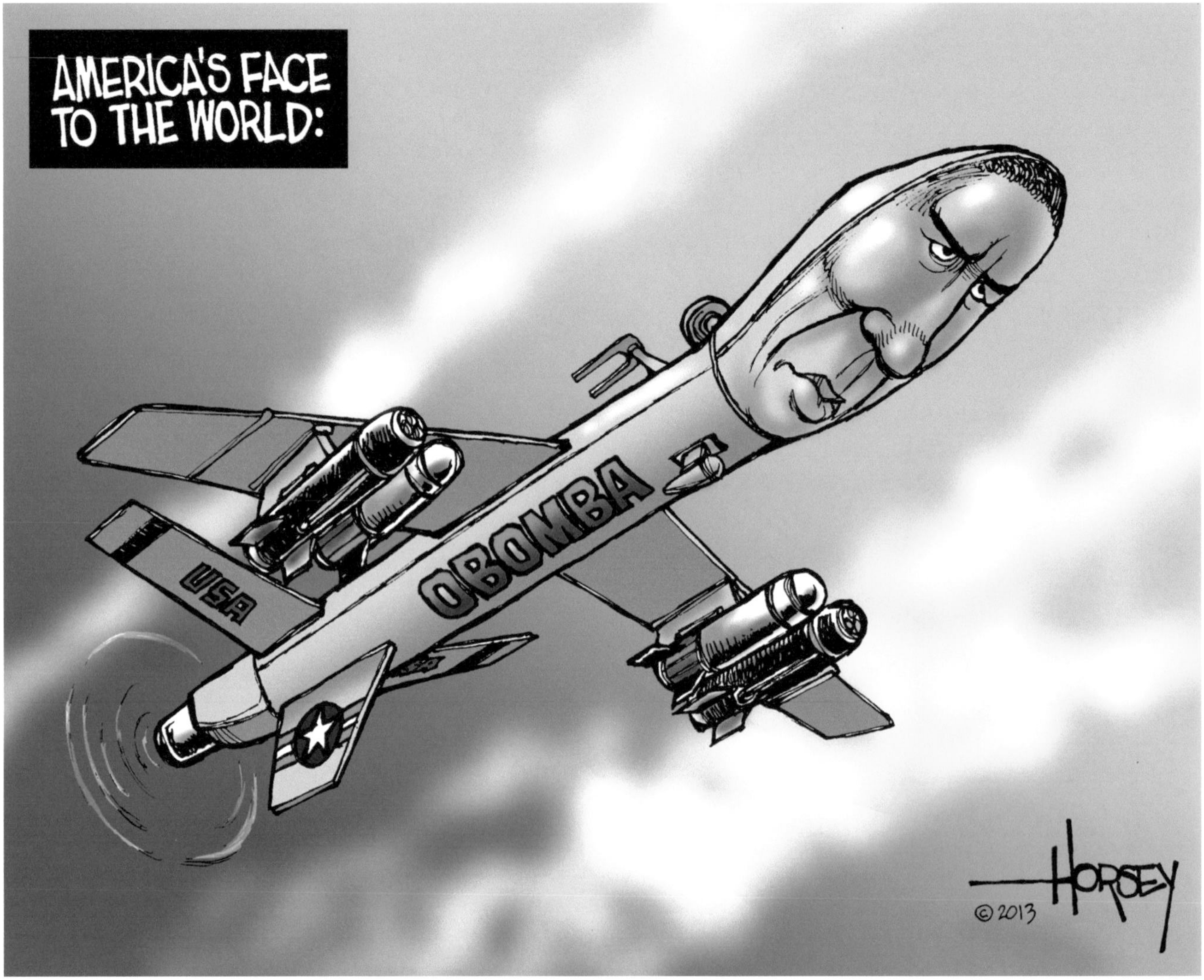
AMERICA'S FACE TO THE WORLD:
OBOMBA
USA
HORSEY
©2013

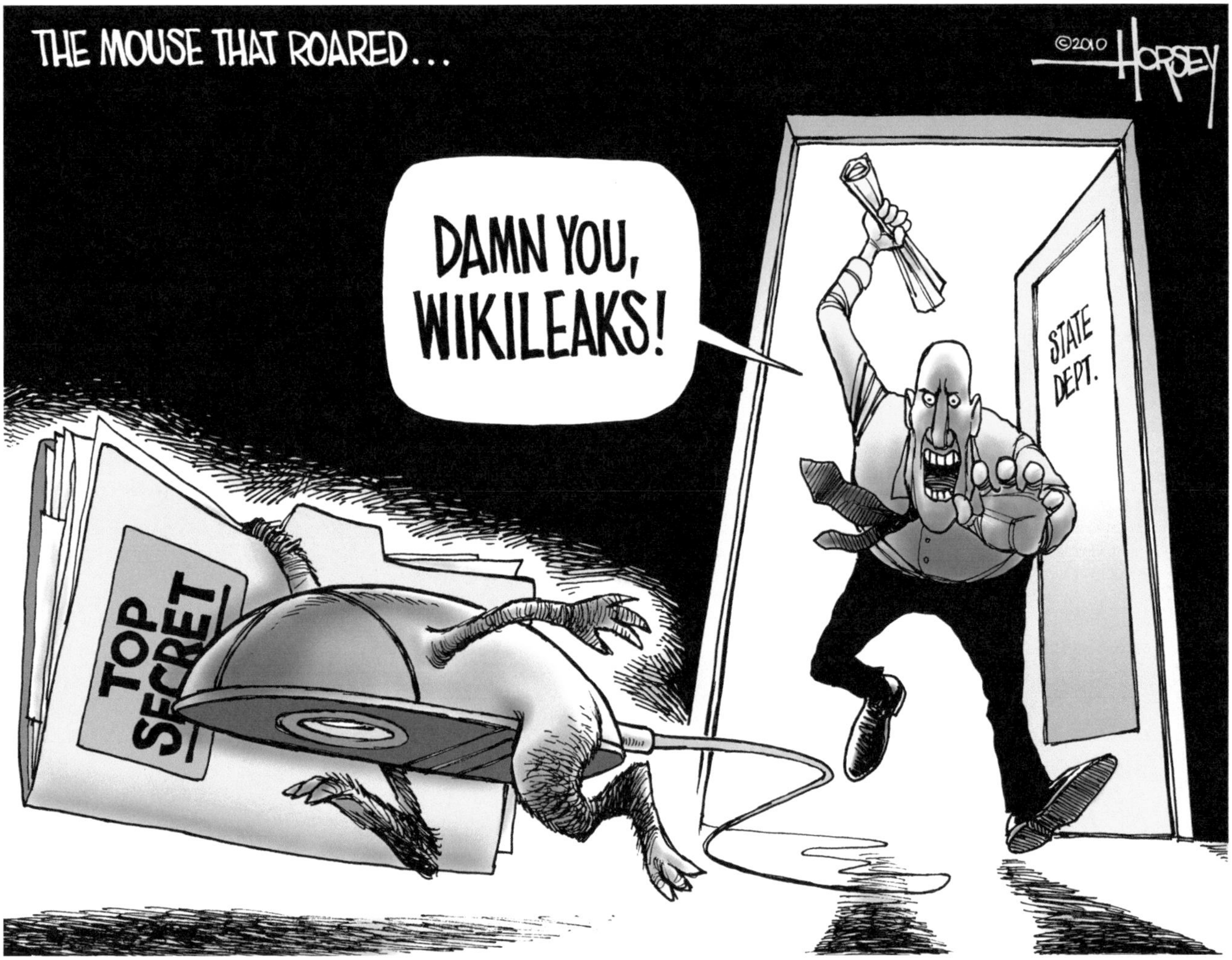
THE MOUSE THAT ROARED...
©2010 HORSEY
DAMN YOU, WIKILEAKS!
STATE DEPT.
TOP SECRET

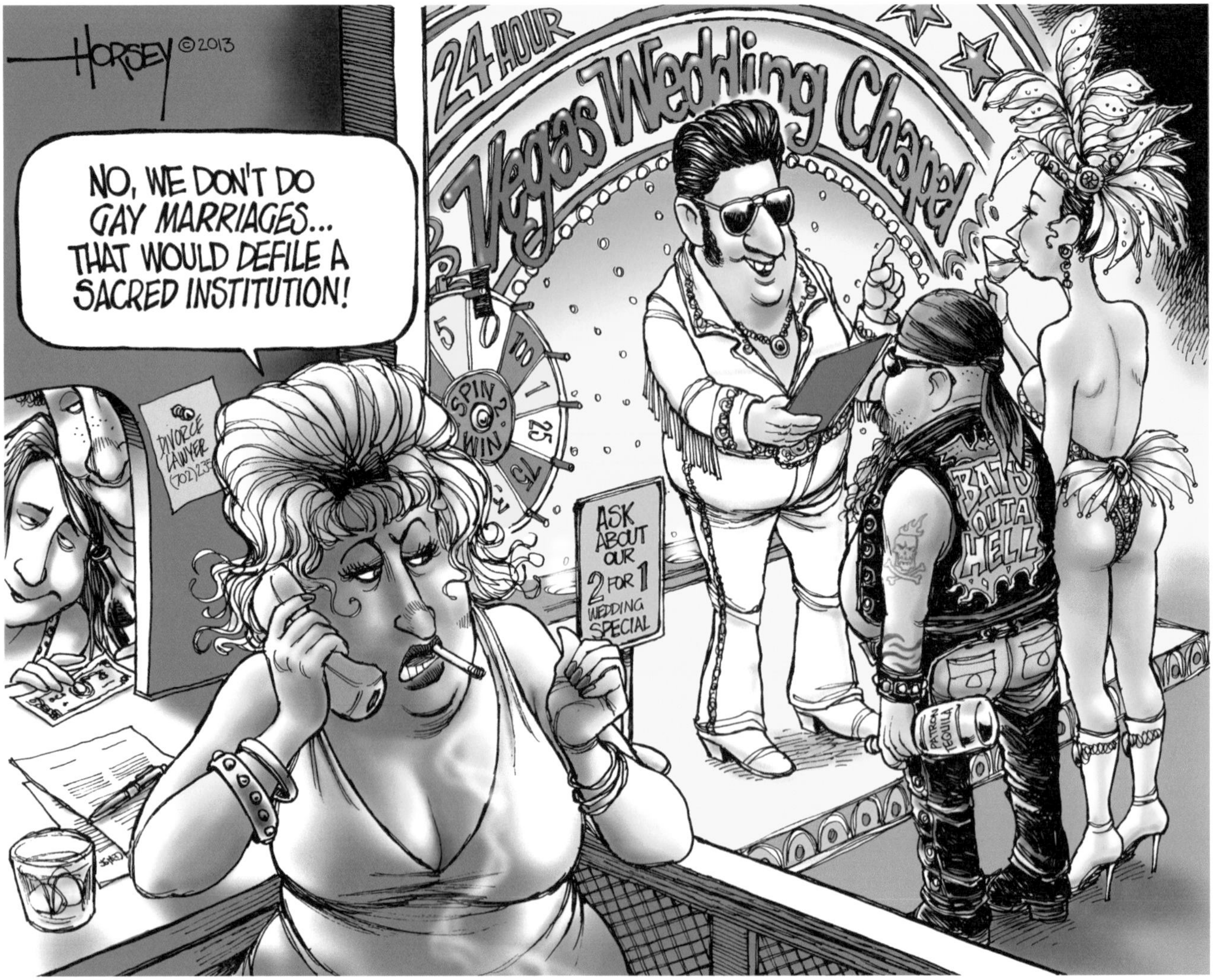
HORSEY ©2013
NO, WE DON'T DO GAY MARRIAGES... THAT WOULD DEFILE A SACRED INSTITUTION!
24 HOUR
Vegas Wedding Chapel
SPIN 2 WIN
DIVORCE LAWYER
ASK ABOUT OUR 2 FOR 1 WEDDING SPECIAL
BATS OUTA HELL
PATRON TEQUILA

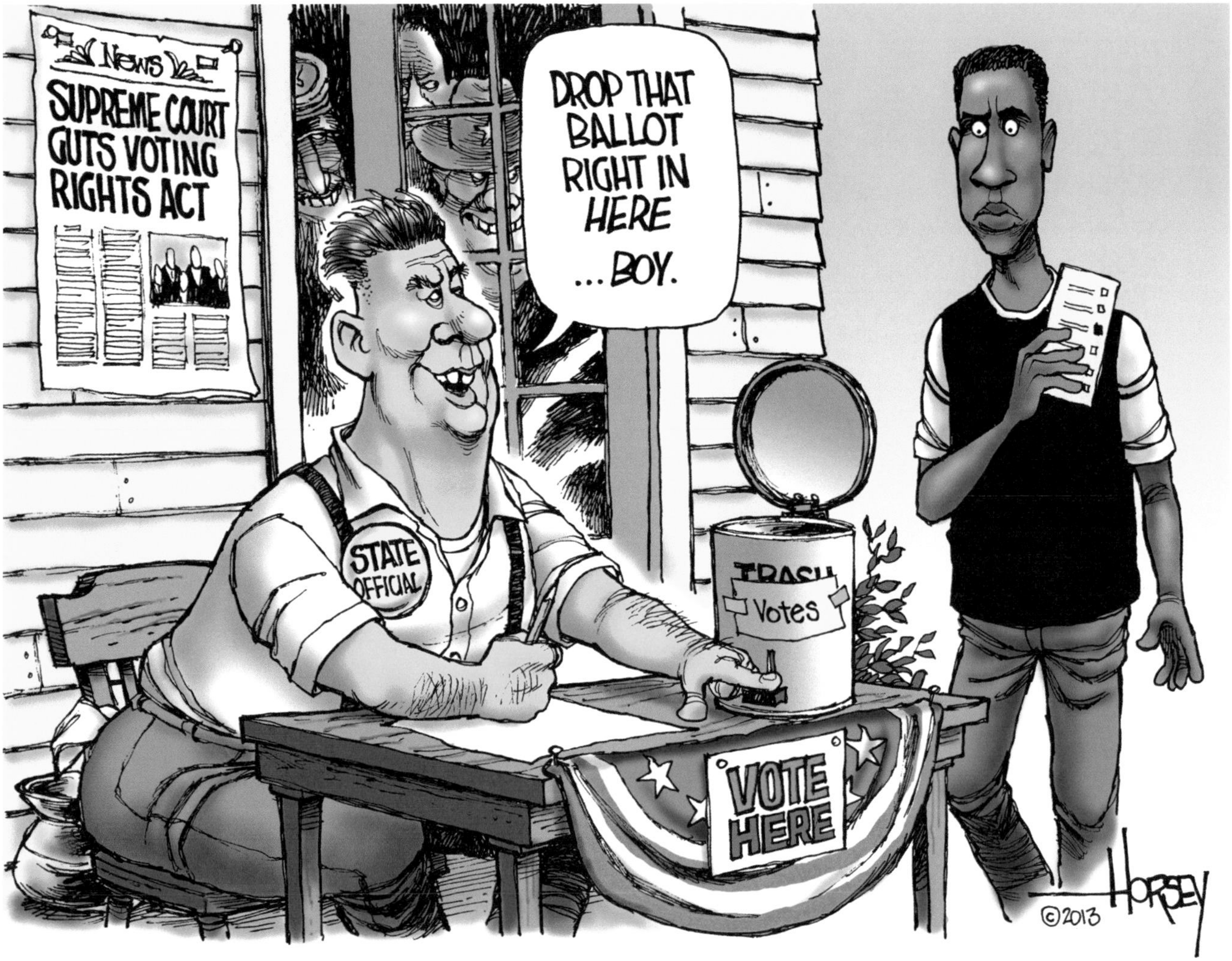
News
SUPREME COURT GUTS VOTING RIGHTS ACT
DROP THAT BALLOT RIGHT IN *HERE*
...BOY.
STATE OFFICIAL
TRASH
Votes
VOTE HERE
HORSEY
©2013

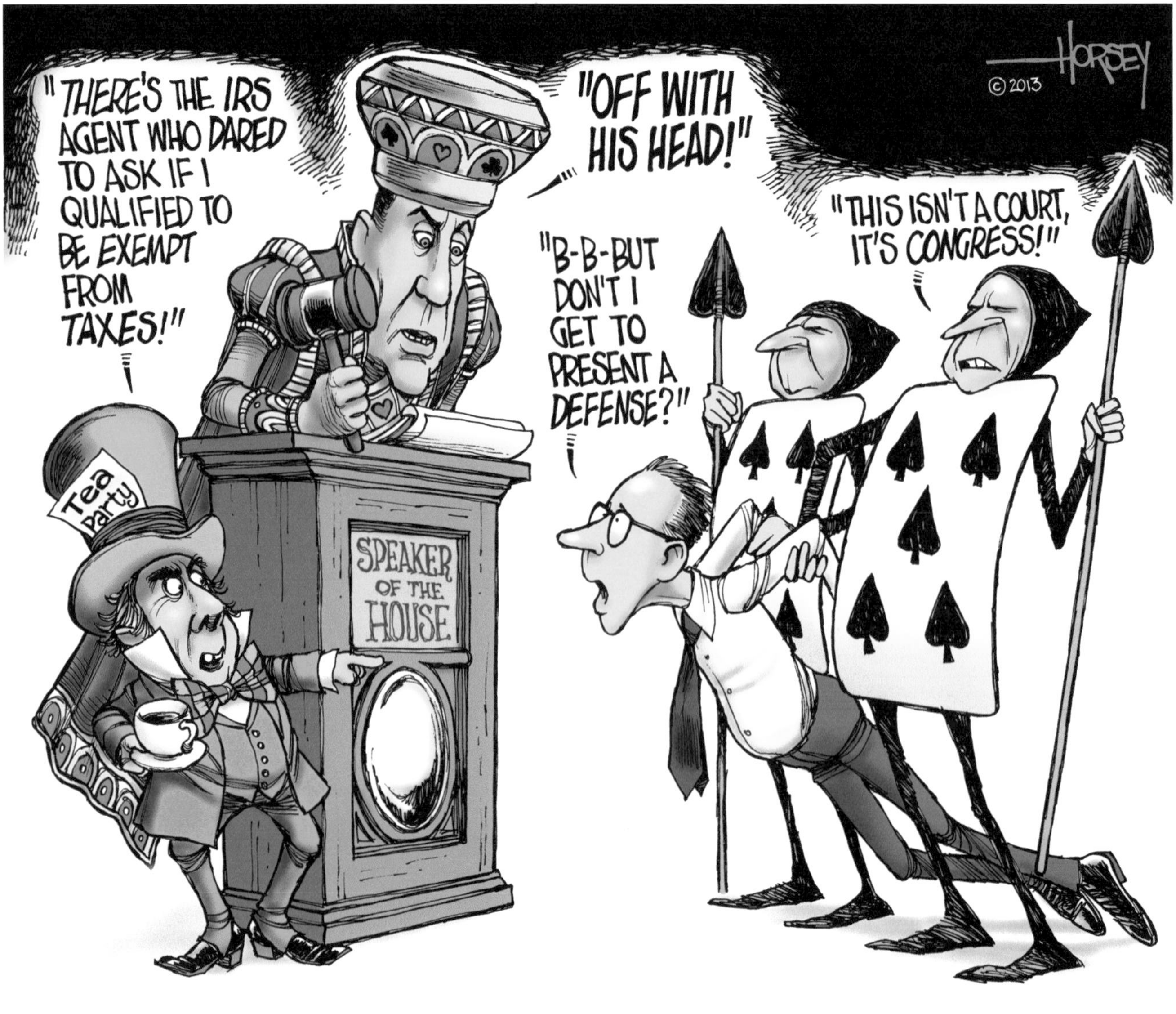
"THERE'S THE IRS AGENT WHO DARED TO ASK IF I QUALIFIED TO BE EXEMPT FROM TAXES!"
"OFF WITH HIS HEAD!"
HORSEY
© 2013
"B-B-BUT DON'T I GET TO PRESENT A DEFENSE?"
"THIS ISN'T A COURT, IT'S CONGRESS!"
Tea party
SPEAKER OF THE HOUSE

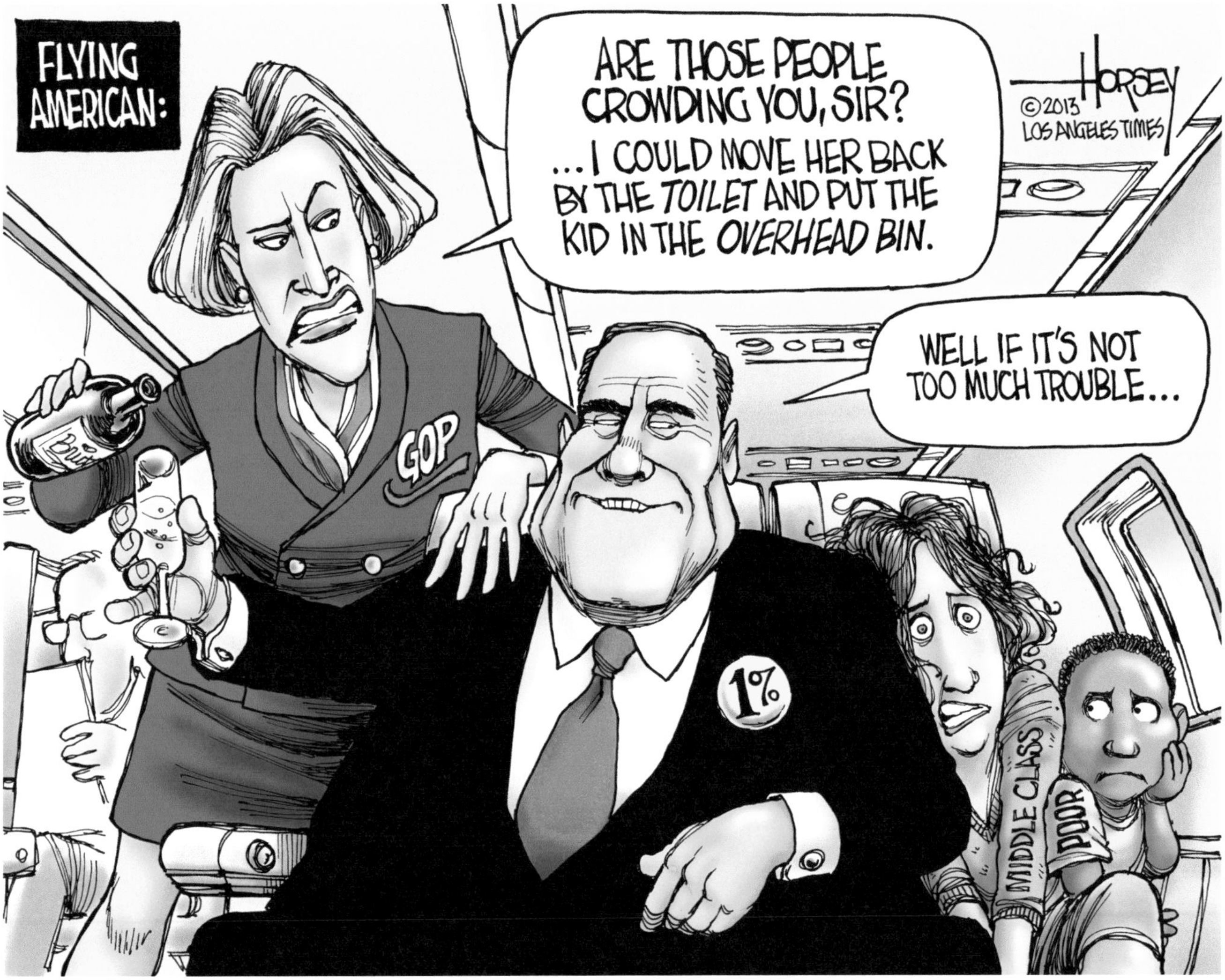
FLYING AMERICAN:
ARE THOSE PEOPLE CROWDING YOU, SIR?
...I COULD MOVE HER BACK BY THE *TOILET* AND PUT THE KID IN THE *OVERHEAD BIN*.
WELL IF IT'S NOT TOO MUCH TROUBLE...
HORSEY
©2013 LOS ANGELES TIMES
GOP
1%
MIDDLE CLASS
POOR

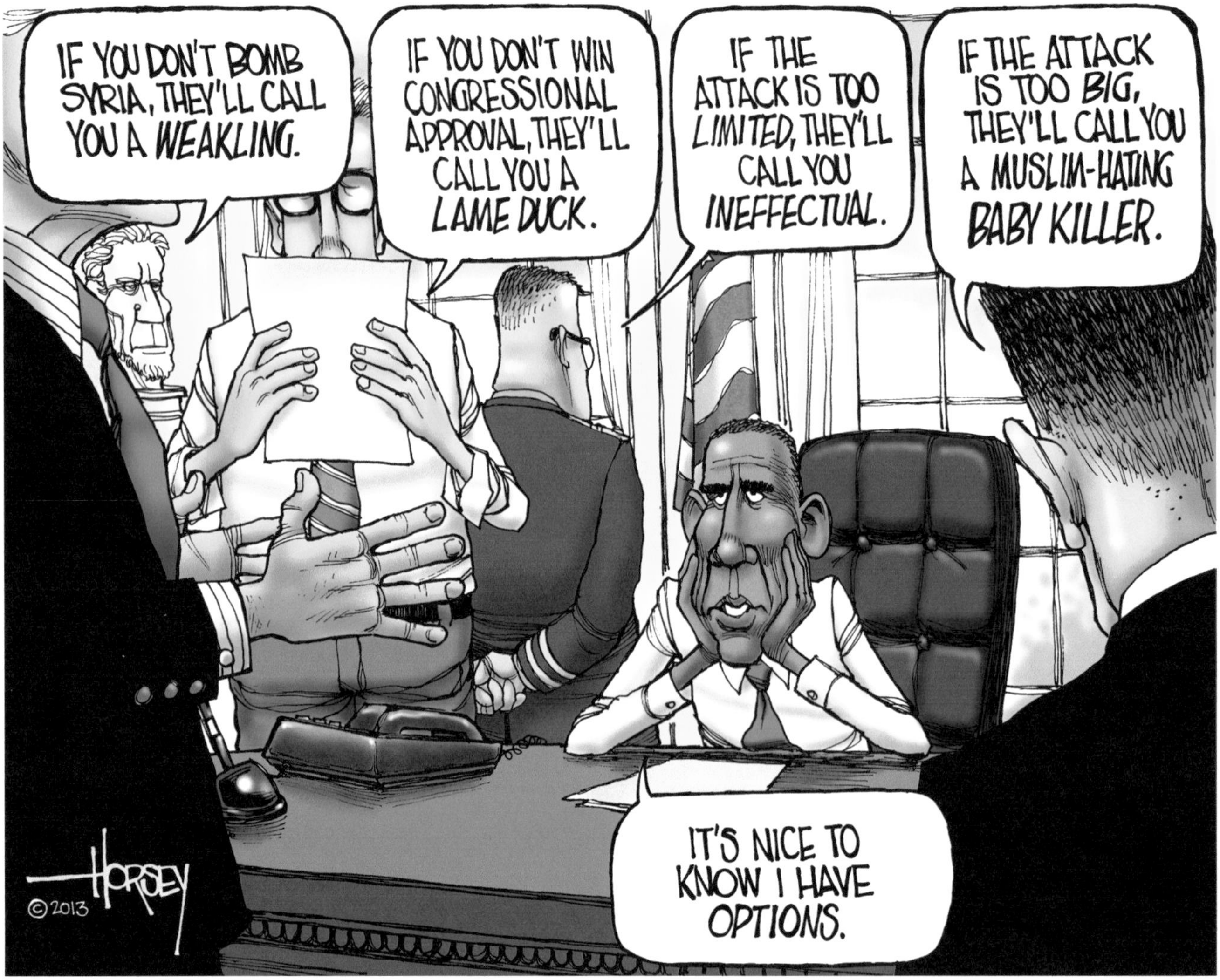
IF YOU DON'T BOMB SYRIA, THEY'LL CALL YOU A WEAKLING.
IF YOU DON'T WIN CONGRESSIONAL APPROVAL, THEY'LL CALL YOU A LAME DUCK.
IF THE ATTACK IS TOO LIMITED, THEY'LL CALL YOU INEFFECTUAL.
IF THE ATTACK IS TOO BIG, THEY'LL CALL YOU A MUSLIM-HATING BABY KILLER.
IT'S NICE TO KNOW I HAVE OPTIONS.
HORSEY
©2013

SYRIA
"NO WAR, GUYS...WE TALKED IT OUT AND THEY'RE GIVING UP THEIR WEAPONS."
WHAT?! TALK?! NO WAR?!!
THIS IS A DEBACLE!
I KNEW HE WAS GAY!
WIMP!
CHICKEN HAWKS
Neo cons
FOX NEWS
BUSH ADMINISTRATION VETS
HORSEY
©2013 LOS ANGELES TIMES

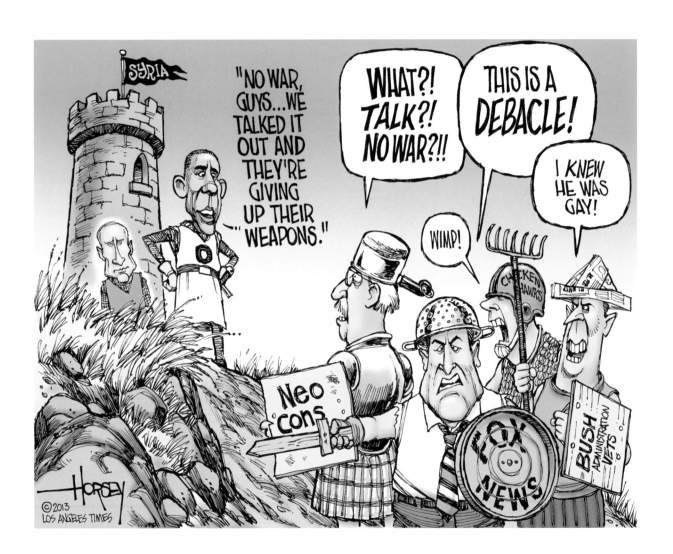

TREASURY OF THE UNITED STATES
NO COMPROMISE! I'LL BLOW IT ALL UP!
OMIGOD! HE'S A SUICIDE BOMBER!
WORSE... HE'S A TEA PARTY REPUBLICAN REFUSING TO RAISE THE DEBT CEILING!
©2011 HORSEY

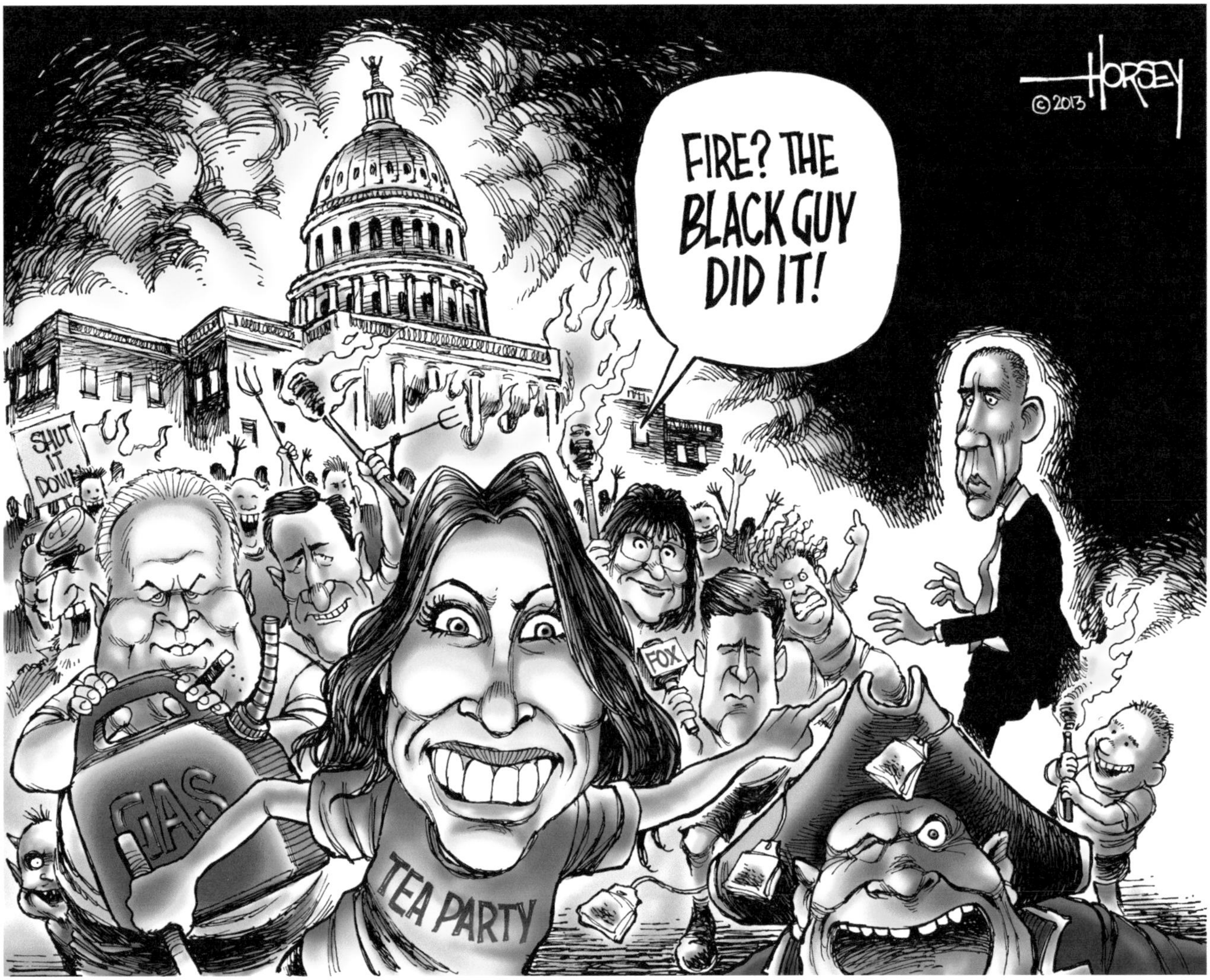
HORSEY
©2013
FIRE? THE BLACK GUY DID IT!
SHUT IT DOWN
FOX
GAS
TEA PARTY

ABOUT DAVID HORSEY

Photo by Nancy LeVine

In 2012, after a long career at the Seattle Post-Intelligencer,
David Horsey became a political cartoonist and columnist for the Los Angeles Times.
He has twice won the Pulitzer Prize for Editorial Cartooning, as well as many other accolades,
including The Berryman Award from the National Press Foundation and a Best of the West first
prize for his columns about the 2008 presidential election. His cartoons and columns are
syndicated to more than 200 newspapers by Tribune Media Services.

Made in United States
Troutdale, OR
01/21/2024

17045947R00076